DOCTOR WHO
THE TENTH DOCTOR

VOL 3: THE FOUNTAINS OF FOREVER

"If possible, I'm even more excited for the next issue than I was last time. In my eyes, Abadzis and co. can do no wrong."
BIG COMIC PAGE

"One of the best stories to be told via the comic book medium."
SNAP POW

"The artwork remains the high quality stuff we've come to expect. The characters come to life wonderfully and the effects, mood and emotions flow freely. Titan Comics has taken the Doctor to places we've not seen from anyone else."
READING WITH A FLIGHT RING

"Go buy this!"
COMICS VERSE

"The best of Titan Comics' slate of Doctor Who comics."
GIANT FREAKING ROBOT

"Perfectly captures the spirit of Doctor Who!"
KABOOOOOM!

"Fully embracing the spirit of the series, all Whovians will find themselves shouting, 'Allons-y!'"
NEWSARAMA

"Abadzis should be commended for how masterfully he spins the story and at how well he has utilized the mythology of the classic series while still expanding it with his own tale."
MY GEEKY GEEKY WAYS

"Injects a massive jolt of excitement and nostalgia. A blockbuster epic."
POP CULTURE BANDIT

"Doctor Who fans are well-served."
SOUNDS ON SIGHT

"The Doctor Who comic fans have always deserved."
BLOODY DISGUSTING

"If you've missed the skinny one with the sandshoes, then you'll enjoy this."
SCIFI BULLETIN

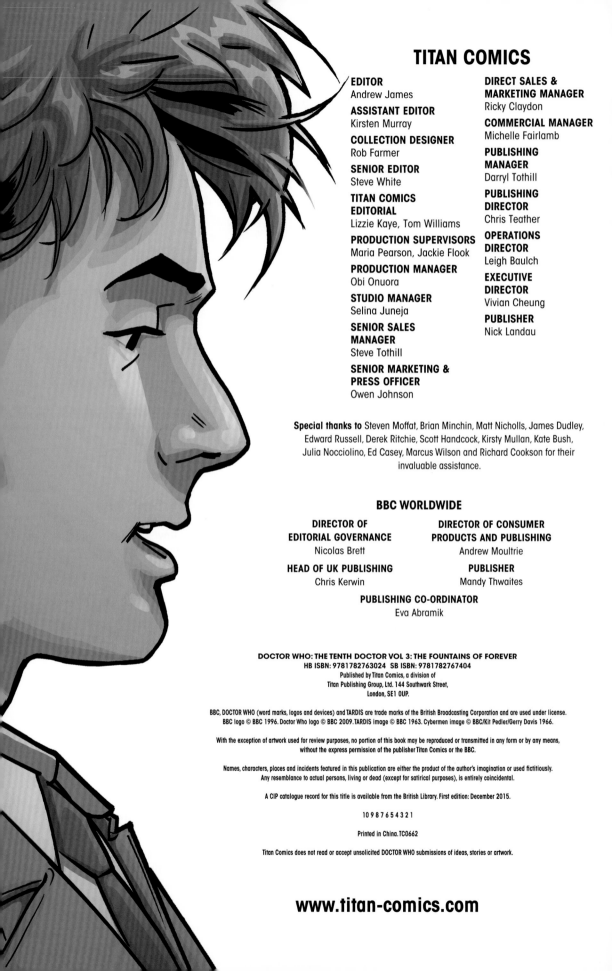

TITAN COMICS

EDITOR
Andrew James

ASSISTANT EDITOR
Kirsten Murray

COLLECTION DESIGNER
Rob Farmer

SENIOR EDITOR
Steve White

TITAN COMICS EDITORIAL
Lizzie Kaye, Tom Williams

PRODUCTION SUPERVISORS
Maria Pearson, Jackie Flook

PRODUCTION MANAGER
Obi Onuora

STUDIO MANAGER
Selina Juneja

SENIOR SALES MANAGER
Steve Tothill

SENIOR MARKETING & PRESS OFFICER
Owen Johnson

DIRECT SALES & MARKETING MANAGER
Ricky Claydon

COMMERCIAL MANAGER
Michelle Fairlamb

PUBLISHING MANAGER
Darryl Tothill

PUBLISHING DIRECTOR
Chris Teather

OPERATIONS DIRECTOR
Leigh Baulch

EXECUTIVE DIRECTOR
Vivian Cheung

PUBLISHER
Nick Landau

Special thanks to Steven Moffat, Brian Minchin, Matt Nicholls, James Dudley, Edward Russell, Derek Ritchie, Scott Handcock, Kirsty Mullan, Kate Bush, Julia Nocciolino, Ed Casey, Marcus Wilson and Richard Cookson for their invaluable assistance.

BBC WORLDWIDE

DIRECTOR OF EDITORIAL GOVERNANCE
Nicolas Brett

HEAD OF UK PUBLISHING
Chris Kerwin

DIRECTOR OF CONSUMER PRODUCTS AND PUBLISHING
Andrew Moultrie

PUBLISHER
Mandy Thwaites

PUBLISHING CO-ORDINATOR
Eva Abramik

DOCTOR WHO: THE TENTH DOCTOR VOL 3: THE FOUNTAINS OF FOREVER
HB ISBN: 9781782763024 SB ISBN: 9781782767404
Published by Titan Comics, a division of
Titan Publishing Group, Ltd. 144 Southwark Street,
London, SE1 0UP.

A CIP catalogue record for this title is available from the British Library. First edition: December 2015.

10 9 8 7 6 5 4 3 2 1

Printed in China. TC0662

Titan Comics does not read or accept unsolicited DOCTOR WHO submissions of ideas, stories or artwork.

www.titan-comics.com

BBC

DOCTOR WHO

THE TENTH DOCTOR

VOL 3: THE FOUNTAINS OF FOREVER

WRITER: NICK ABADZIS

ARTISTS: ELENA CASAGRANDE, ELEONORA CARLINI, RACHAEL STOTT & LEONARDO ROMERO

COLORISTS: ARIANNA FLOREAN & HI-FI

LETTERS: RICHARD STARKINGS AND COMICRAFT'S JIMMY BETANCOURT

TITAN COMICS · BBC

BBC

DOCTOR WHO

THE TENTH DOCTOR

THE DOCTOR

An alien who walks like a man. Last of the Time Lords of Gallifrey. Never cruel or cowardly, he champions the oppressed across time and space. Forever traveling, the Doctor lives to see the universe anew through the eyes of his human companions!

GABBY GONZALEZ

Gabriella Gonzalez is a would-be artist, stuck working in her father's laundromat until she met the Doctor. Having impressed him with her courage and creativity during her first voyage through time and space, Gabby has been welcomed aboard the TARDIS to accompany the Time Lord on his latest adventures!

THE TARDIS

'Time and Relative Dimension in Space'. Bigger on the inside, this unassuming blue box is your ticket to unforgettable adventure!

The Doctor likes to think he's in control, but more often than not, the TARDIS takes him where and when he needs to be...

PREVIOUSLY...

After journeying through time and space at the Doctor's side – on adventures that took her to an alien art gallery on a world as beautiful as it was strange, then back to the war-torn, Weeping Angel-strewn trenches of World War I – Gabby is back home in New York City!

Yesterday, the pair drove off an alien invasion. Before Gabby makes time for her best friend, Cindy Wu... it's time for the Doctor to do some laundry!

When you've finished reading this collection, please email your thoughts to doctorwhocomic@titanemail.com

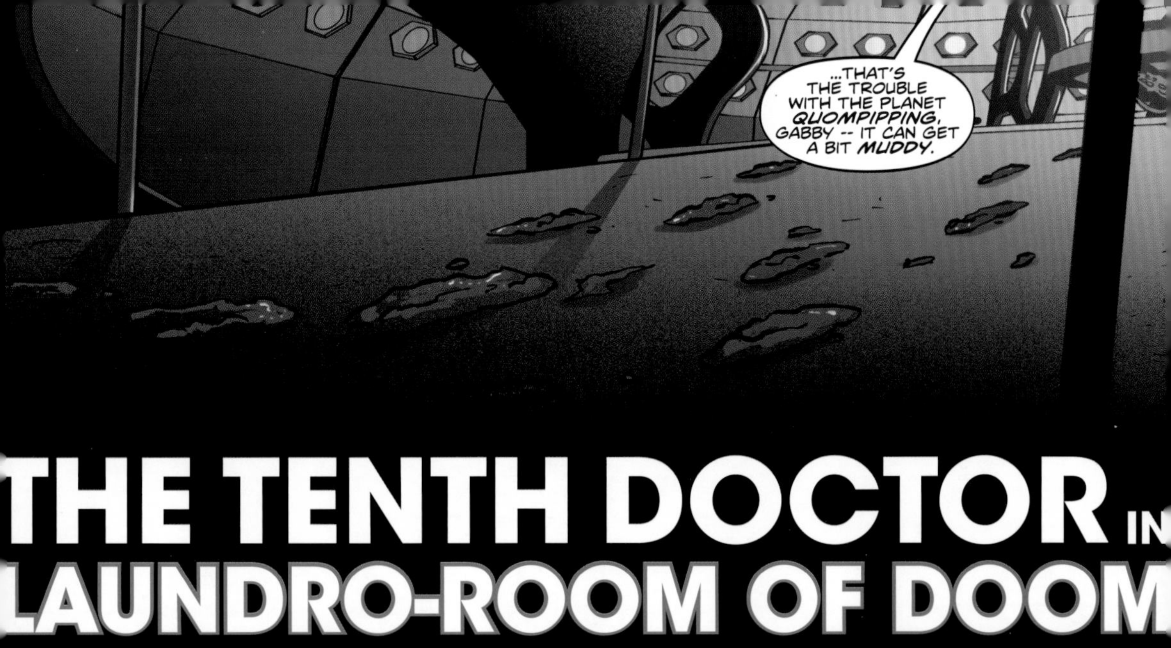
...THAT'S THE TROUBLE WITH THE PLANET QUOMPIPPING, GABBY -- IT CAN GET A BIT MUDDY.

THE TENTH DOCTOR IN LAUNDRO-ROOM OF DOOM

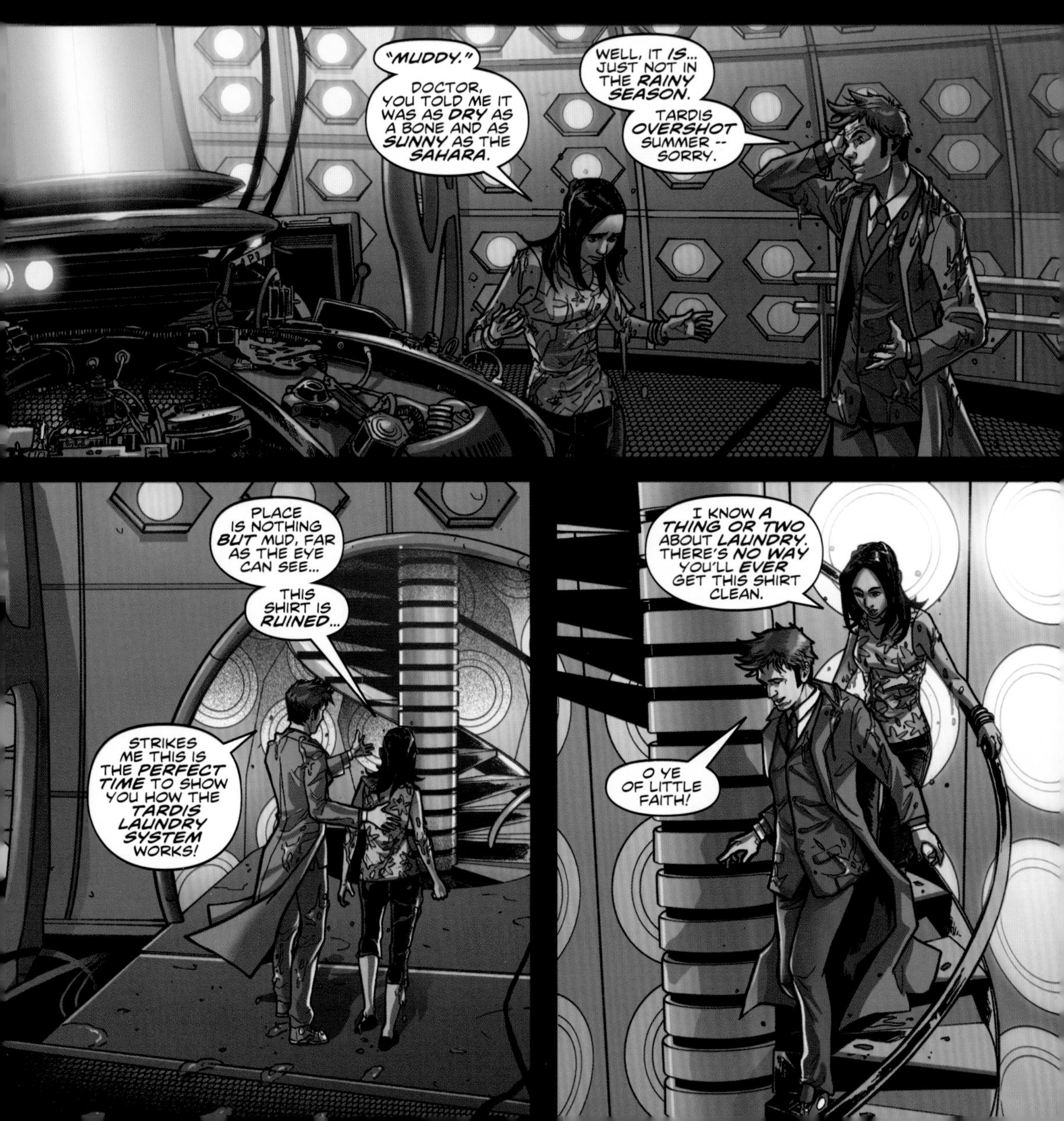
"MUDDY."
DOCTOR, YOU TOLD ME IT WAS AS DRY AS A BONE AND AS SUNNY AS THE SAHARA.
WELL, IT IS... JUST NOT IN THE RAINY SEASON.
TARDIS OVERSHOT SUMMER -- SORRY.
PLACE IS NOTHING BUT MUD, FAR AS THE EYE CAN SEE...
THIS SHIRT IS RUINED...
STRIKES ME THIS IS THE PERFECT TIME TO SHOW YOU HOW THE TARDIS LAUNDRY SYSTEM WORKS!
I KNOW A THING OR TWO ABOUT LAUNDRY. THERE'S NO WAY YOU'LL EVER GET THIS SHIRT CLEAN.
O YE OF LITTLE FAITH!

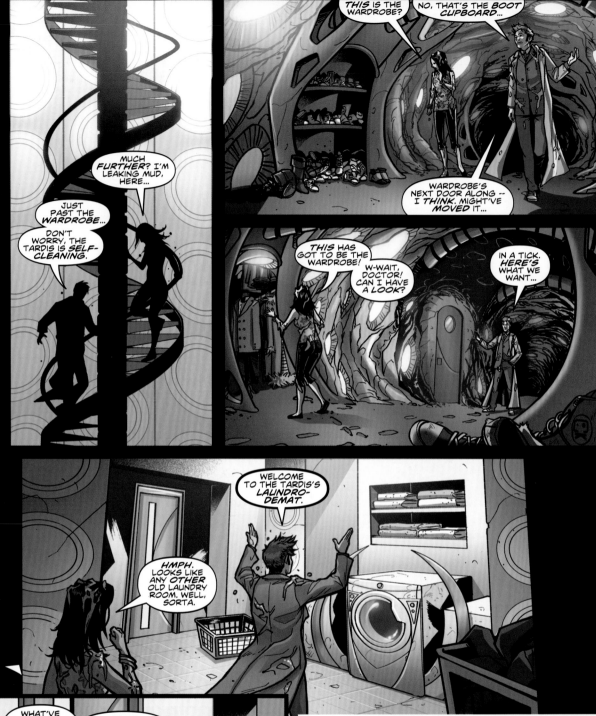

THIS IS THE WARDROBE?

NO, THAT'S THE *BOOT CUPBOARD*...

MUCH *FURTHER*? I'M LEAKING MUD, HERE...

JUST PAST THE *WARDROBE*...

DON'T WORRY, THE TARDIS IS *SELF-CLEANING*.

WARDROBE'S NEXT DOOR ALONG -- I *THINK*. MIGHT'VE *MOVED* IT...

THIS HAS GOT TO BE THE WARDROBE!

W-WAIT, DOCTOR! CAN I HAVE A *LOOK*?

IN A TICK. *HERE'S* WHAT WE WANT...

WELCOME TO THE TARDIS'S *LAUNDRODEMAT*.

HMPH. LOOKS LIKE ANY *OTHER* OLD LAUNDRY ROOM. WELL, SORTA.

WHAT'VE I TOLD YOU? APPEARANCES CAN BE *DECEPTIVE*.

SPA'S THROUGH *THERE* -- NICE HOT BATH'LL SORT YOU OUT, *GRUMPILOCKS*.

GET CHANGED AND I'LL SHOW YOU HOW IT *WORKS*...

"...THEN YOU CAN PICK *SOMETHING NICE* FROM THE WARDROBE."

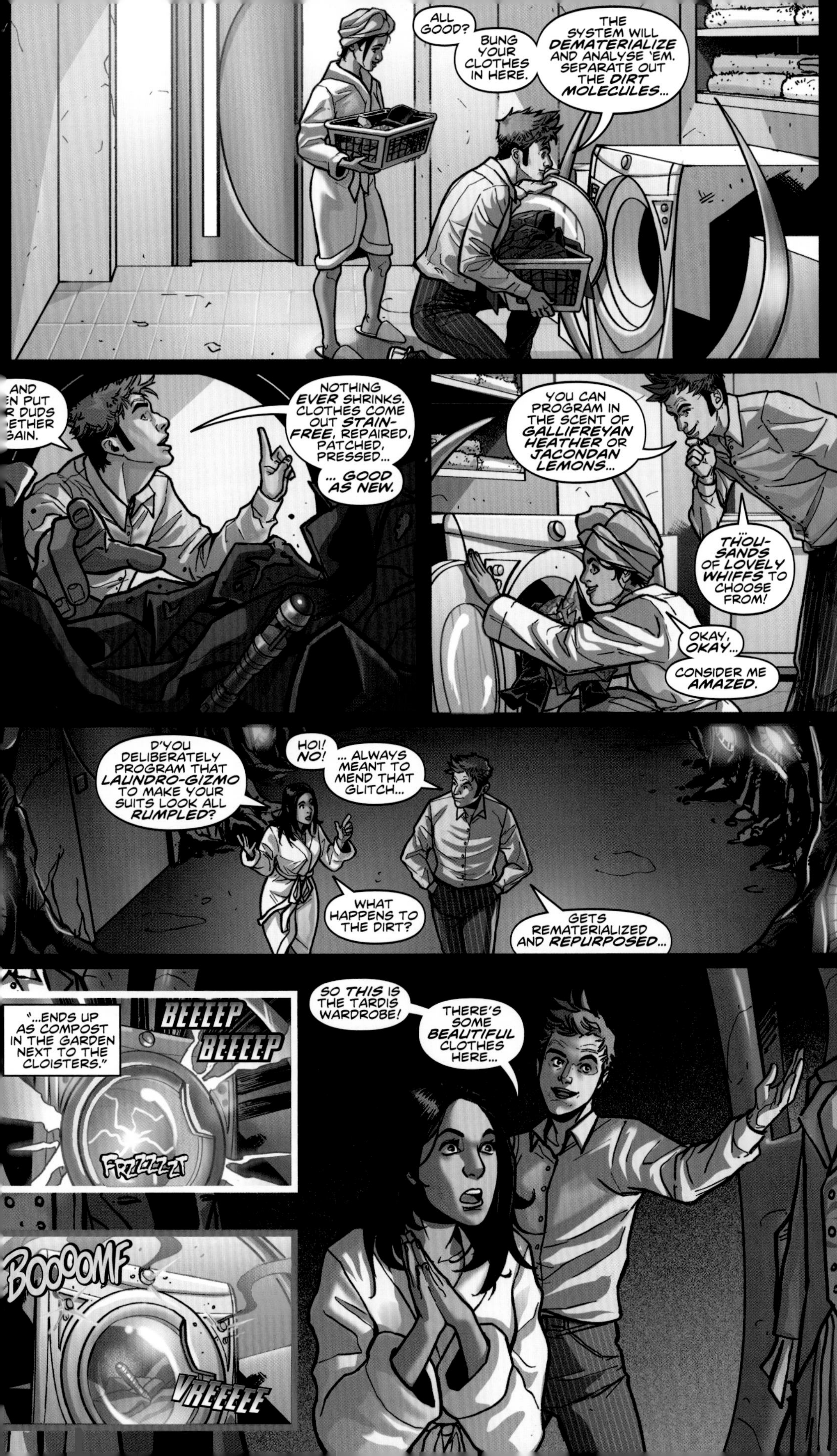
ALL GOOD?
BUNG YOUR CLOTHES IN HERE.
THE SYSTEM WILL DEMATERIALIZE AND ANALYSE 'EM. SEPARATE OUT THE DIRT MOLECULES...
AND ...EN PUT ...R DUDS ...GETHER ...GAIN.
NOTHING EVER SHRINKS. CLOTHES COME OUT STAIN-FREE, REPAIRED, PATCHED, PRESSED...
...GOOD AS NEW.
YOU CAN PROGRAM IN THE SCENT OF GALLIFREYAN HEATHER OR JACONDAN LEMONS...
...THOU-SANDS OF LOVELY WHIFFS TO CHOOSE FROM!
OKAY, OKAY...
CONSIDER ME AMAZED.
D'YOU DELIBERATELY PROGRAM THAT LAUNDRO-GIZMO TO MAKE YOUR SUITS LOOK ALL RUMPLED?
HOI! NO!
... ALWAYS MEANT TO MEND THAT GLITCH...
WHAT HAPPENS TO THE DIRT?
GETS REMATERIALIZED AND REPURPOSED...
"...ENDS UP AS COMPOST IN THE GARDEN NEXT TO THE CLOISTERS."
BEEEEP
BEEEEP
FRZZZZZZT
BOOOOMF
VREEEEE
SO THIS IS THE TARDIS WARDROBE!
THERE'S SOME BEAUTIFUL CLOTHES HERE...

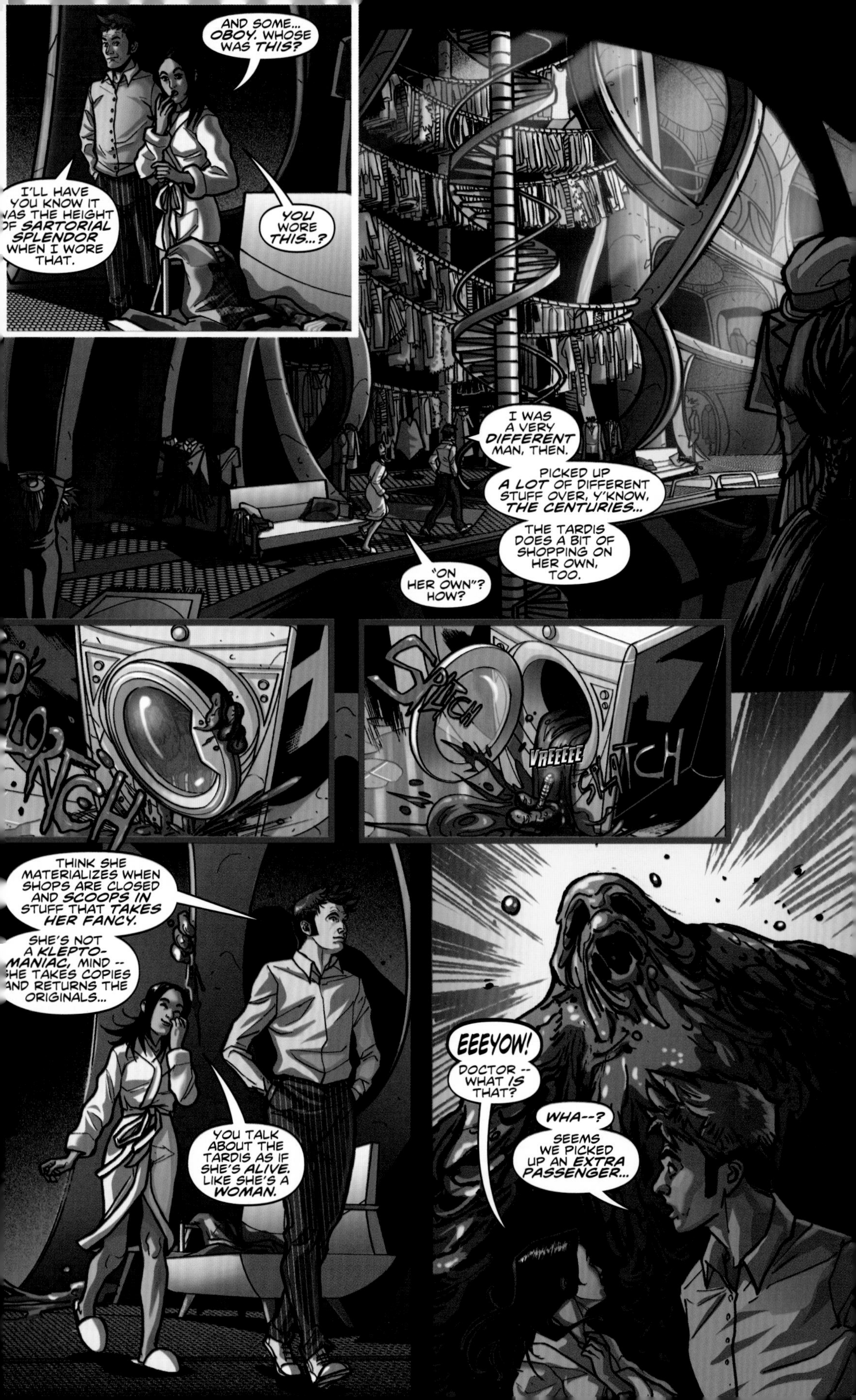
AND SOME... OBOY. WHOSE WAS THIS?
I'LL HAVE YOU KNOW IT WAS THE HEIGHT OF SARTORIAL SPLENDOR WHEN I WORE THAT.
YOU WORE THIS...?
I WAS A VERY DIFFERENT MAN, THEN.
PICKED UP A LOT OF DIFFERENT STUFF OVER, Y'KNOW, THE CENTURIES...
THE TARDIS DOES A BIT OF SHOPPING ON HER OWN, TOO.
"ON HER OWN"? HOW?
SPLORTCH
SPLATCH
VREEEEE
SPLATCH
THINK SHE MATERIALIZES WHEN SHOPS ARE CLOSED AND SCOOPS IN STUFF THAT TAKES HER FANCY.
SHE'S NOT A KLEPTO-MANIAC, MIND -- SHE TAKES COPIES AND RETURNS THE ORIGINALS...
YOU TALK ABOUT THE TARDIS AS IF SHE'S ALIVE. LIKE SHE'S A WOMAN.
EEEYOW!
DOCTOR -- WHAT IS THAT?
WHA--?
SEEMS WE PICKED UP AN EXTRA PASSENGER...

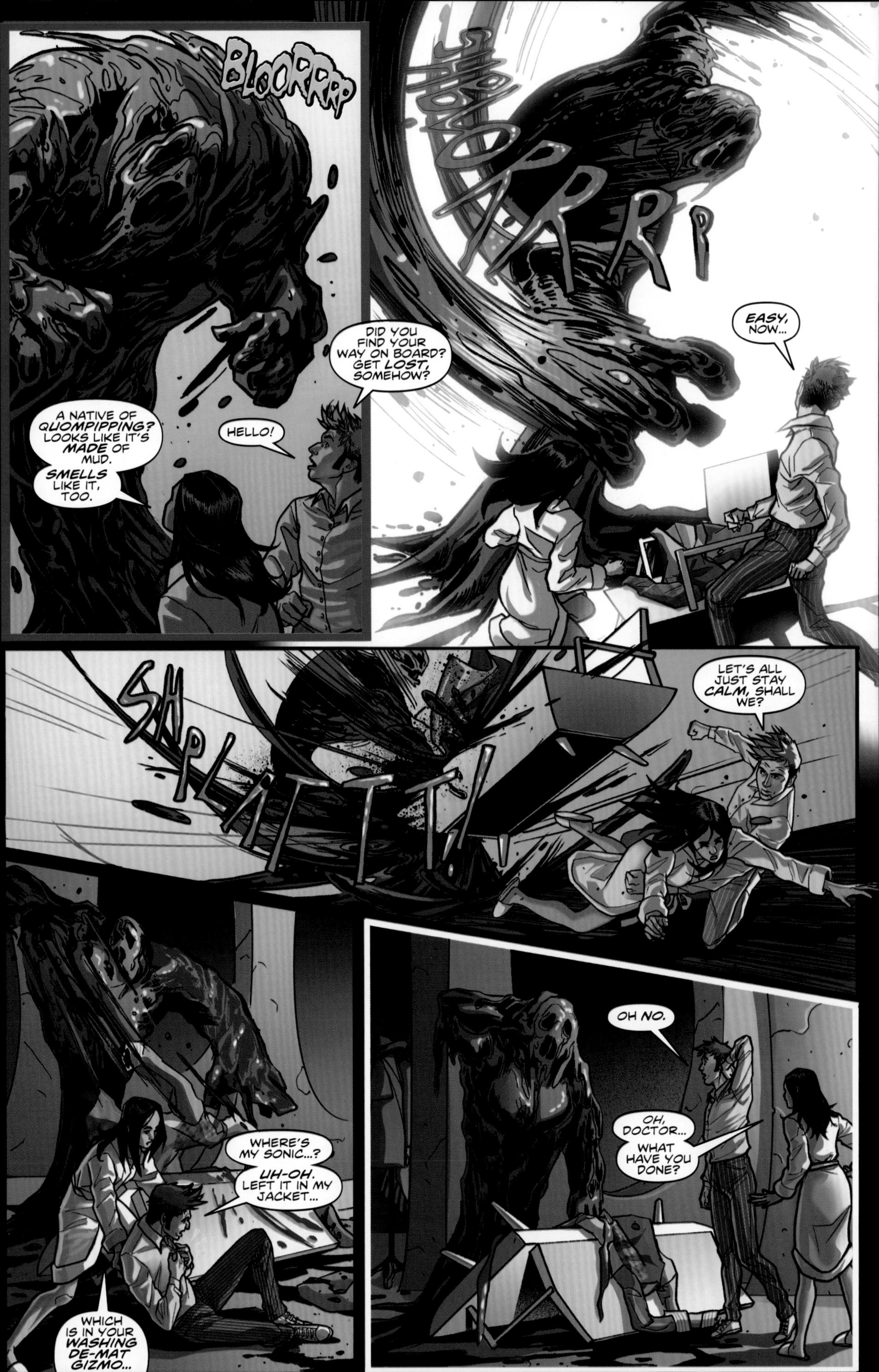
BLOORRRP
A NATIVE OF QUOMPIPPING? LOOKS LIKE IT'S MADE OF MUD.
SMELLS LIKE IT, TOO.
HELLO!
DID YOU FIND YOUR WAY ON BOARD? GET LOST, SOMEHOW?
SHLOOORRRP
EASY, NOW...
SHPLATT!
LET'S ALL JUST STAY CALM, SHALL WE?
WHERE'S MY SONIC...?
UH-OH. LEFT IT IN MY JACKET...
WHICH IS IN YOUR WASHING DE-MAT GIZMO...
OH NO.
OH, DOCTOR... WHAT HAVE YOU DONE?

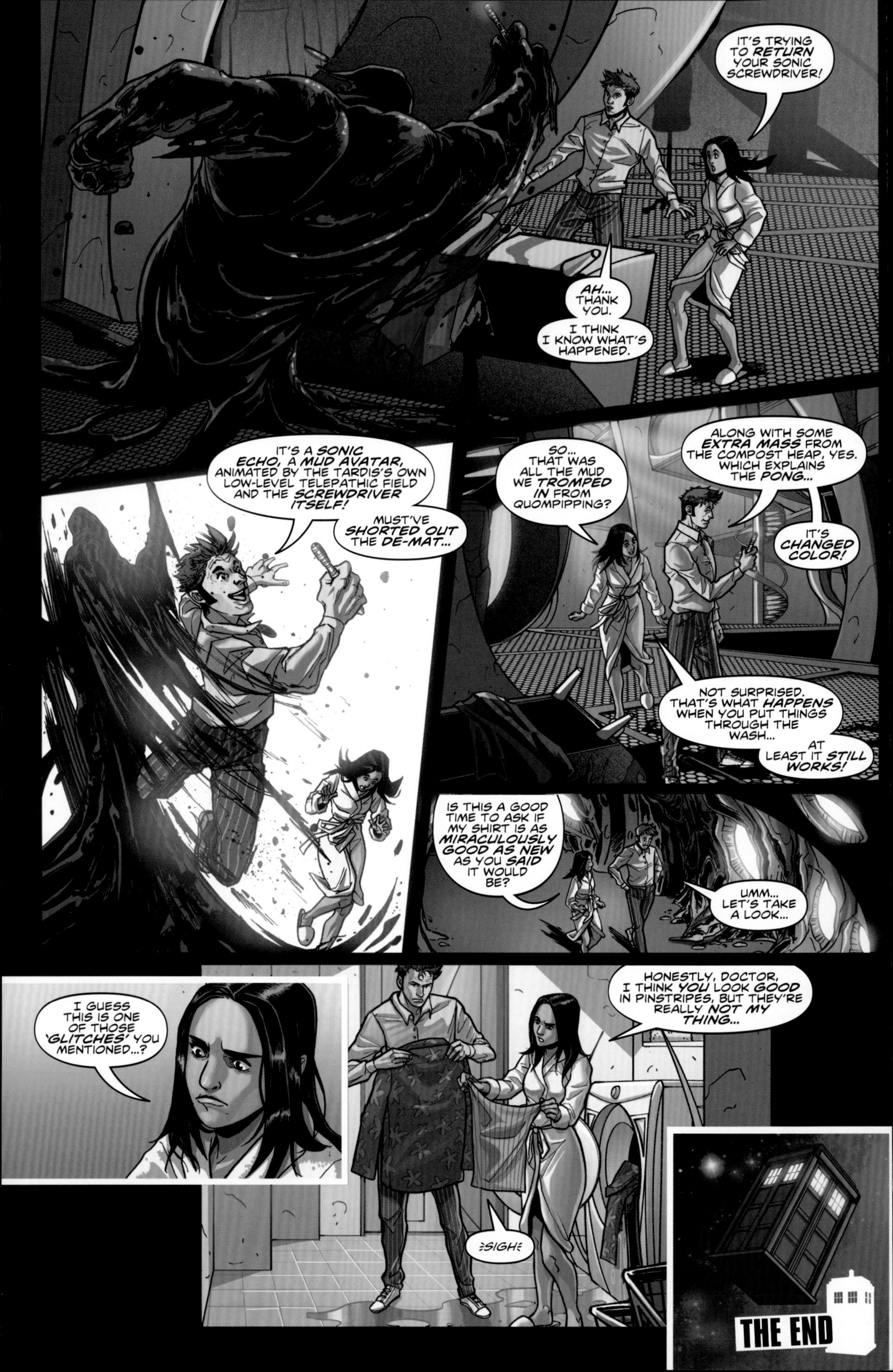
IT'S TRYING TO RETURN YOUR SONIC SCREWDRIVER!
AH... THANK YOU.
I THINK I KNOW WHAT'S HAPPENED.
IT'S A SONIC ECHO, A MUD AVATAR, ANIMATED BY THE TARDIS'S OWN LOW-LEVEL TELEPATHIC FIELD AND THE SCREWDRIVER ITSELF!
MUST'VE SHORTED OUT THE DE-MAT...
SO... THAT WAS ALL THE MUD WE TROMPED IN FROM QUOMPIPPING?
ALONG WITH SOME EXTRA MASS FROM THE COMPOST HEAP, YES. WHICH EXPLAINS THE PONG...
IT'S CHANGED COLOR!
NOT SURPRISED. THAT'S WHAT HAPPENS WHEN YOU PUT THINGS THROUGH THE WASH...
AT LEAST IT STILL WORKS!
IS THIS A GOOD TIME TO ASK IF MY SHIRT IS AS MIRACULOUSLY GOOD AS NEW AS YOU SAID IT WOULD BE?
UMM... LET'S TAKE A LOOK...
I GUESS THIS IS ONE OF THOSE 'GLITCHES' YOU MENTIONED...?
HONESTLY, DOCTOR, I THINK YOU LOOK GOOD IN PINSTRIPES, BUT THEY'RE REALLY NOT MY THING...
SIGH
THE END

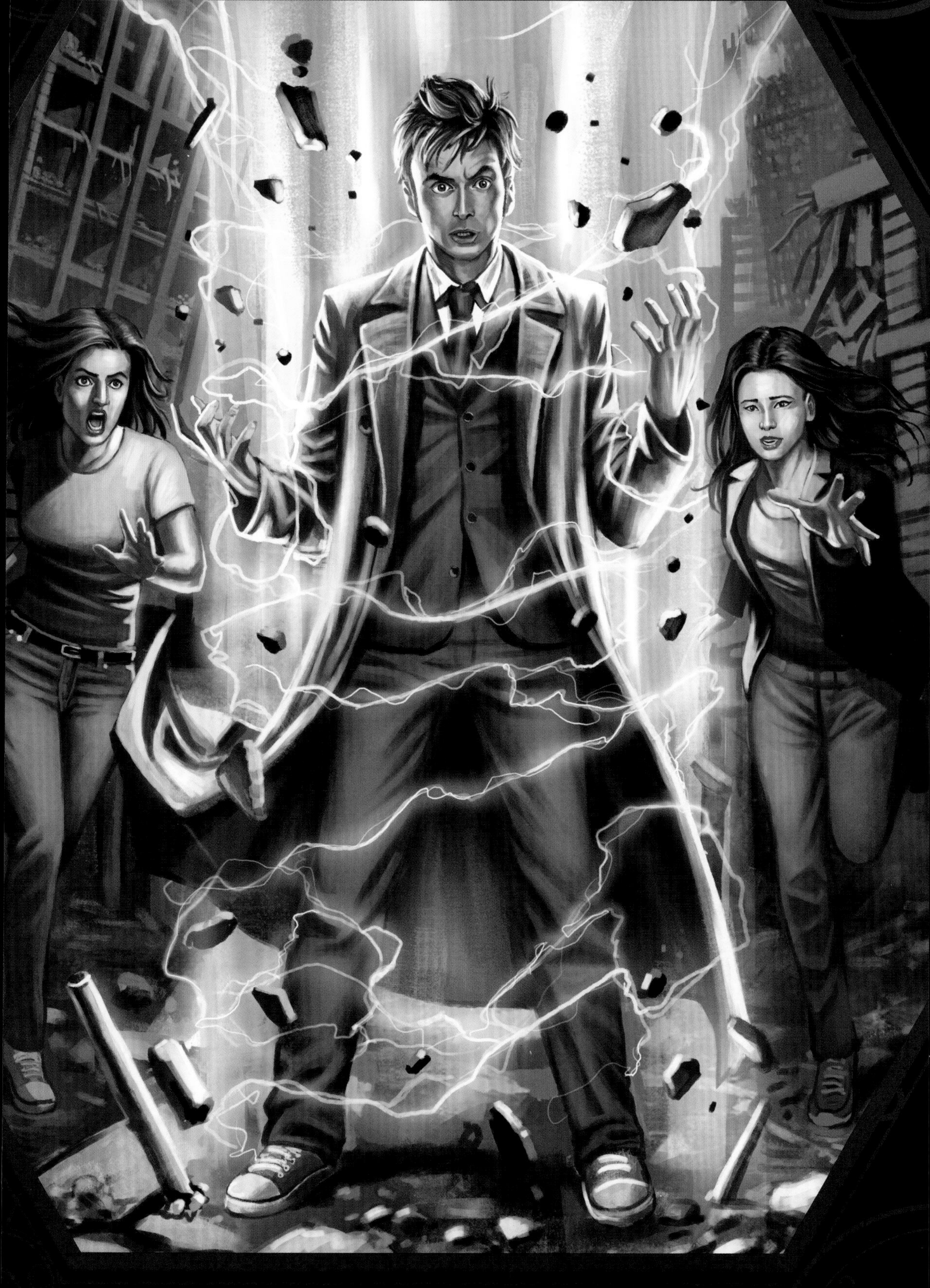

Cover: MARIANO LACLAUSTRA

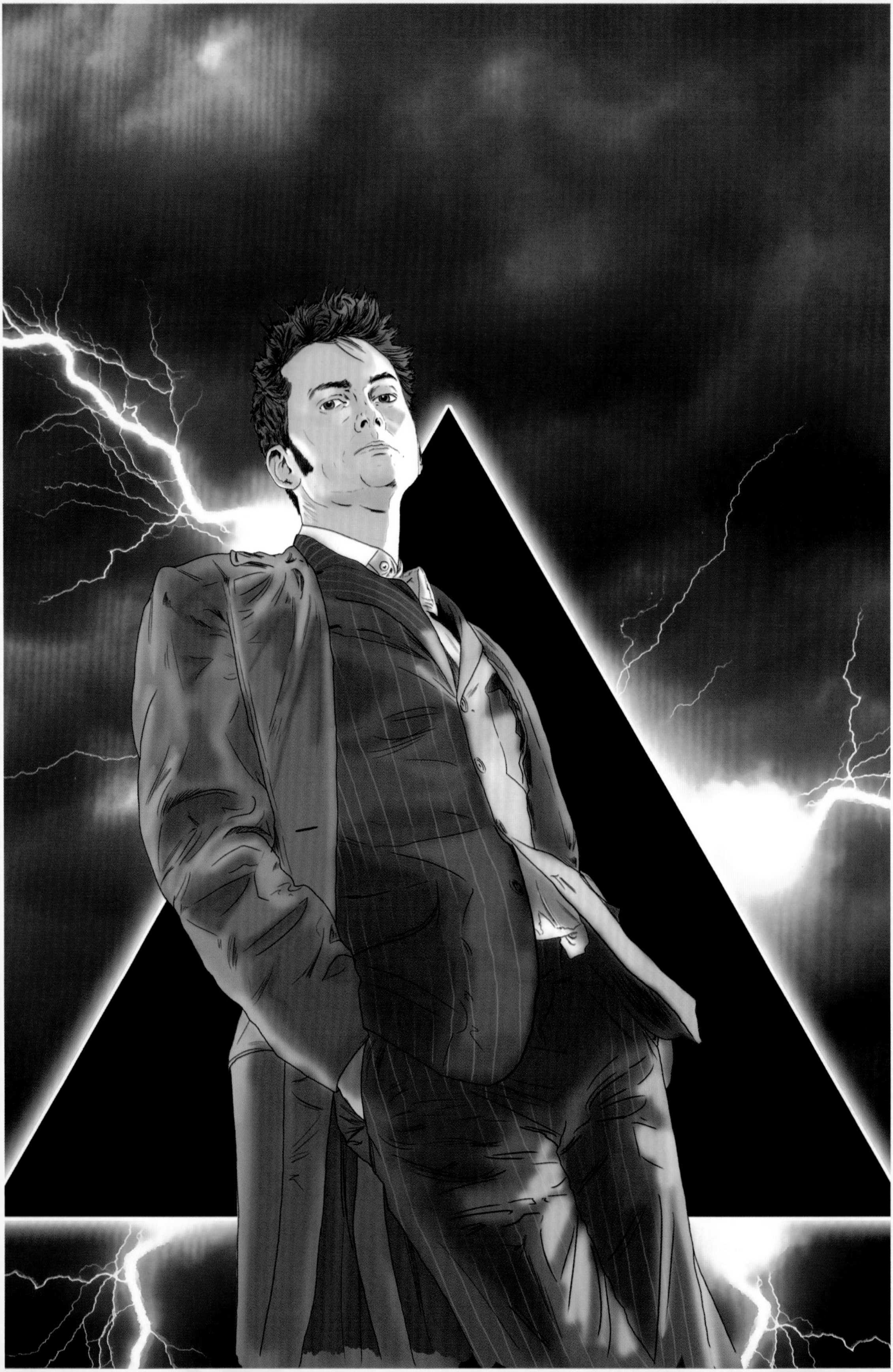

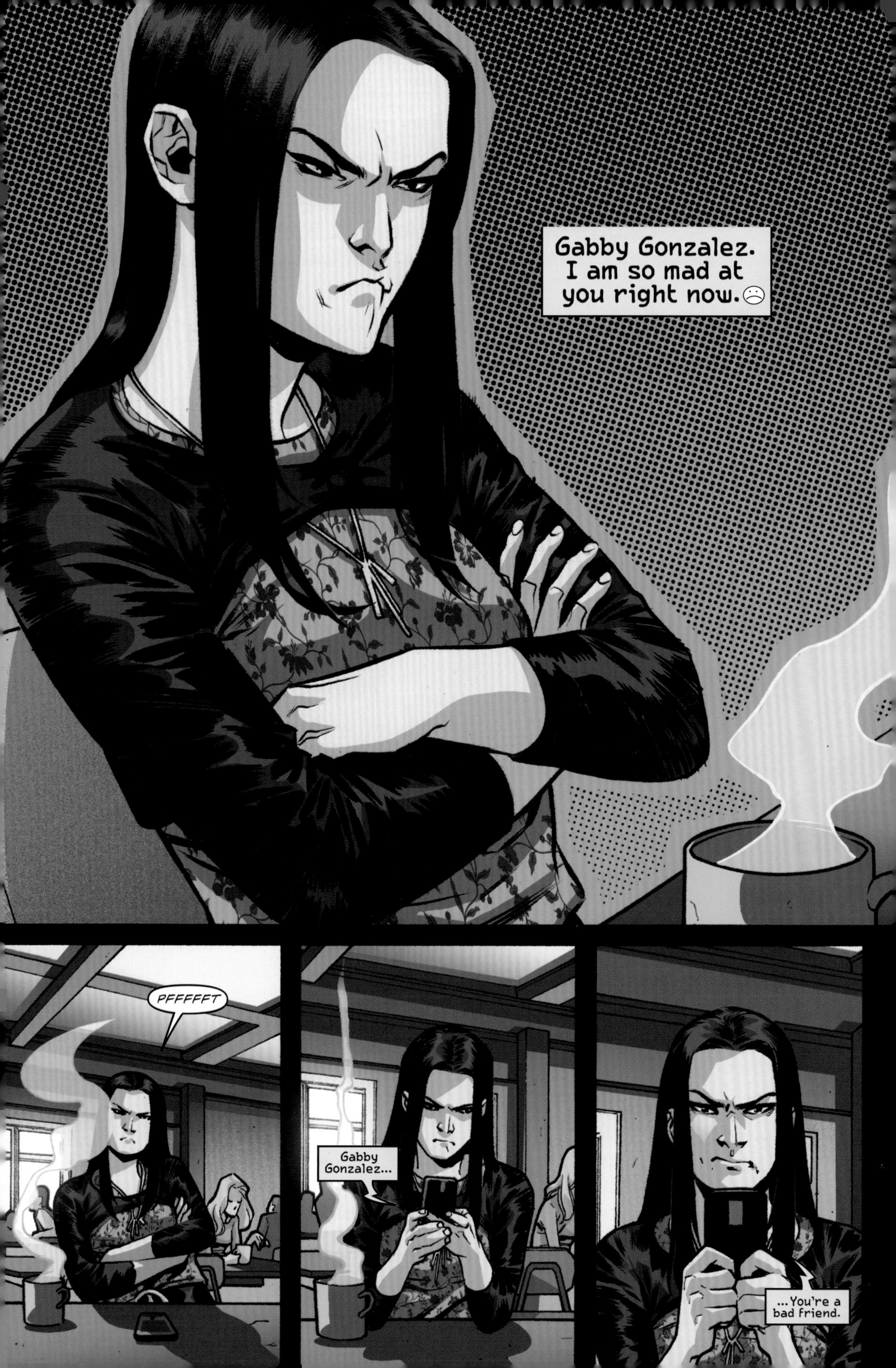

Gabby Gonzalez. I am so mad at you right now. ☹
PFFFFFT
Gabby Gonzalez...
...You're a bad friend.

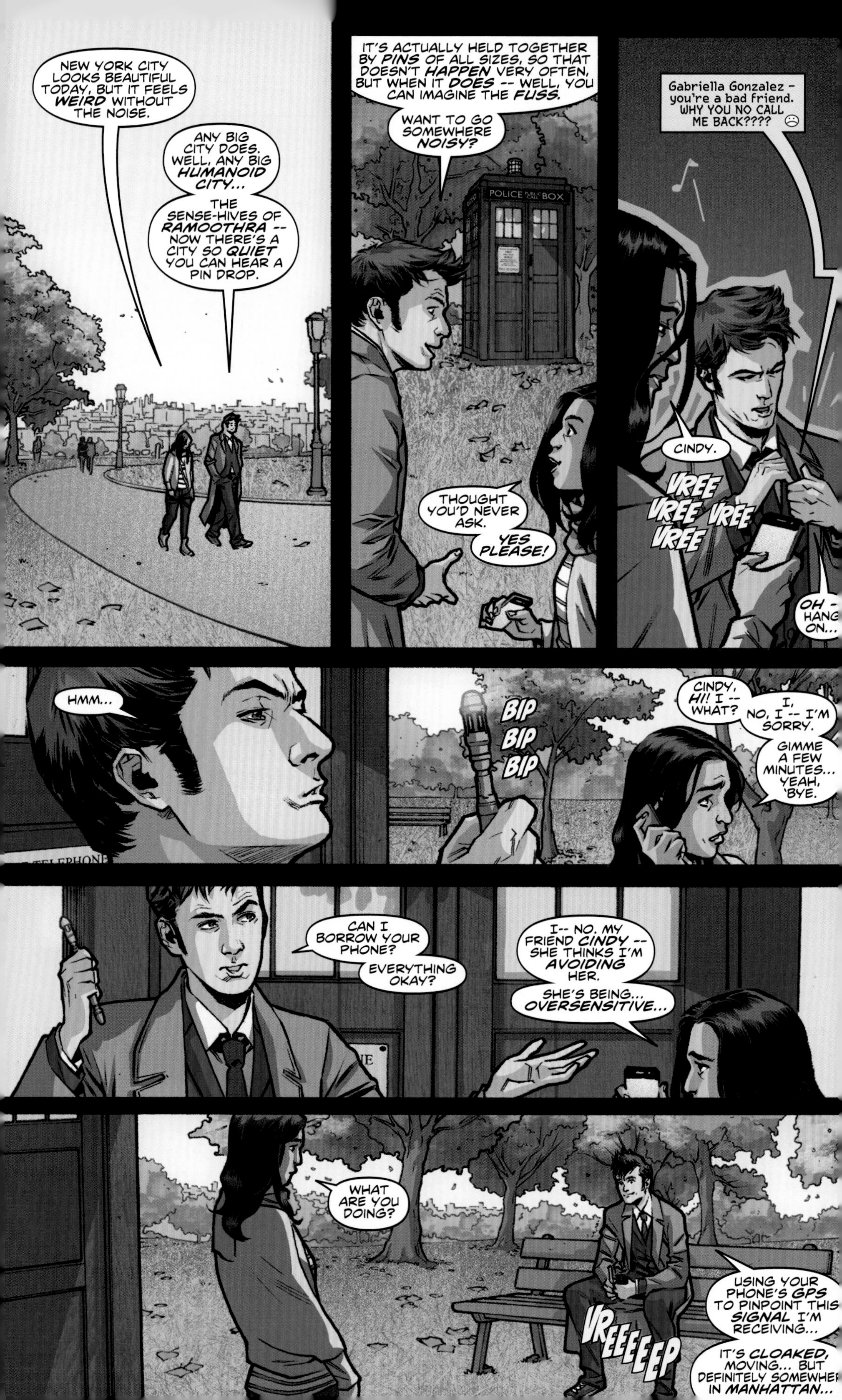
NEW YORK CITY LOOKS BEAUTIFUL TODAY, BUT IT FEELS WEIRD WITHOUT THE NOISE.
ANY BIG CITY DOES. WELL, ANY BIG HUMANOID CITY...
THE SENSE-HIVES OF RAMOOTHRA -- NOW THERE'S A CITY SO QUIET YOU CAN HEAR A PIN DROP.
IT'S ACTUALLY HELD TOGETHER BY PINS OF ALL SIZES, SO THAT DOESN'T HAPPEN VERY OFTEN, BUT WHEN IT DOES -- WELL, YOU CAN IMAGINE THE FUSS.
WANT TO GO SOMEWHERE NOISY?
POLICE PUBLIC CALL BOX
THOUGHT YOU'D NEVER ASK.
YES PLEASE!
Gabriella Gonzalez – you're a bad friend. WHY YOU NO CALL ME BACK????
CINDY.
VREE VREE VREE VREE
OH – HANG ON...
HMM...
BIP BIP BIP
CINDY, HI! I -- WHAT?
I, NO, I -- I'M SORRY.
GIMME A FEW MINUTES... YEAH, 'BYE.
CAN I BORROW YOUR PHONE?
EVERYTHING OKAY?
I-- NO. MY FRIEND CINDY -- SHE THINKS I'M AVOIDING HER.
SHE'S BEING... OVERSENSITIVE...
WHAT ARE YOU DOING?
VREEEEEEP
USING YOUR PHONE'S GPS TO PINPOINT THIS SIGNAL I'M RECEIVING...
IT'S CLOAKED, MOVING... BUT DEFINITELY SOMEWHER IN MANHATTAN...

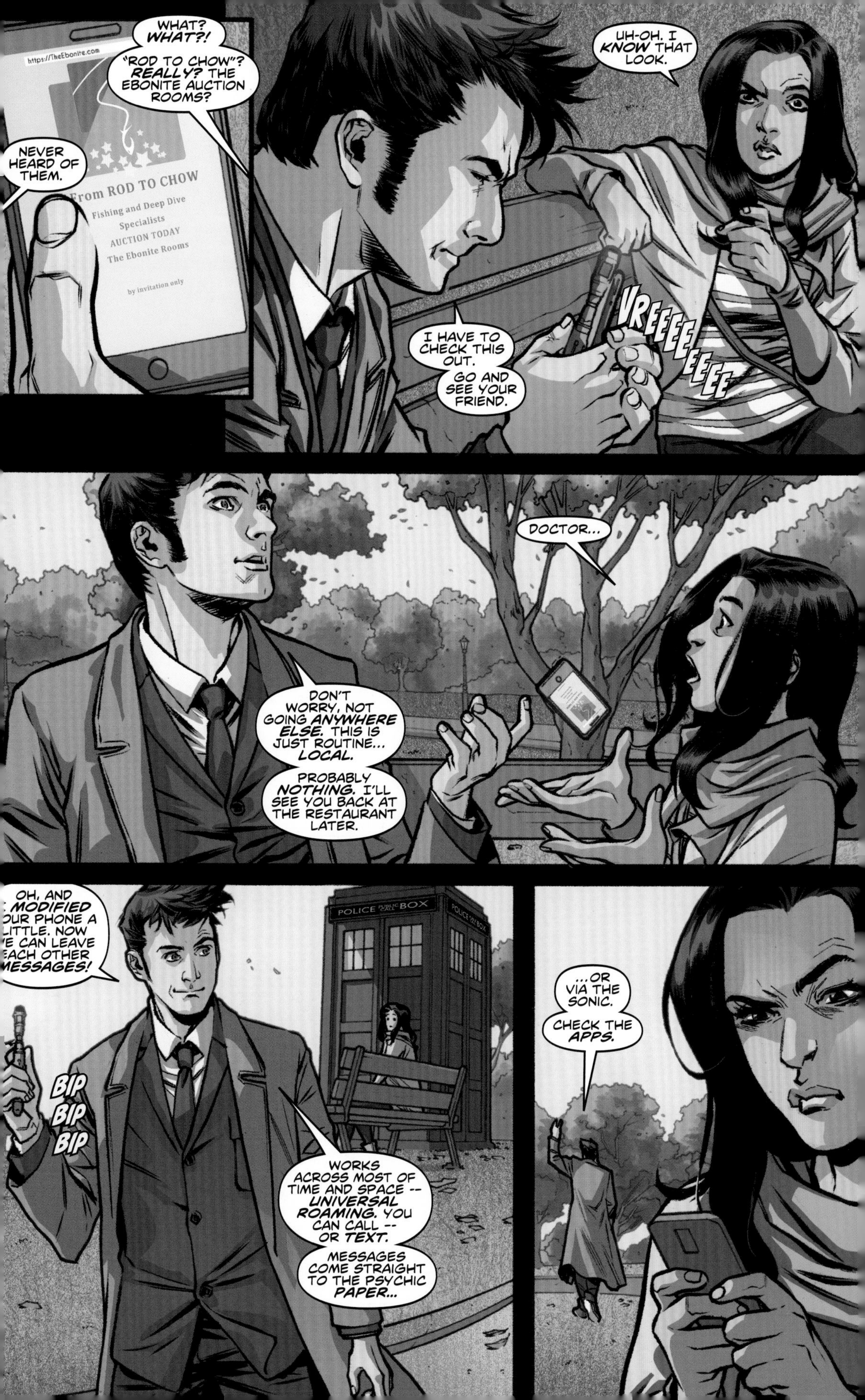
https://TheEbonite.com
From ROD TO CHOW
Fishing and Deep Dive Specialists
AUCTION TODAY
The Ebonite Rooms
by invitation only
WHAT? WHAT?!
"ROD TO CHOW"? REALLY? THE EBONITE AUCTION ROOMS?
NEVER HEARD OF THEM.
UH-OH. I KNOW THAT LOOK.
I HAVE TO CHECK THIS OUT.
GO AND SEE YOUR FRIEND.
VREEEEEEEEE
DOCTOR...
DON'T WORRY, NOT GOING ANYWHERE ELSE. THIS IS JUST ROUTINE... LOCAL.
PROBABLY NOTHING. I'LL SEE YOU BACK AT THE RESTAURANT LATER.
OH, AND MODIFIED OUR PHONE A LITTLE. NOW E CAN LEAVE EACH OTHER MESSAGES!
POLICE PUBLIC CALL BOX
BIP BIP BIP
WORKS ACROSS MOST OF TIME AND SPACE -- UNIVERSAL ROAMING. YOU CAN CALL -- OR TEXT.
MESSAGES COME STRAIGHT TO THE PSYCHIC PAPER...
...OR VIA THE SONIC.
CHECK THE APPS.

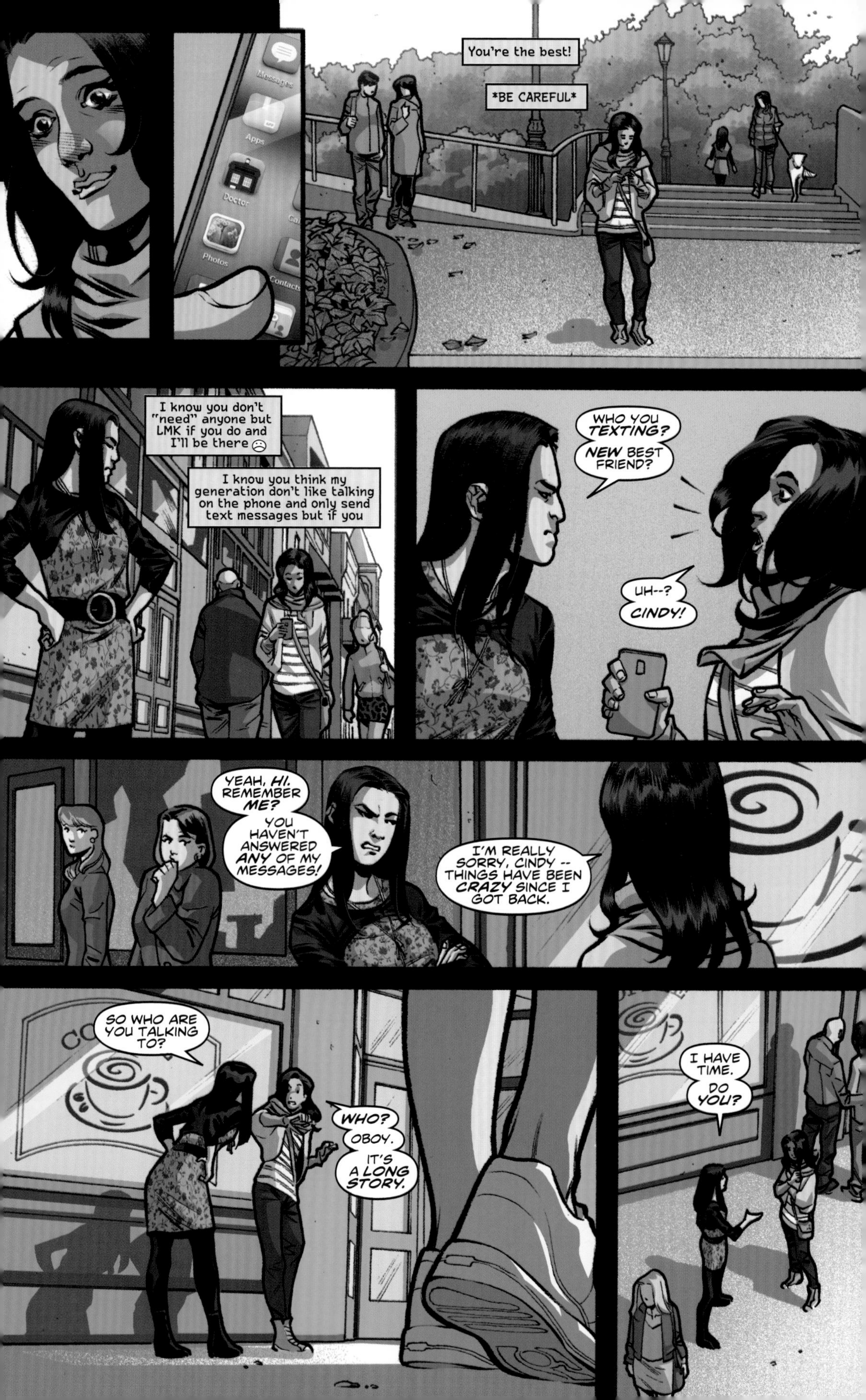
You're the best!
BE CAREFUL
I know you don't "need" anyone but LMK if you do and I'll be there ☹
I know you think my generation don't like talking on the phone and only send text messages but if you
WHO YOU TEXTING? NEW BEST FRIEND?
UH--? CINDY!
YEAH, HI. REMEMBER ME?
YOU HAVEN'T ANSWERED ANY OF MY MESSAGES!
I'M REALLY SORRY, CINDY -- THINGS HAVE BEEN CRAZY SINCE I GOT BACK.
SO WHO ARE YOU TALKING TO?
WHO?
OBOY.
IT'S A LONG STORY.
I HAVE TIME.
DO YOU?

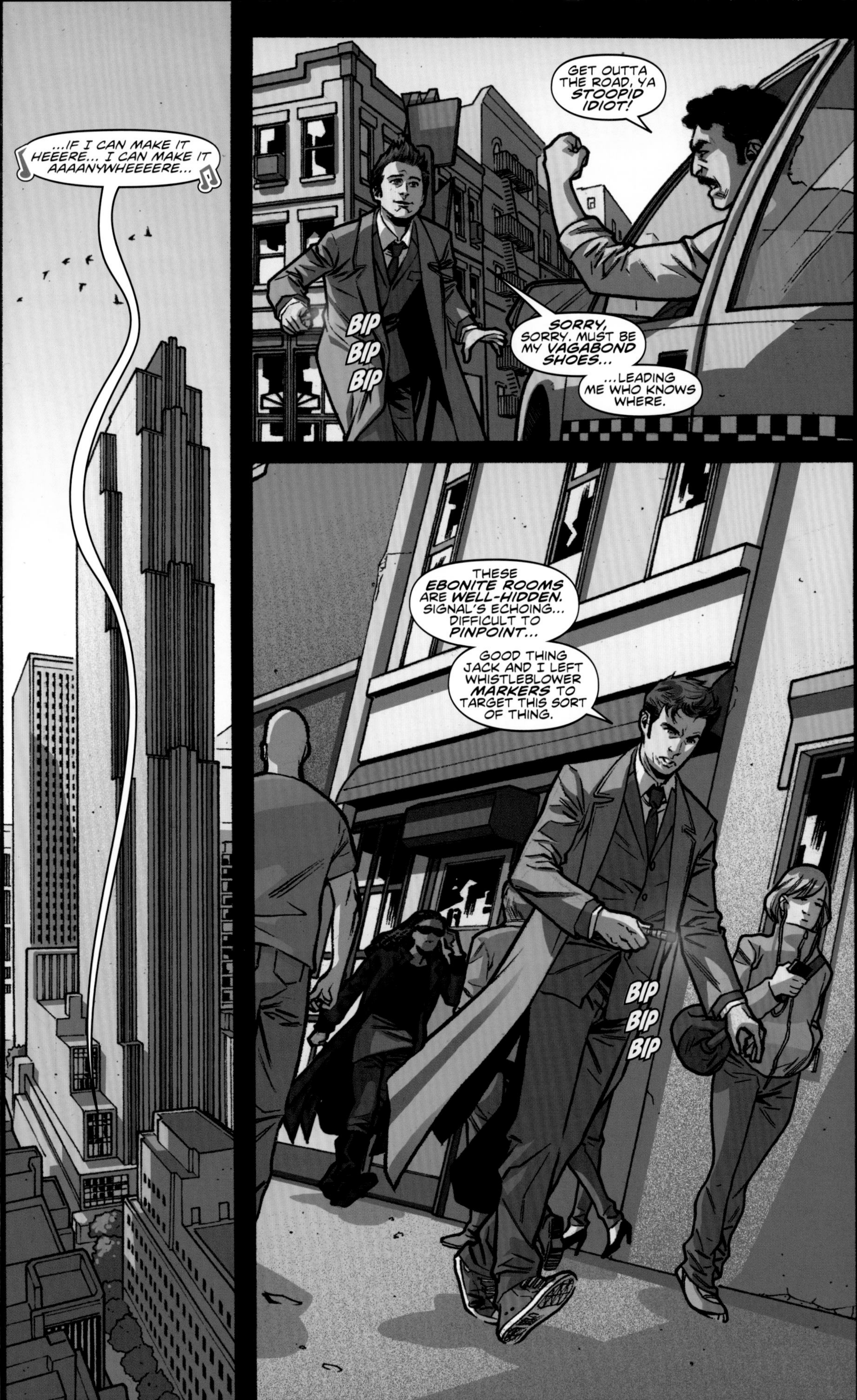

...IF I CAN MAKE IT HEEEERE... I CAN MAKE IT AAAANYWHEEEERE...
GET OUTTA THE ROAD, YA STOOPID IDIOT!
BIP BIP BIP
SORRY, SORRY. MUST BE MY VAGABOND SHOES...
...LEADING ME WHO KNOWS WHERE.
THESE EBONITE ROOMS ARE WELL-HIDDEN. SIGNAL'S ECHOING... DIFFICULT TO PINPOINT...
GOOD THING JACK AND I LEFT WHISTLEBLOWER MARKERS TO TARGET THIS SORT OF THING.
BIP BIP BIP

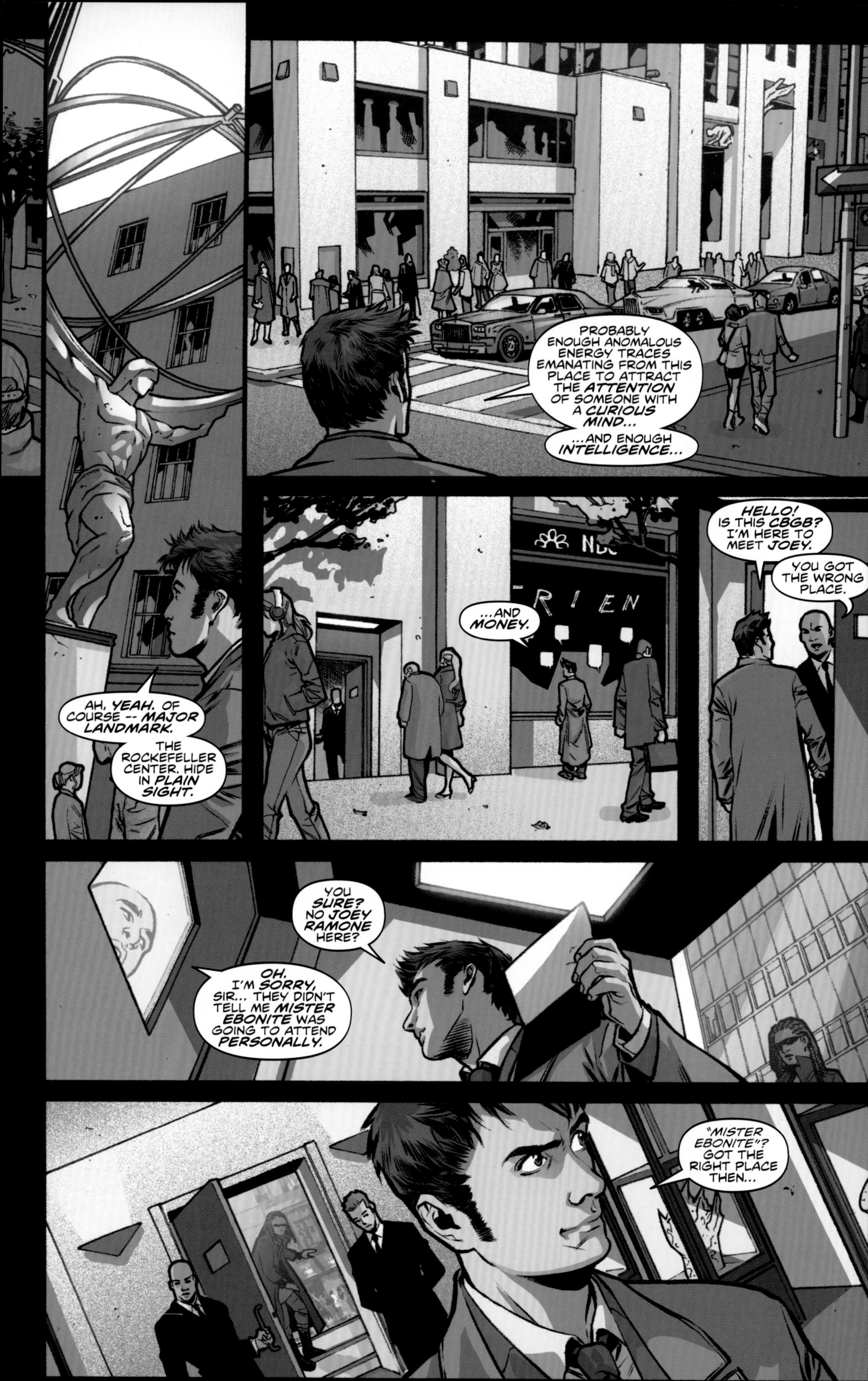
PROBABLY ENOUGH ANOMALOUS ENERGY TRACES EMANATING FROM THIS PLACE TO ATTRACT THE ATTENTION OF SOMEONE WITH A CURIOUS MIND...
...AND ENOUGH INTELLIGENCE...
AH, YEAH. OF COURSE -- MAJOR LANDMARK.
THE ROCKEFELLER CENTER. HIDE IN PLAIN SIGHT.
...AND MONEY.
HELLO! IS THIS CBGB? I'M HERE TO MEET JOEY.
YOU GOT THE WRONG PLACE.
YOU SURE? NO JOEY RAMONE HERE?
OH. I'M SORRY, SIR... THEY DIDN'T TELL ME MISTER EBONITE WAS GOING TO ATTEND PERSONALLY.
"MISTER EBONITE"? GOT THE RIGHT PLACE THEN...

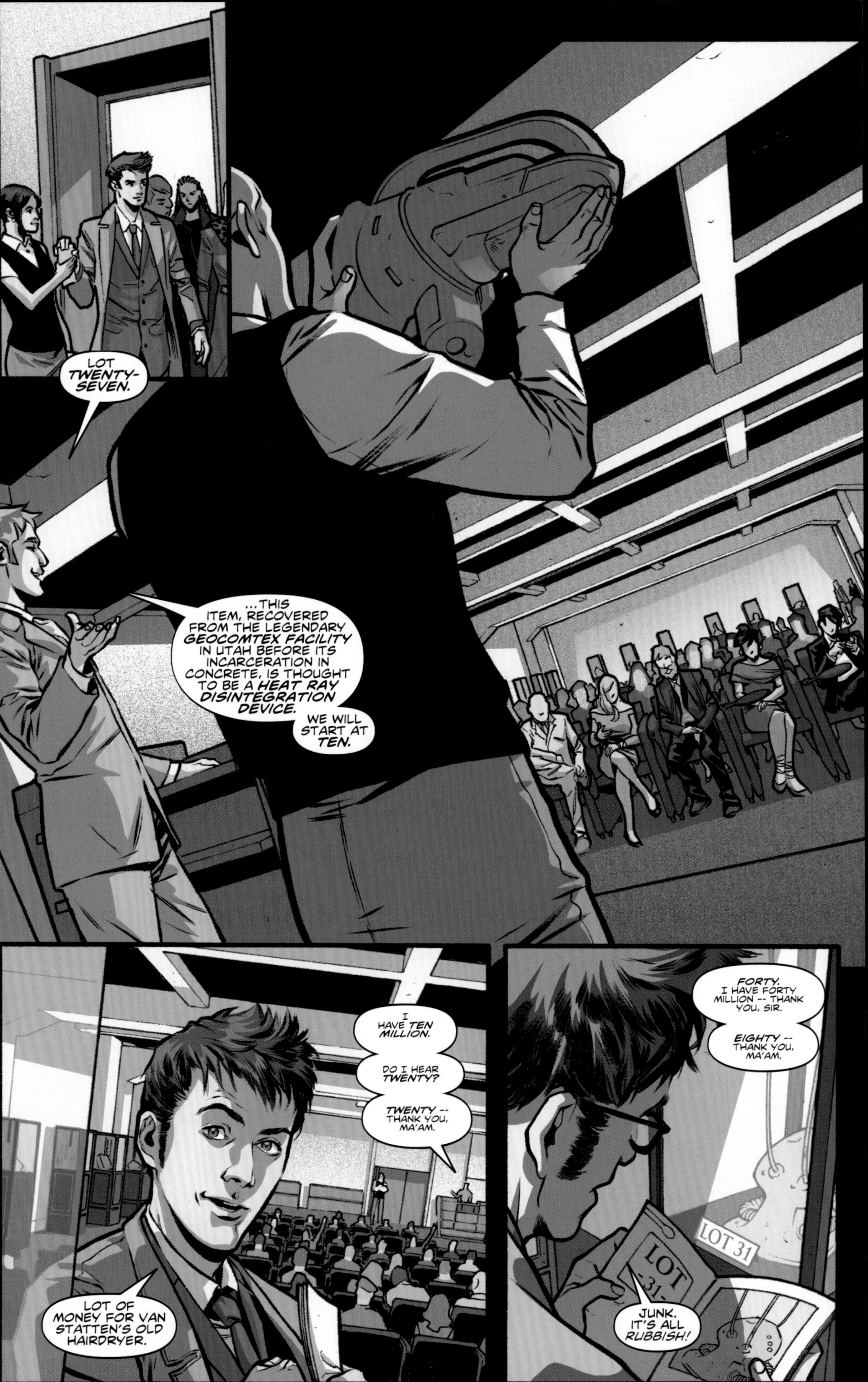
LOT TWENTY-SEVEN.
...THIS ITEM, RECOVERED FROM THE LEGENDARY GEOCOMTEX FACILITY IN UTAH BEFORE ITS INCARCERATION IN CONCRETE, IS THOUGHT TO BE A HEAT RAY DISINTEGRATION DEVICE.
WE WILL START AT TEN.
I HAVE TEN MILLION.
DO I HEAR TWENTY?
TWENTY -- THANK YOU, MA'AM.
LOT OF MONEY FOR VAN STATTEN'S OLD HAIRDRYER.
FORTY. I HAVE FORTY MILLION -- THANK YOU, SIR.
EIGHTY -- THANK YOU, MA'AM.
LOT 31
LOT -31-
JUNK. IT'S ALL RUBBISH!

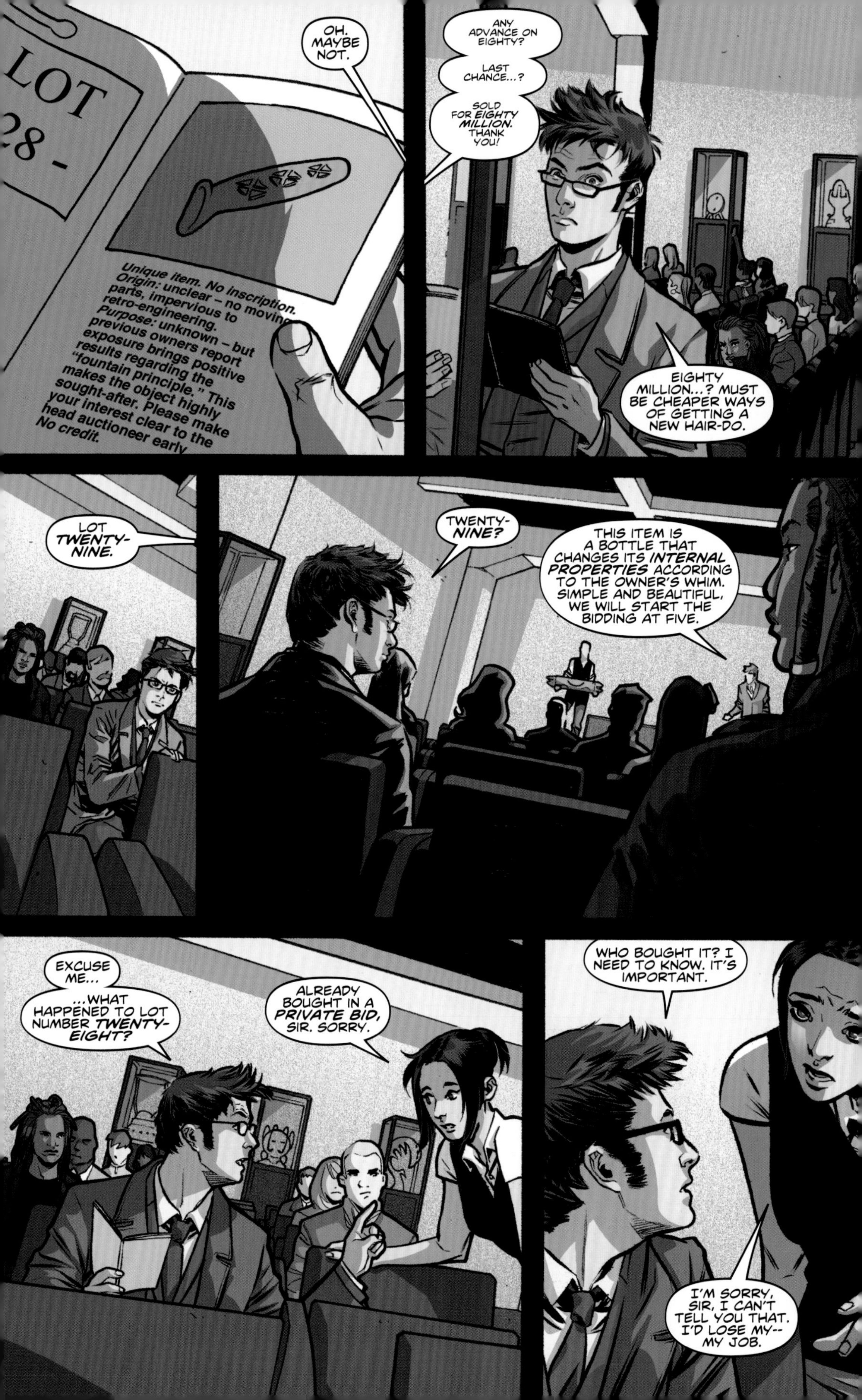
LOT
Unique item. No inscription. Origin: unclear – no movin parts, impervious to retro-engineering. Purpose: unknown – but previous owners report exposure brings positive results regarding the "fountain principle." This makes the object highly sought-after. Please make your interest clear to the head auctioneer early No credit.
OH. MAYBE NOT.
ANY ADVANCE ON EIGHTY?
LAST CHANCE...?
SOLD FOR EIGHTY MILLION. THANK YOU!
EIGHTY MILLION...? MUST BE CHEAPER WAYS OF GETTING A NEW HAIR-DO.
LOT TWENTY-NINE.
TWENTY-NINE?
THIS ITEM IS A BOTTLE THAT CHANGES ITS INTERNAL PROPERTIES ACCORDING TO THE OWNER'S WHIM. SIMPLE AND BEAUTIFUL, WE WILL START THE BIDDING AT FIVE.
EXCUSE ME...
...WHAT HAPPENED TO LOT NUMBER TWENTY-EIGHT?
ALREADY BOUGHT IN A PRIVATE BID, SIR. SORRY.
WHO BOUGHT IT? I NEED TO KNOW. IT'S IMPORTANT.
I'M SORRY, SIR, I CAN'T TELL YOU THAT. I'D LOSE MY-- MY JOB.

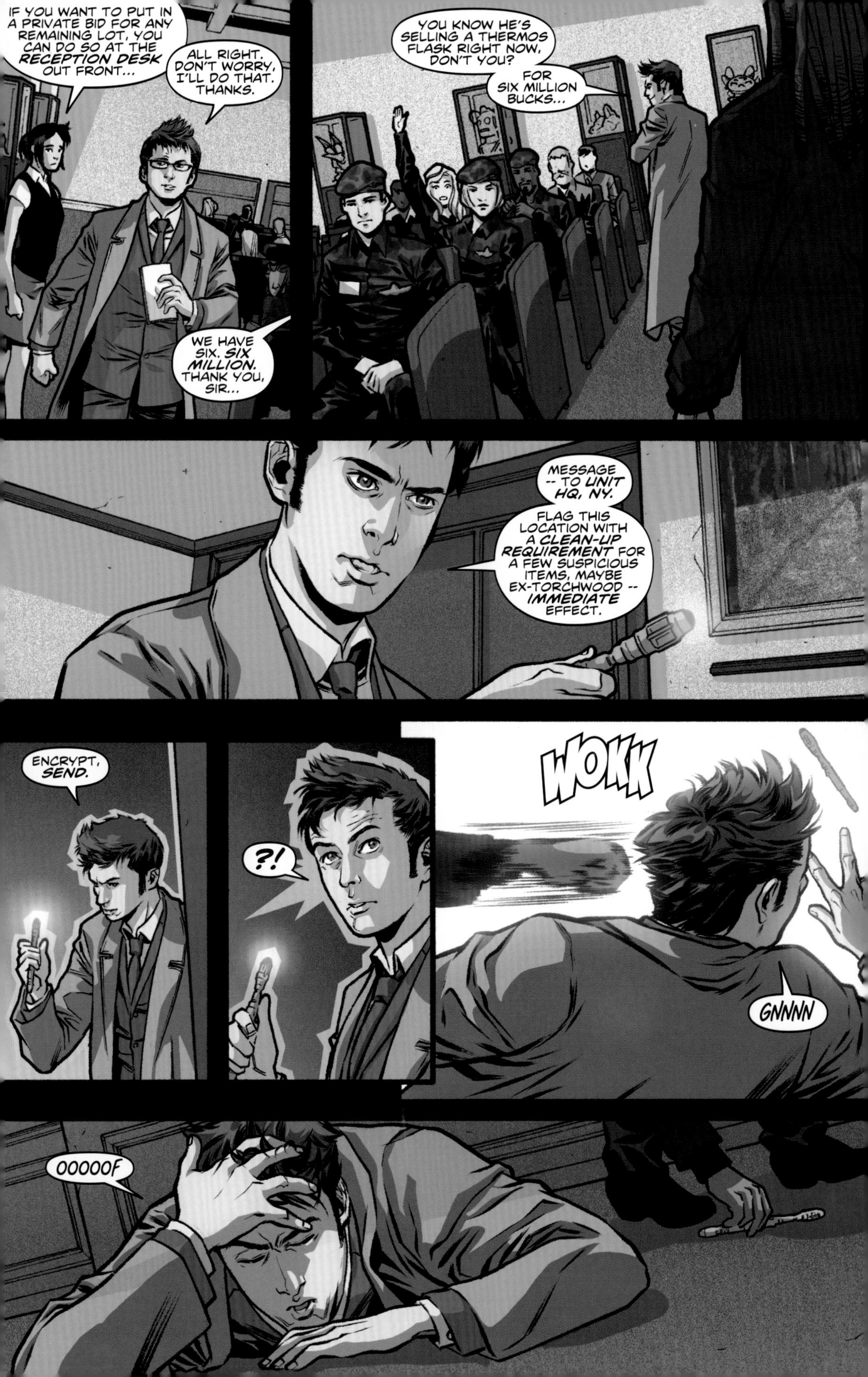
IF YOU WANT TO PUT IN A PRIVATE BID FOR ANY REMAINING LOT, YOU CAN DO SO AT THE RECEPTION DESK OUT FRONT...
ALL RIGHT. DON'T WORRY, I'LL DO THAT. THANKS.
WE HAVE SIX. SIX MILLION. THANK YOU, SIR...
YOU KNOW HE'S SELLING A THERMOS FLASK RIGHT NOW, DON'T YOU?
FOR SIX MILLION BUCKS...
MESSAGE -- TO UNIT HQ, NY.
FLAG THIS LOCATION WITH A CLEAN-UP REQUIREMENT FOR A FEW SUSPICIOUS ITEMS, MAYBE EX-TORCHWOOD -- IMMEDIATE EFFECT.
ENCRYPT, SEND.
?!
WOKK
GNNNN
OOOOOF

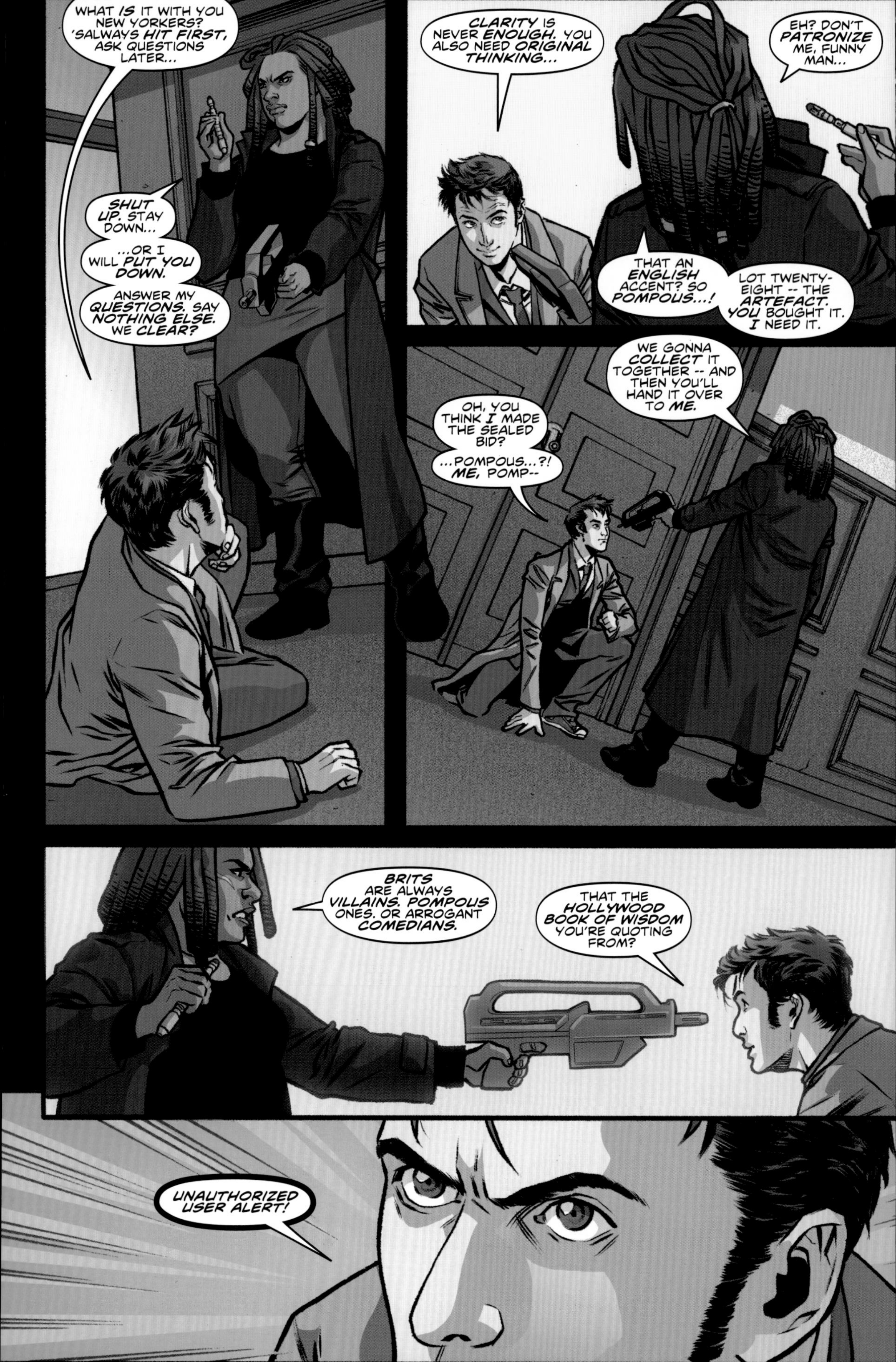
WHAT IS IT WITH YOU NEW YORKERS? 'SALWAYS HIT FIRST, ASK QUESTIONS LATER...
SHUT UP. STAY DOWN...
...OR I WILL PUT YOU DOWN.
ANSWER MY QUESTIONS. SAY NOTHING ELSE. WE CLEAR?
CLARITY IS NEVER ENOUGH. YOU ALSO NEED ORIGINAL THINKING...
EH? DON'T PATRONIZE ME, FUNNY MAN...
THAT AN ENGLISH ACCENT? SO POMPOUS...!
LOT TWENTY-EIGHT -- THE ARTEFACT. YOU BOUGHT IT. I NEED IT.
WE GONNA COLLECT IT TOGETHER -- AND THEN YOU'LL HAND IT OVER TO ME.
OH, YOU THINK I MADE THE SEALED BID?
...POMPOUS...?! ME, POMP--
BRITS ARE ALWAYS VILLAINS. POMPOUS ONES. OR ARROGANT COMEDIANS.
THAT THE HOLLYWOOD BOOK OF WISDOM YOU'RE QUOTING FROM?
UNAUTHORIZED USER ALERT!

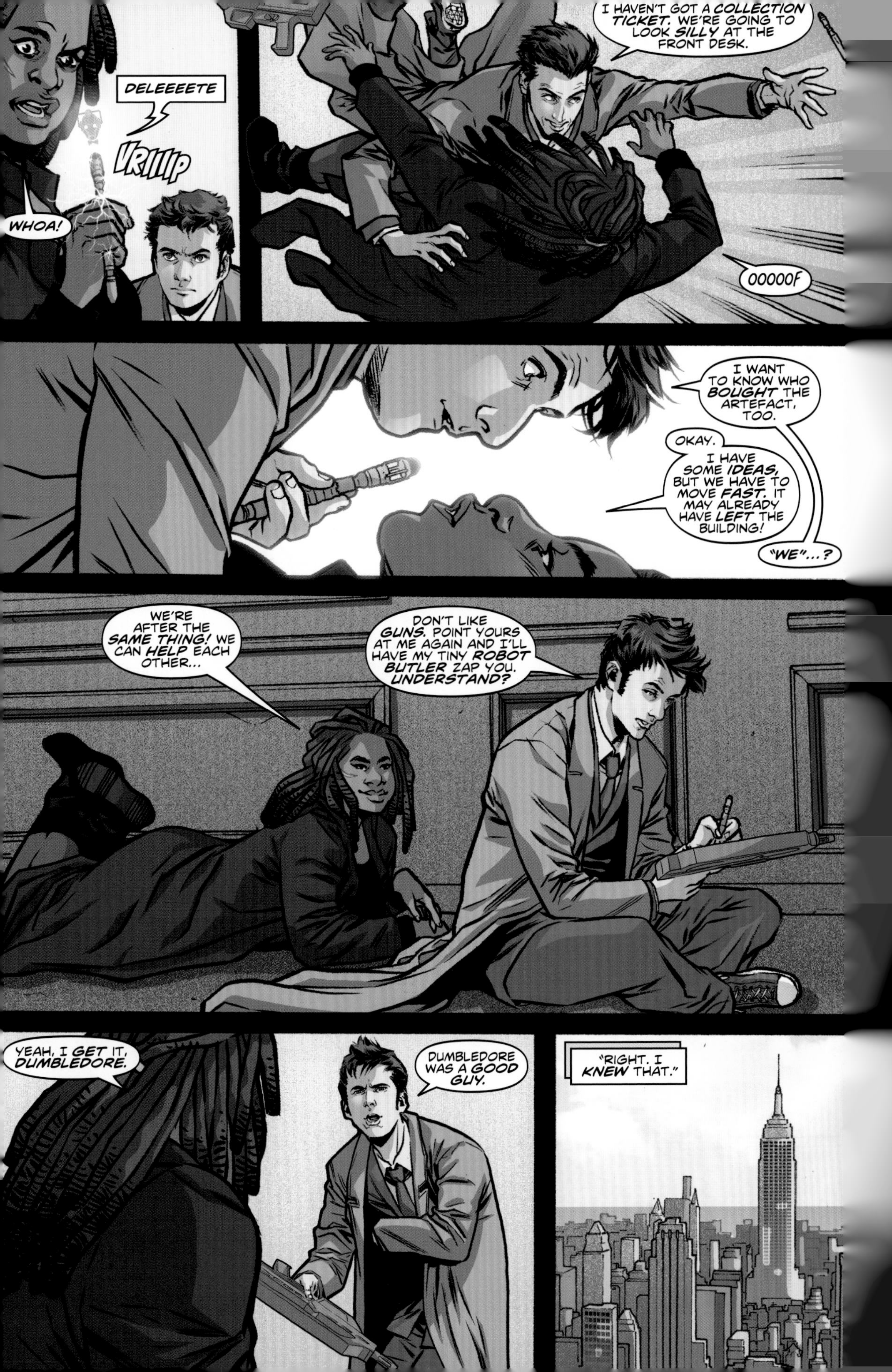

DELEEEETE
VRIIIP
WHOA!
I HAVEN'T GOT A COLLECTION TICKET. WE'RE GOING TO LOOK SILLY AT THE FRONT DESK.
OOOOOF
I WANT TO KNOW WHO BOUGHT THE ARTEFACT, TOO.
OKAY. I HAVE SOME IDEAS, BUT WE HAVE TO MOVE FAST. IT MAY ALREADY HAVE LEFT THE BUILDING!
"WE"...?
WE'RE AFTER THE SAME THING! WE CAN HELP EACH OTHER...
DON'T LIKE GUNS. POINT YOURS AT ME AGAIN AND I'LL HAVE MY TINY ROBOT BUTLER ZAP YOU. UNDERSTAND?
YEAH, I GET IT, DUMBLEDORE.
DUMBLEDORE WAS A GOOD GUY.
"RIGHT. I KNEW THAT."

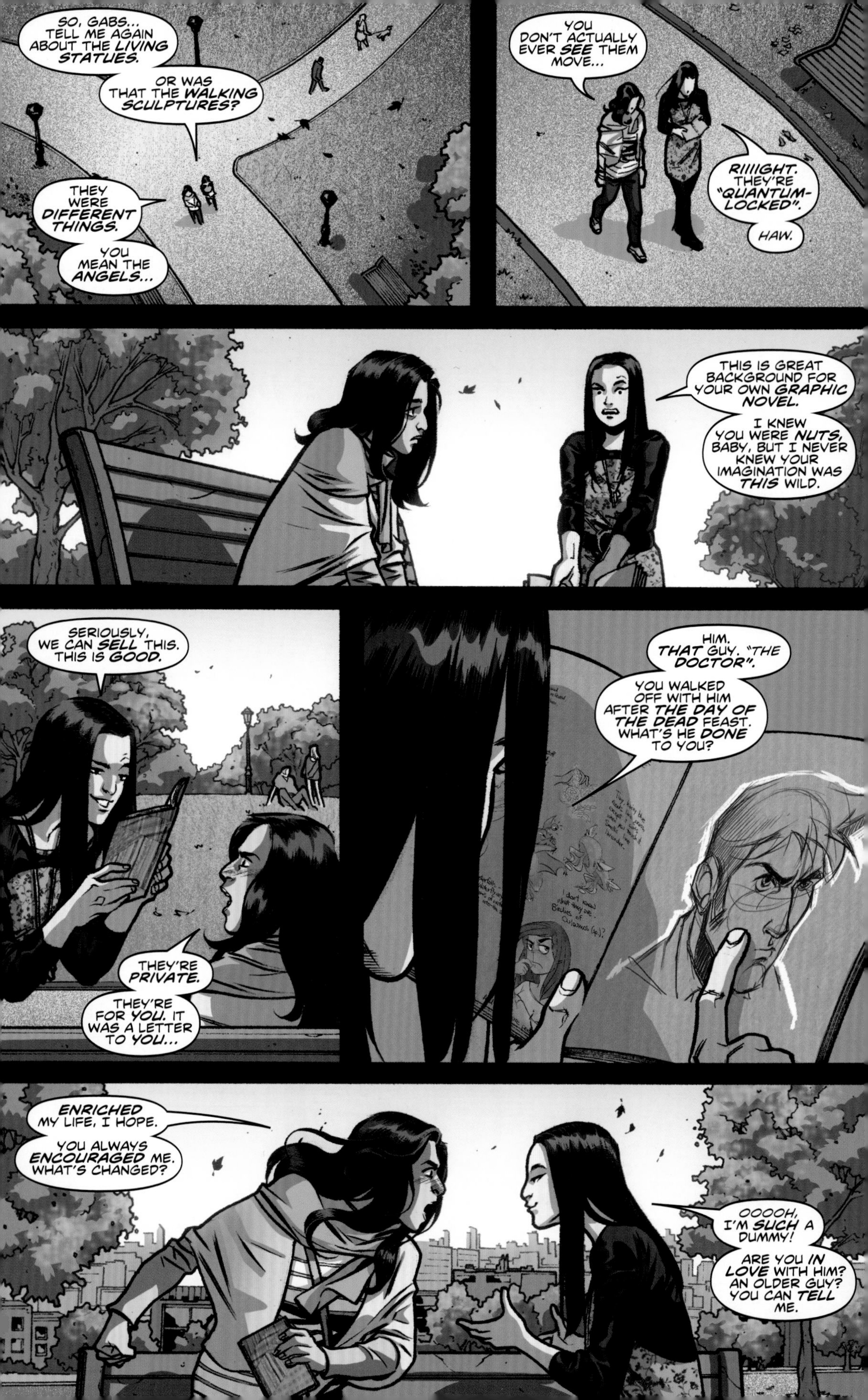
SO, GABS... TELL ME AGAIN ABOUT THE LIVING STATUES.
OR WAS THAT THE WALKING SCULPTURES?
THEY WERE DIFFERENT THINGS.
YOU MEAN THE ANGELS...
YOU DON'T ACTUALLY EVER SEE THEM MOVE...
RIIIGHT. THEY'RE "QUANTUM-LOCKED".
HAW.
THIS IS GREAT BACKGROUND FOR YOUR OWN GRAPHIC NOVEL.
I KNEW YOU WERE NUTS, BABY, BUT I NEVER KNEW YOUR IMAGINATION WAS THIS WILD.
SERIOUSLY, WE CAN SELL THIS. THIS IS GOOD.
THEY'RE PRIVATE.
THEY'RE FOR YOU. IT WAS A LETTER TO YOU...
HIM. THAT GUY. "THE DOCTOR".
YOU WALKED OFF WITH HIM AFTER THE DAY OF THE DEAD FEAST. WHAT'S HE DONE TO YOU?
ENRICHED MY LIFE, I HOPE.
YOU ALWAYS ENCOURAGED ME. WHAT'S CHANGED?
OOOOH, I'M SUCH A DUMMY!
ARE YOU IN LOVE WITH HIM? AN OLDER GUY? YOU CAN TELL ME.

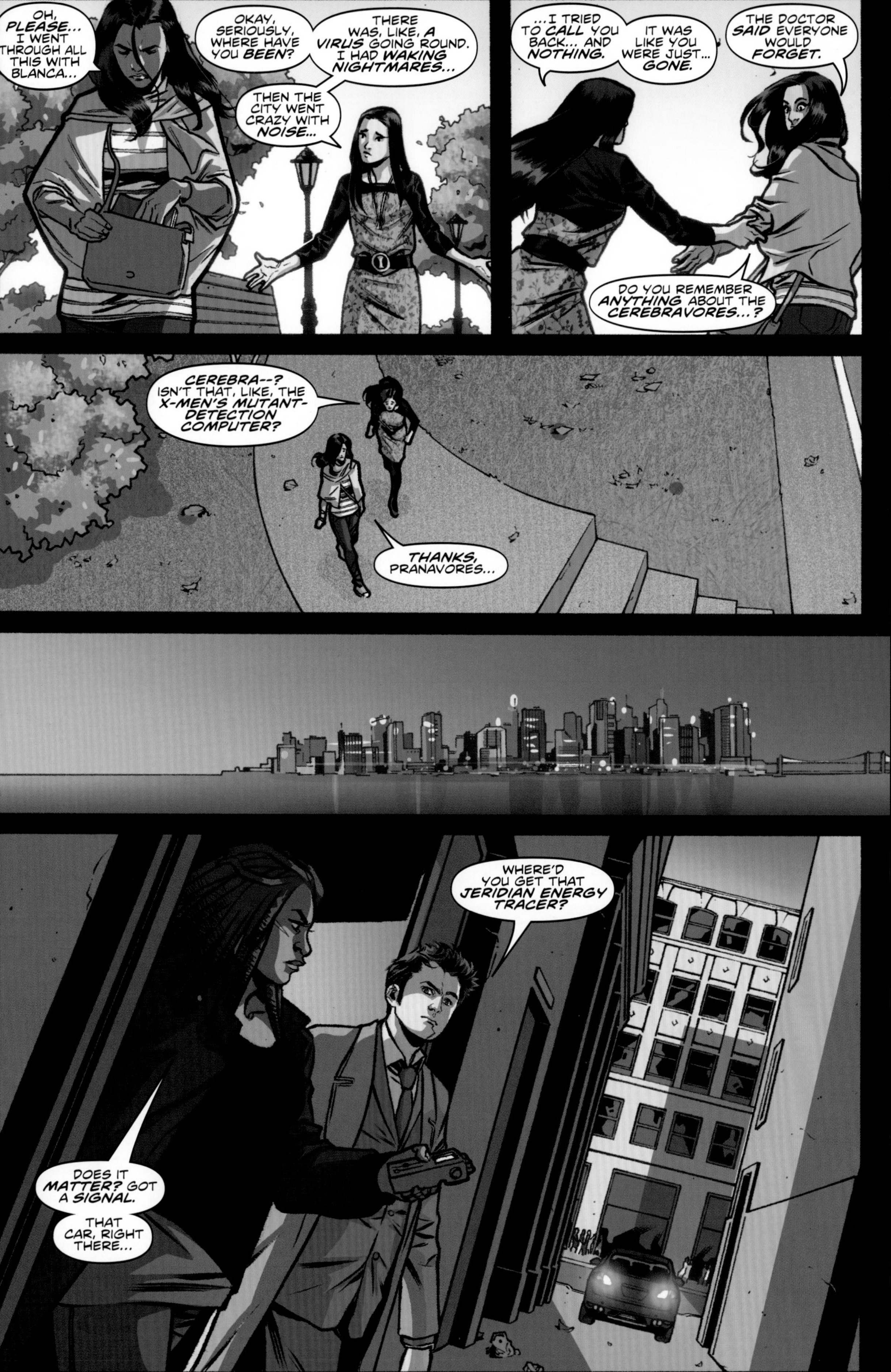
OH, PLEASE... I WENT THROUGH ALL THIS WITH BLANCA...
OKAY, SERIOUSLY, WHERE HAVE YOU BEEN?
THERE WAS, LIKE, A VIRUS GOING ROUND. I HAD WAKING NIGHTMARES...
THEN THE CITY WENT CRAZY WITH NOISE...
...I TRIED TO CALL YOU BACK... AND NOTHING.
IT WAS LIKE YOU WERE JUST... GONE.
THE DOCTOR SAID EVERYONE WOULD FORGET.
DO YOU REMEMBER ANYTHING ABOUT THE CEREBRAVORES...?
CEREBRA--? ISN'T THAT, LIKE, THE X-MEN'S MUTANT-DETECTION COMPUTER?
THANKS, PRANAVORES...
WHERE'D YOU GET THAT JERIDIAN ENERGY TRACER?
DOES IT MATTER? GOT A SIGNAL.
THAT CAR, RIGHT THERE...

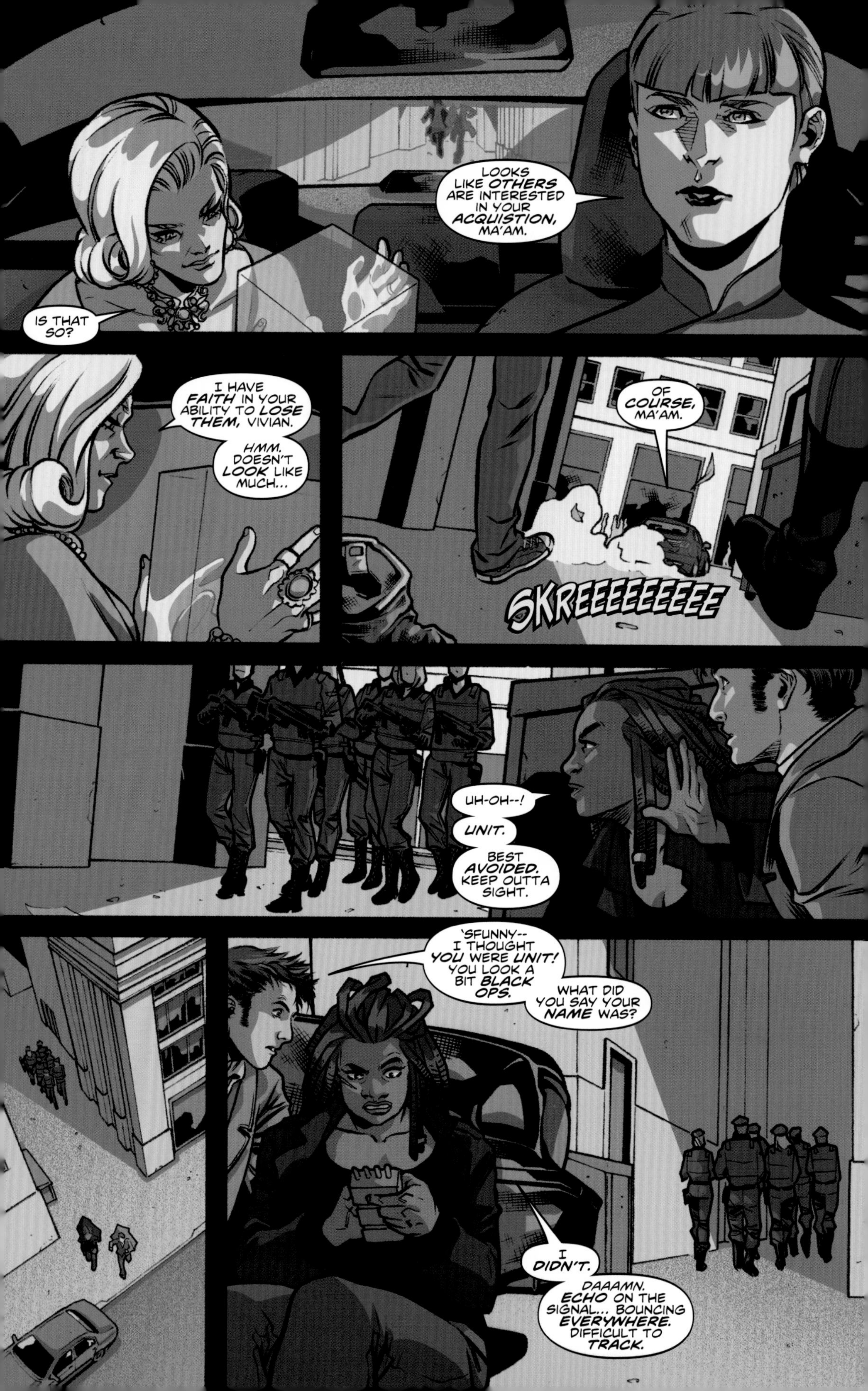

LOOKS LIKE OTHERS ARE INTERESTED IN YOUR ACQUISTION, MA'AM.
IS THAT SO?
I HAVE FAITH IN YOUR ABILITY TO LOSE THEM, VIVIAN.
HMM. DOESN'T LOOK LIKE MUCH...
OF COURSE, MA'AM.
SKREEEEEEEEE
UH-OH--!
UNIT.
BEST AVOIDED. KEEP OUTTA SIGHT.
'SFUNNY-- I THOUGHT YOU WERE UNIT! YOU LOOK A BIT BLACK OPS.
WHAT DID YOU SAY YOUR NAME WAS?
I DIDN'T.
DAAAMN. ECHO ON THE SIGNAL... BOUNCING EVERYWHERE. DIFFICULT TO TRACK.

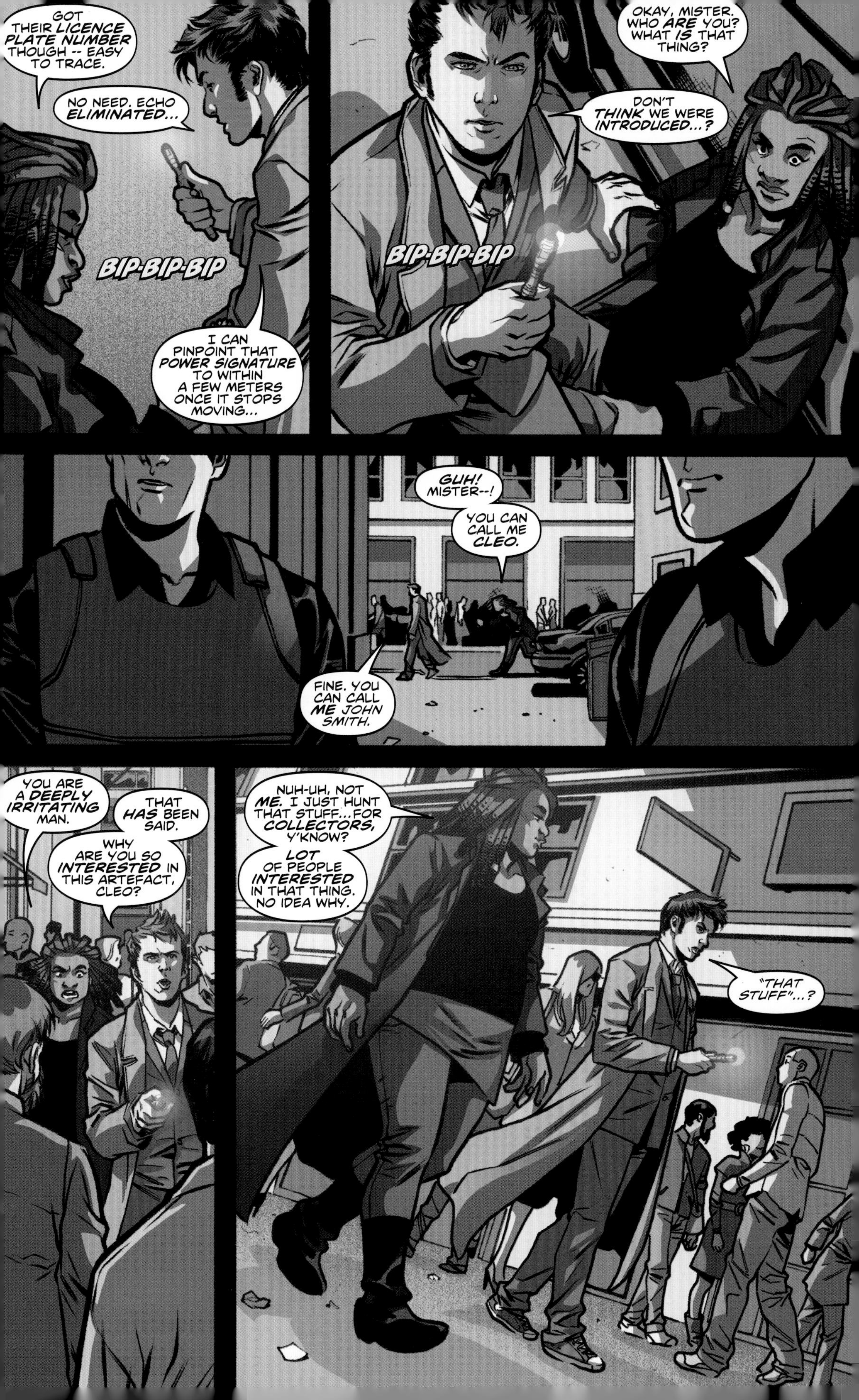

GOT THEIR LICENCE PLATE NUMBER THOUGH -- EASY TO TRACE.
NO NEED. ECHO ELIMINATED...
BIP-BIP-BIP
I CAN PINPOINT THAT POWER SIGNATURE TO WITHIN A FEW METERS ONCE IT STOPS MOVING...
OKAY, MISTER. WHO ARE YOU? WHAT IS THAT THING?
DON'T THINK WE WERE INTRODUCED...?
BIP-BIP-BIP
GUH! MISTER--!
YOU CAN CALL ME CLEO.
FINE. YOU CAN CALL ME JOHN SMITH.
YOU ARE A DEEPLY IRRITATING MAN.
THAT HAS BEEN SAID.
WHY ARE YOU SO INTERESTED IN THIS ARTEFACT, CLEO?
NUH-UH, NOT ME. I JUST HUNT THAT STUFF...FOR COLLECTORS, Y'KNOW?
LOT OF PEOPLE INTERESTED IN THAT THING. NO IDEA WHY.
"THAT STUFF"...?

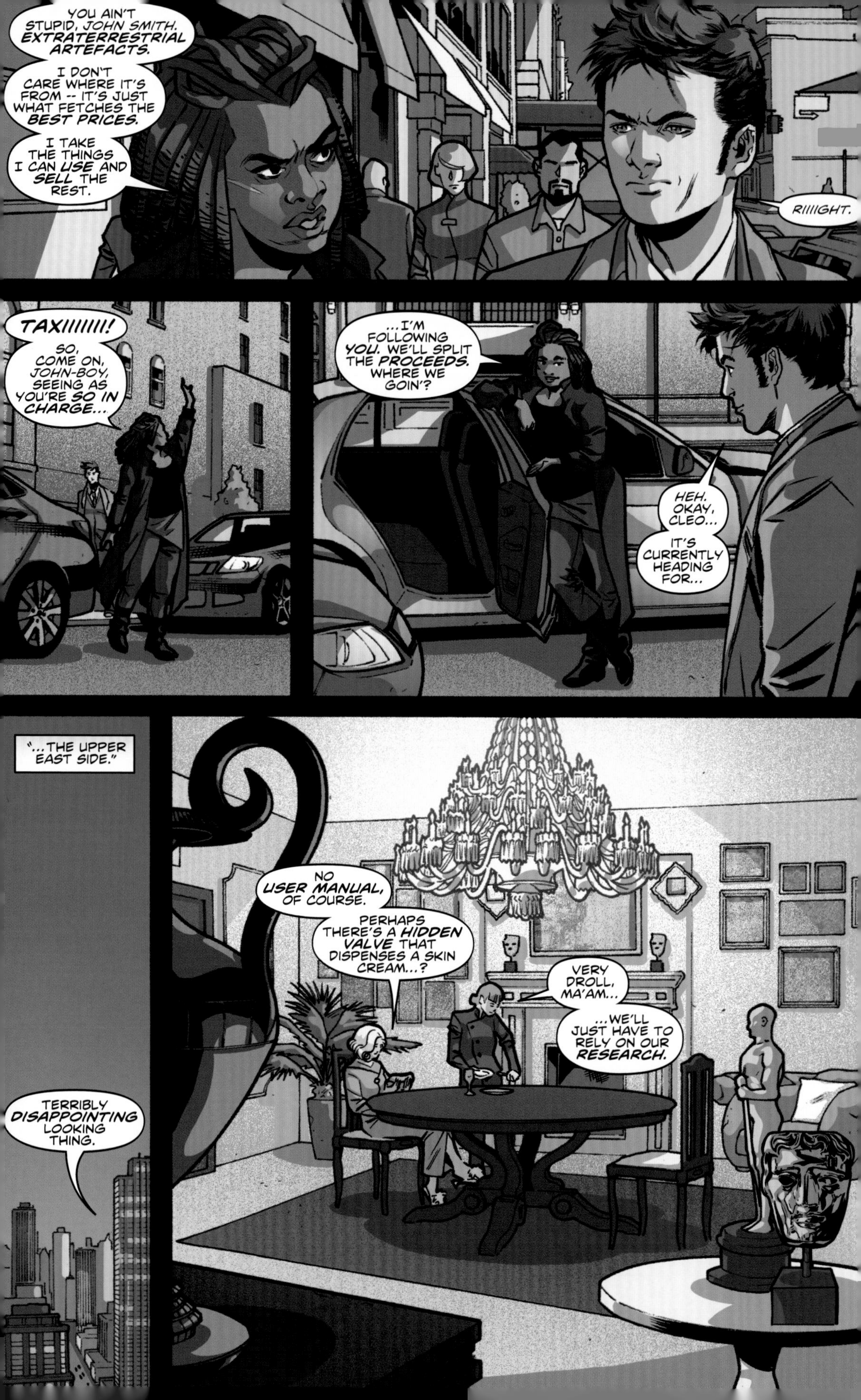
YOU AIN'T STUPID, JOHN SMITH. EXTRATERRESTRIAL ARTEFACTS.
I DON'T CARE WHERE IT'S FROM -- IT'S JUST WHAT FETCHES THE BEST PRICES.
I TAKE THE THINGS I CAN USE AND SELL THE REST.
RIIIIGHT.
TAXIIIIIII!
SO, COME ON, JOHN-BOY, SEEING AS YOU'RE SO IN CHARGE...
...I'M FOLLOWING YOU. WE'LL SPLIT THE PROCEEDS. WHERE WE GOIN'?
HEH. OKAY, CLEO...
IT'S CURRENTLY HEADING FOR...
"...THE UPPER EAST SIDE."
TERRIBLY DISAPPOINTING LOOKING THING.
NO USER MANUAL, OF COURSE.
PERHAPS THERE'S A HIDDEN VALVE THAT DISPENSES A SKIN CREAM...?
VERY DROLL, MA'AM...
...WE'LL JUST HAVE TO RELY ON OUR RESEARCH.

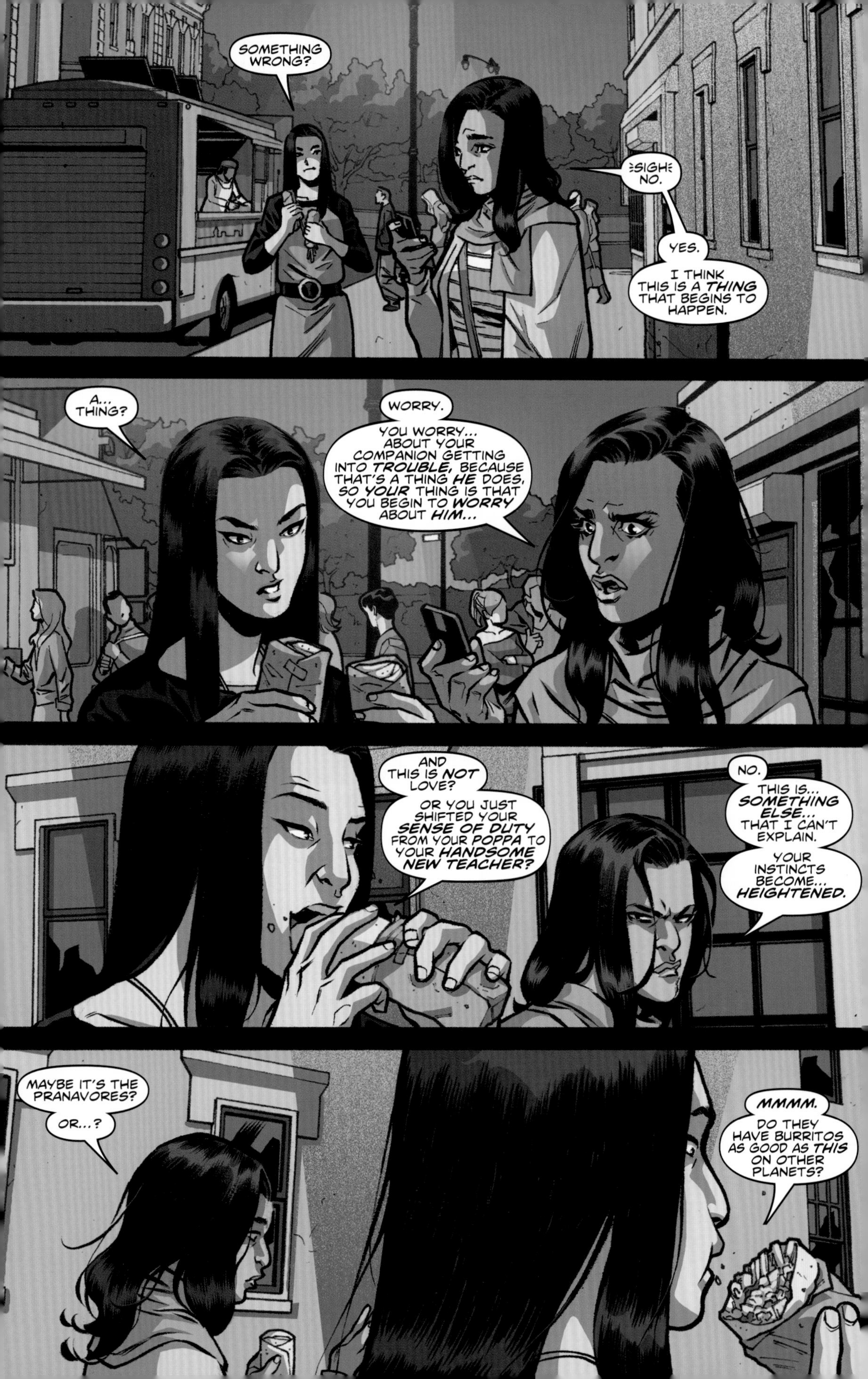
SOMETHING WRONG?
SIGH
NO.
YES.
I THINK THIS IS A *THING* THAT BEGINS TO HAPPEN.
A... THING?
WORRY.
YOU WORRY... ABOUT YOUR COMPANION GETTING INTO *TROUBLE,* BECAUSE THAT'S A THING *HE* DOES, SO *YOUR* THING IS THAT YOU BEGIN TO *WORRY* ABOUT *HIM...*
AND THIS IS *NOT* LOVE?
OR YOU JUST SHIFTED YOUR *SENSE OF DUTY* FROM YOUR *POPPA* TO YOUR *HANDSOME NEW TEACHER?*
NO.
THIS IS... *SOMETHING ELSE...* THAT I CAN'T EXPLAIN.
YOUR INSTINCTS BECOME... *HEIGHTENED.*
MAYBE IT'S THE PRANAVORES?
OR...?
MMMM.
DO THEY HAVE BURRITOS AS GOOD AS *THIS* ON OTHER PLANETS?

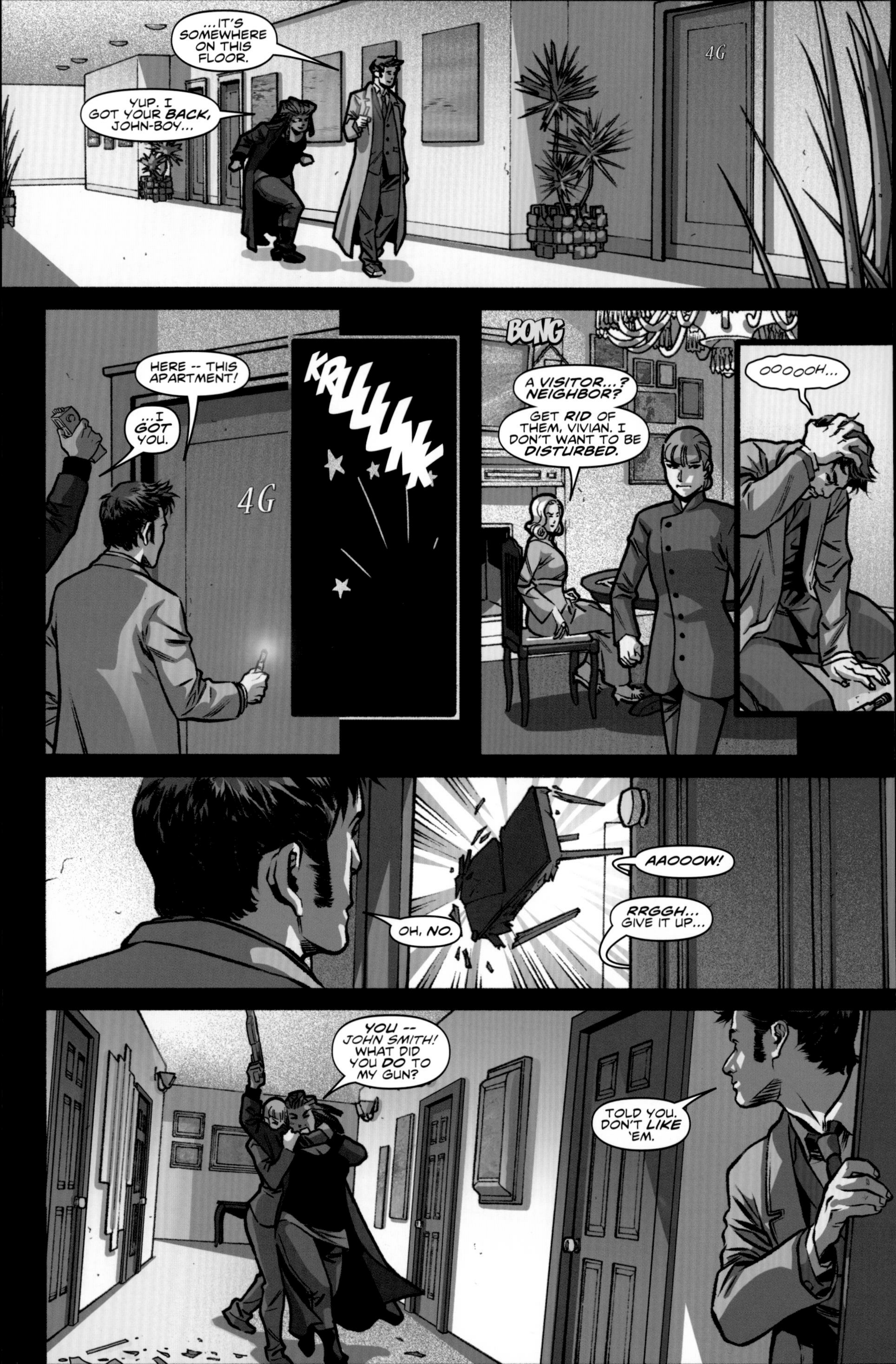
...IT'S SOMEWHERE ON THIS FLOOR.
YUP. I GOT YOUR BACK, JOHN-BOY...
4G
HERE -- THIS APARTMENT!
...I GOT YOU.
4G
KRUUUNK
BONG
A VISITOR...? NEIGHBOR?
GET RID OF THEM, VIVIAN. I DON'T WANT TO BE DISTURBED.
OOOOOH...
OH, NO.
AAOOOW!
RRGGH... GIVE IT UP...
YOU -- JOHN SMITH! WHAT DID YOU DO TO MY GUN?
TOLD YOU. DON'T LIKE 'EM.

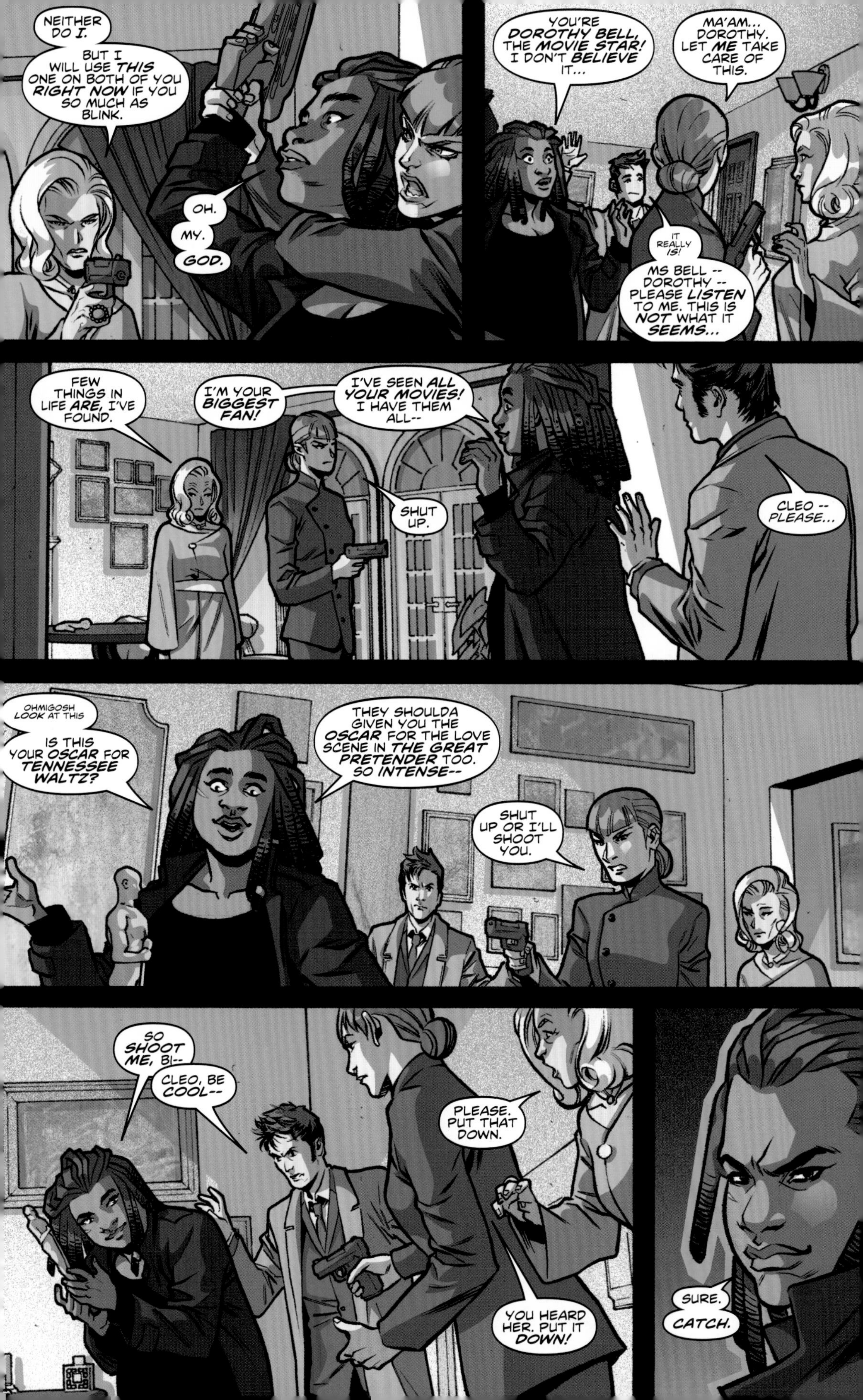
NEITHER DO I.
BUT I WILL USE THIS ONE ON BOTH OF YOU RIGHT NOW IF YOU SO MUCH AS BLINK.
OH.
MY.
GOD.
YOU'RE DOROTHY BELL, THE MOVIE STAR! I DON'T BELIEVE IT...
MA'AM... DOROTHY. LET ME TAKE CARE OF THIS.
IT REALLY IS!
MS BELL -- DOROTHY -- PLEASE LISTEN TO ME. THIS IS NOT WHAT IT SEEMS...
FEW THINGS IN LIFE ARE, I'VE FOUND.
I'M YOUR BIGGEST FAN!
I'VE SEEN ALL YOUR MOVIES! I HAVE THEM ALL--
SHUT UP.
CLEO -- PLEASE...
OHMIGOSH LOOK AT THIS
IS THIS YOUR OSCAR FOR TENNESSEE WALTZ?
THEY SHOULDA GIVEN YOU THE OSCAR FOR THE LOVE SCENE IN THE GREAT PRETENDER TOO. SO INTENSE--
SHUT UP OR I'LL SHOOT YOU.
SO SHOOT ME, BI--
CLEO, BE COOL--
PLEASE. PUT THAT DOWN.
YOU HEARD HER. PUT IT DOWN!
SURE.
CATCH.

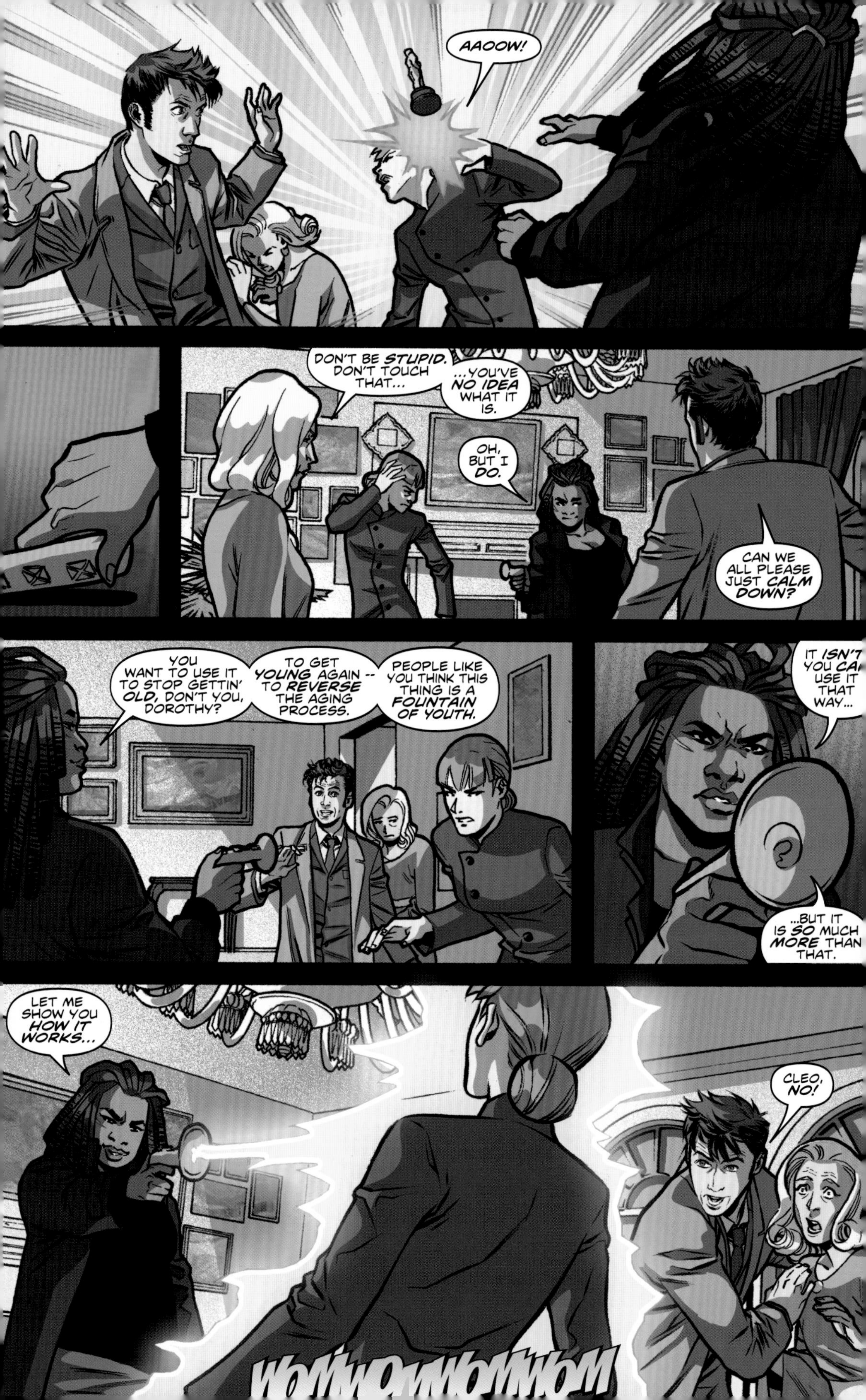
AAOOW!
DON'T BE STUPID. DON'T TOUCH THAT...
...YOU'VE NO IDEA WHAT IT IS.
OH, BUT I DO.
CAN WE ALL PLEASE JUST CALM DOWN?
YOU WANT TO USE IT TO STOP GETTIN' OLD, DON'T YOU, DOROTHY?
TO GET YOUNG AGAIN -- TO REVERSE THE AGING PROCESS.
PEOPLE LIKE YOU THINK THIS THING IS A FOUNTAIN OF YOUTH.
...BUT IT IS SO MUCH MORE THAN THAT.
LET ME SHOW YOU HOW IT WORKS...
CLEO, NO!
WOMWOMWOMWOM

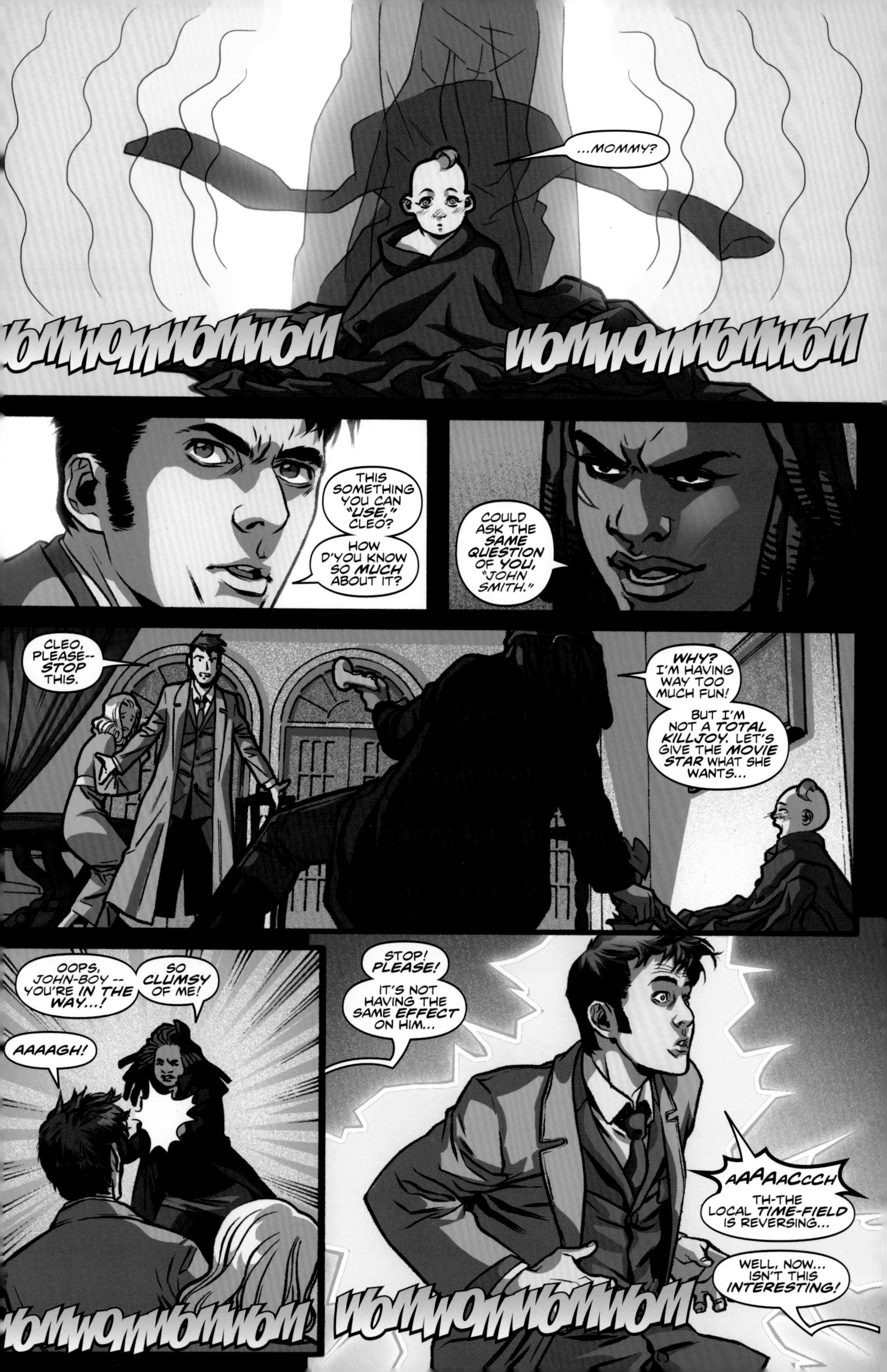
...MOMMY?
WOMWOMWOMWOM
WOMWOMWOMWOMWOM
THIS SOMETHING YOU CAN "USE," CLEO?
HOW D'YOU KNOW SO MUCH ABOUT IT?
COULD ASK THE SAME QUESTION OF YOU, "JOHN SMITH."
CLEO, PLEASE-- STOP THIS.
WHY? I'M HAVING WAY TOO MUCH FUN!
BUT I'M NOT A TOTAL KILLJOY. LET'S GIVE THE MOVIE STAR WHAT SHE WANTS...
OOPS, JOHN-BOY -- YOU'RE IN THE WAY...!
SO CLUMSY OF ME!
AAAAGH!
STOP! PLEASE!
IT'S NOT HAVING THE SAME EFFECT ON HIM...
AAAAACCCH
TH-THE LOCAL TIME-FIELD IS REVERSING...
WELL, NOW... ISN'T THIS INTERESTING!
WOMWOMWOMWOM
WOMWOMWOMWOMWOM

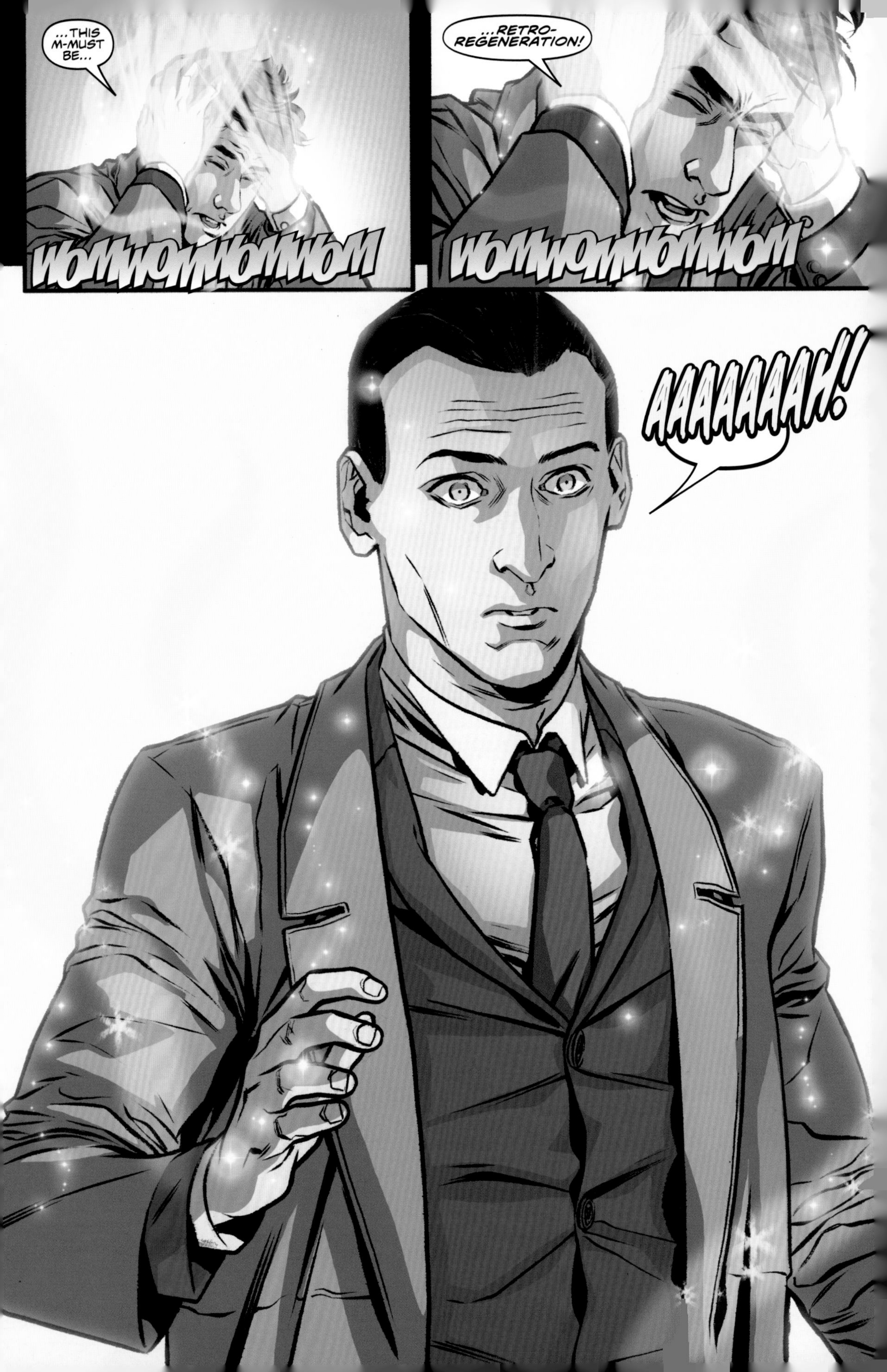
...THIS M-MUST BE...
WOMWOMWOMWOM
...RETRO-REGENERATION!
WOMWOMWOMWOM
AAAAAAAH!

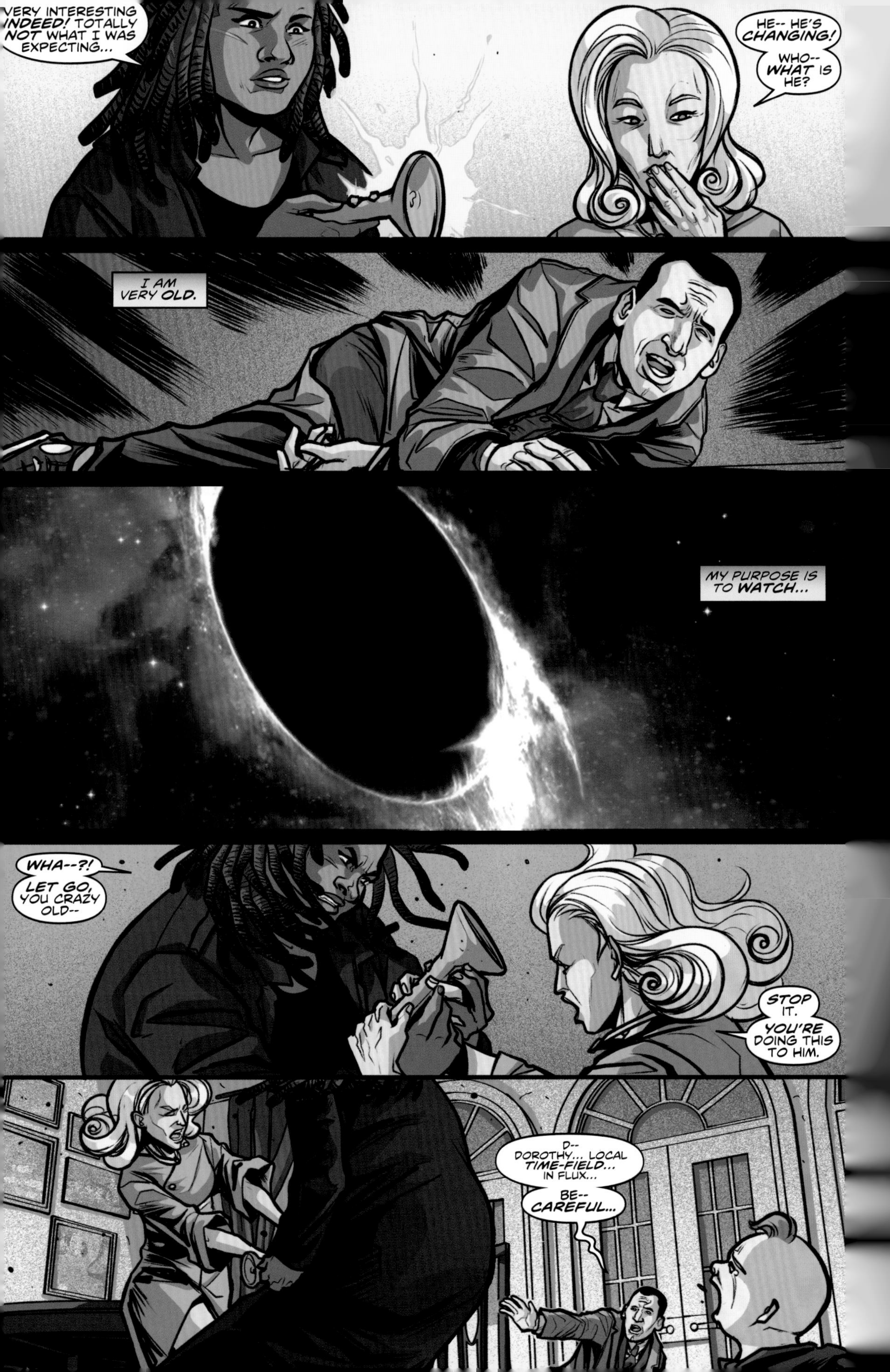
VERY INTERESTING INDEED! TOTALLY NOT WHAT I WAS EXPECTING...
HE-- HE'S CHANGING!
WHO-- WHAT IS HE?
I AM VERY OLD.
MY PURPOSE IS TO WATCH...
WHA--?!
LET GO, YOU CRAZY OLD--
STOP IT.
YOU'RE DOING THIS TO HIM.
D-- DOROTHY... LOCAL TIME-FIELD... IN FLUX...
BE-- CAREFUL...

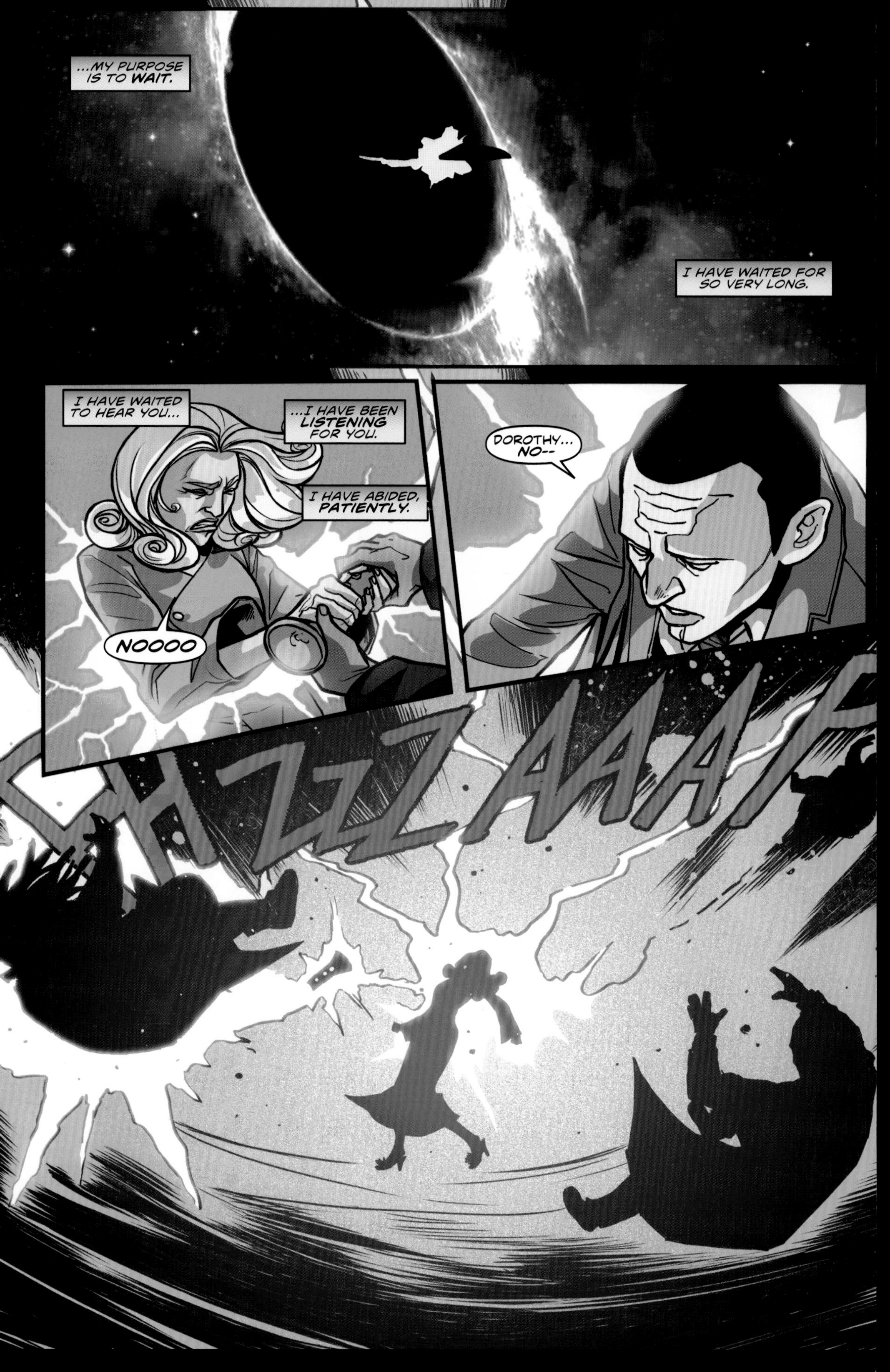

...MY PURPOSE IS TO WAIT.
I HAVE WAITED FOR SO VERY LONG.
I HAVE WAITED TO HEAR YOU...
...I HAVE BEEN LISTENING FOR YOU.
I HAVE ABIDED, PATIENTLY.
NOOOO
DOROTHY... NO--

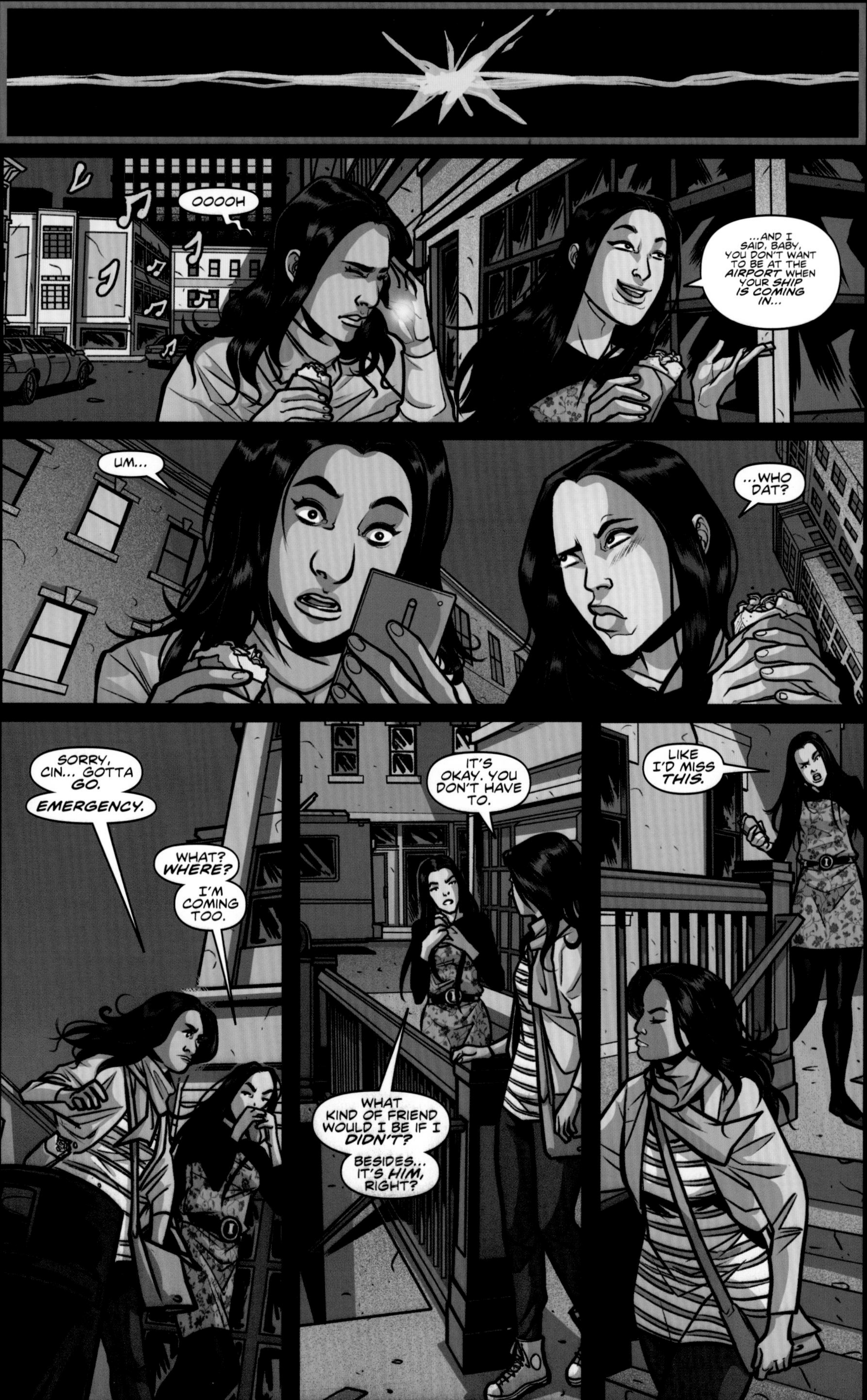
OOOOH
...AND I SAID, BABY, YOU DON'T WANT TO BE AT THE AIRPORT WHEN YOUR SHIP IS COMING IN...
UM...
...WHO DAT?
SORRY, CIN... GOTTA GO.
EMERGENCY.
WHAT? WHERE?
I'M COMING TOO.
IT'S OKAY. YOU DON'T HAVE TO.
WHAT KIND OF FRIEND WOULD I BE IF I DIDN'T?
BESIDES... IT'S HIM, RIGHT?
LIKE I'D MISS THIS.

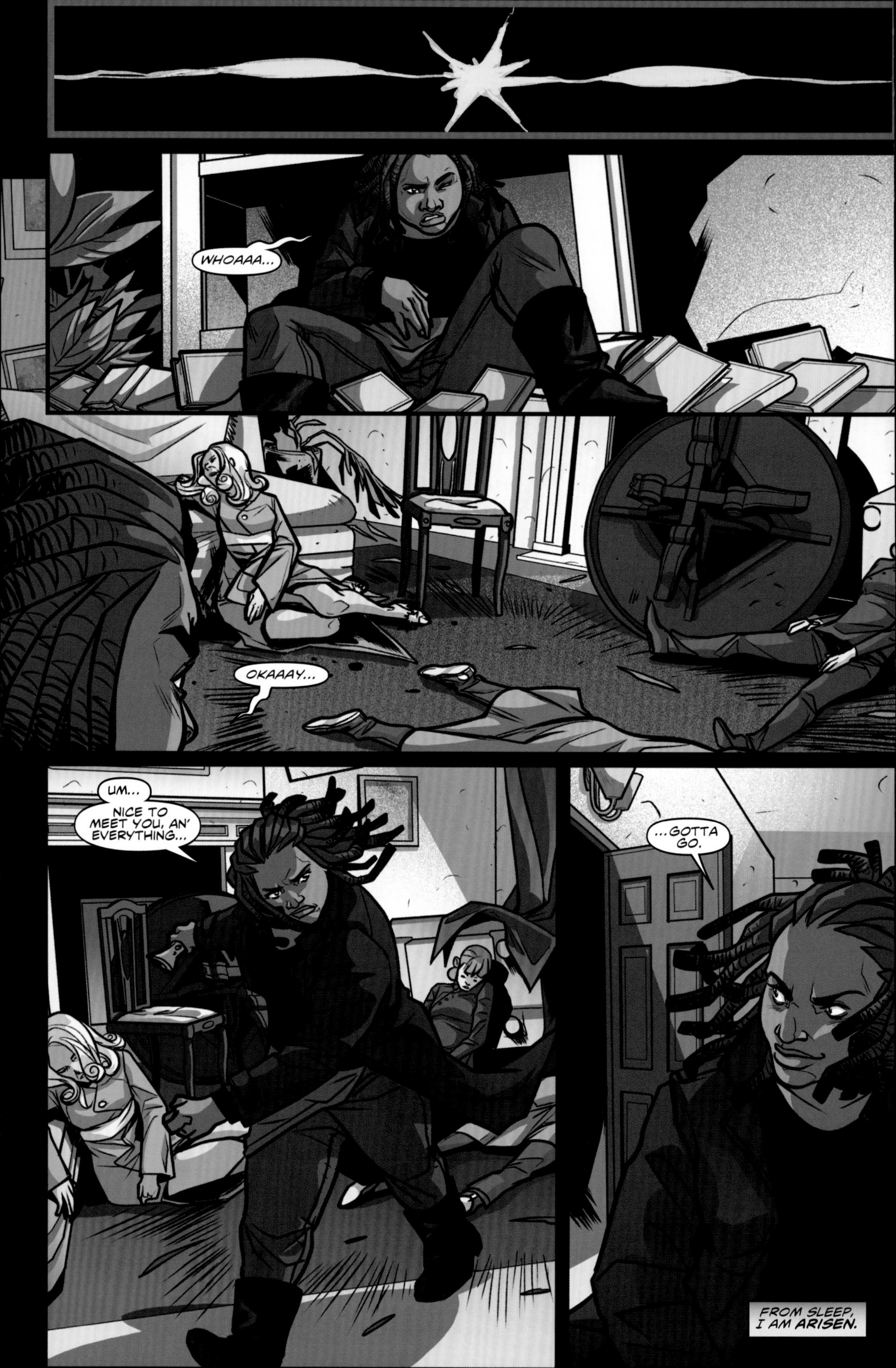
WHOAAA...
OKAAAY...
UM...
NICE TO MEET YOU, AN' EVERYTHING...
...GOTTA GO.
FROM SLEEP, I AM ARISEN.

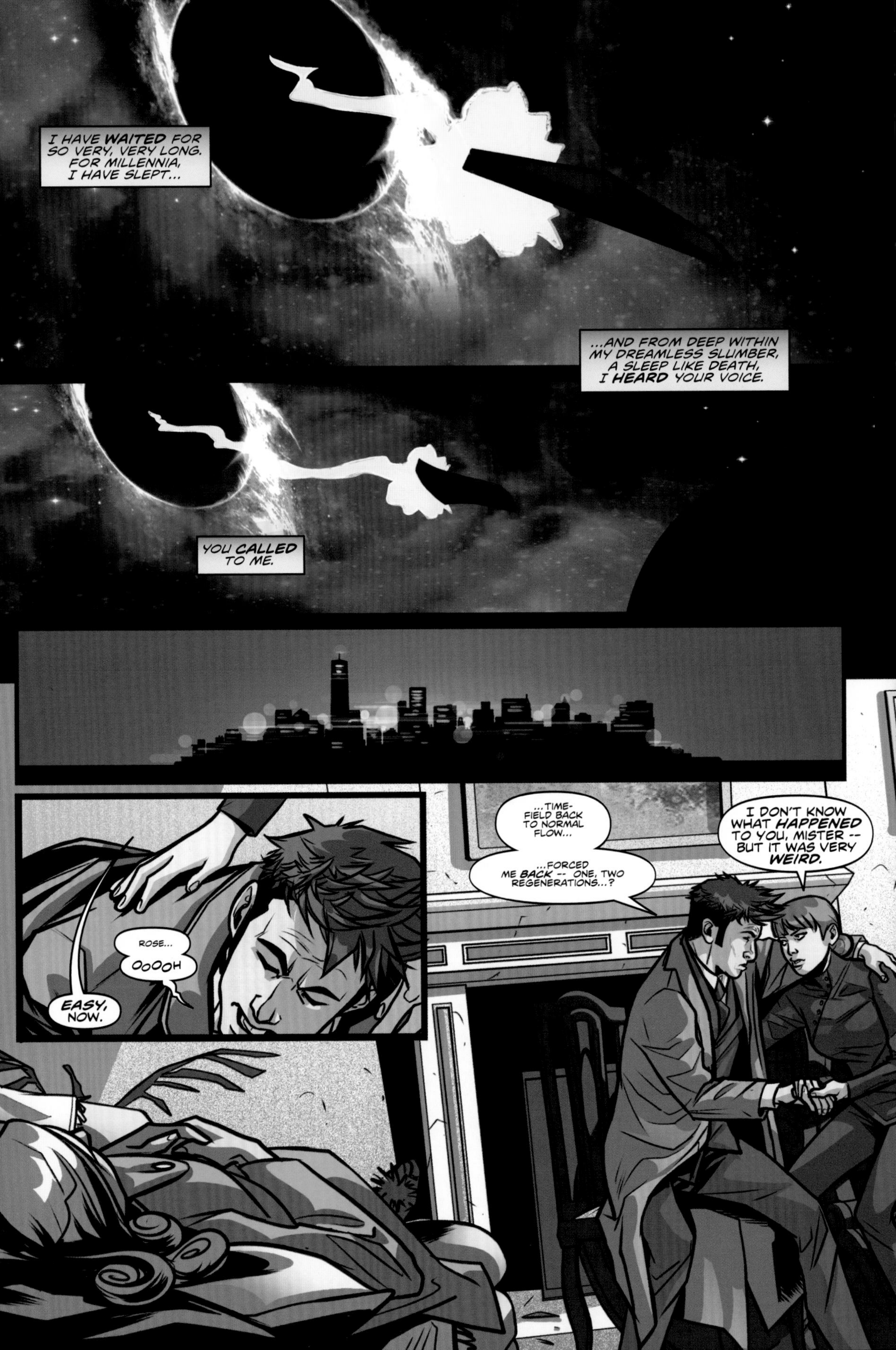
I HAVE **WAITED** FOR SO VERY, VERY LONG. FOR MILLENNIA, I HAVE SLEPT...
...AND FROM DEEP WITHIN MY DREAMLESS SLUMBER, A SLEEP LIKE DEATH, I **HEARD** YOUR VOICE.
YOU **CALLED** TO ME.
ROSE...
OOOOH
EASY, NOW.
...TIME-FIELD BACK TO NORMAL FLOW...
...FORCED ME **BACK** -- ONE, TWO REGENERATIONS...?
I DON'T KNOW WHAT **HAPPENED** TO YOU, MISTER -- BUT IT WAS VERY **WEIRD.**

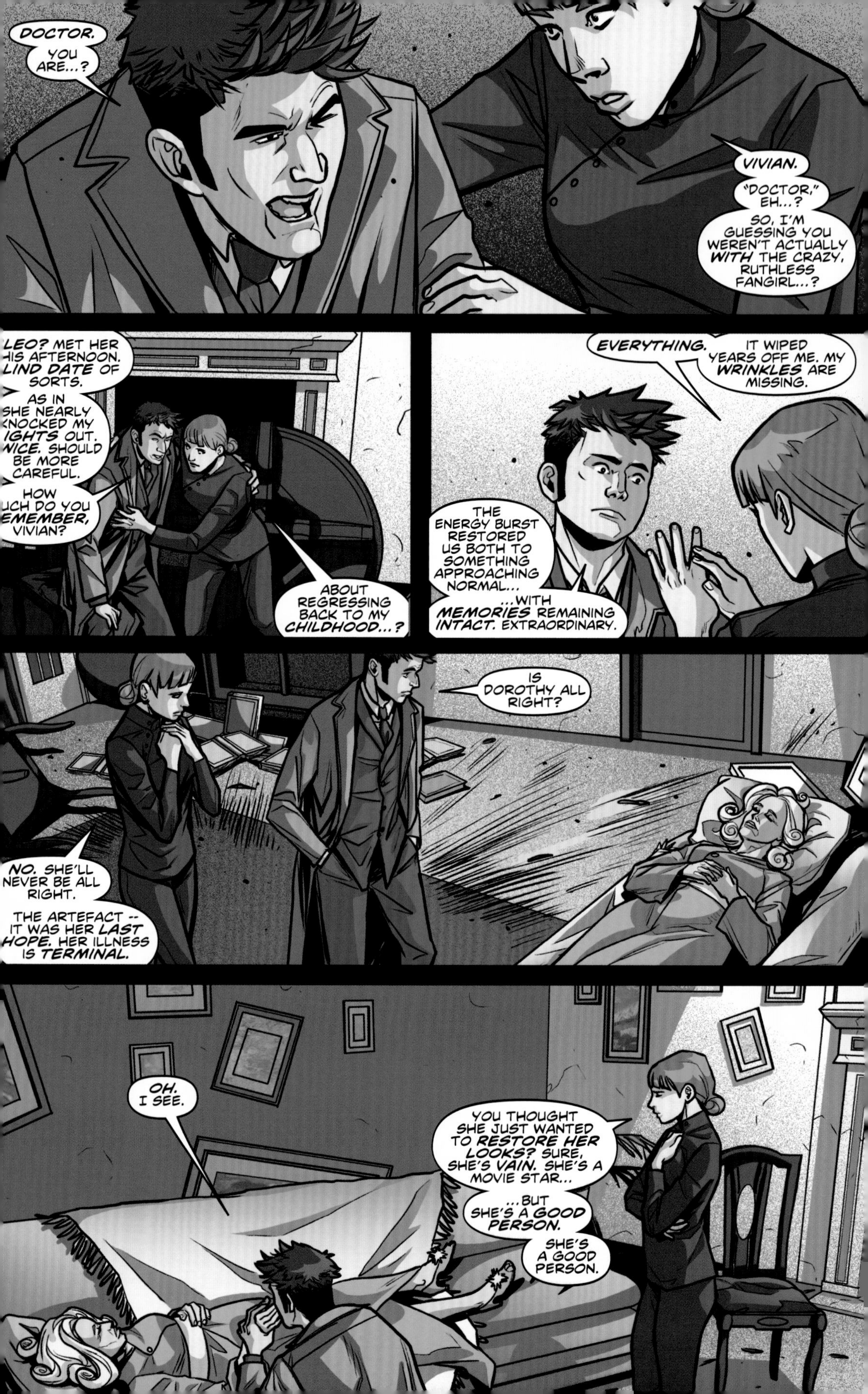
DOCTOR.
YOU ARE...?
VIVIAN.
"DOCTOR," EH...?
SO, I'M GUESSING YOU WEREN'T ACTUALLY WITH THE CRAZY, RUTHLESS FANGIRL...?
LEO? MET HER HIS AFTERNOON. LIND DATE OF SORTS.
AS IN SHE NEARLY KNOCKED MY IGHTS OUT. NICE. SHOULD BE MORE CAREFUL.
HOW UCH DO YOU EMEMBER, VIVIAN?
ABOUT REGRESSING BACK TO MY CHILDHOOD...?
EVERYTHING.
IT WIPED YEARS OFF ME. MY WRINKLES ARE MISSING.
THE ENERGY BURST RESTORED US BOTH TO SOMETHING APPROACHING NORMAL...
...WITH MEMORIES REMAINING INTACT. EXTRAORDINARY.
IS DOROTHY ALL RIGHT?
NO. SHE'LL NEVER BE ALL RIGHT.
THE ARTEFACT -- IT WAS HER LAST HOPE. HER ILLNESS IS TERMINAL.
OH. I SEE.
YOU THOUGHT SHE JUST WANTED TO RESTORE HER LOOKS? SURE, SHE'S VAIN. SHE'S A MOVIE STAR...
...BUT SHE'S A GOOD PERSON.
SHE'S A GOOD PERSON.

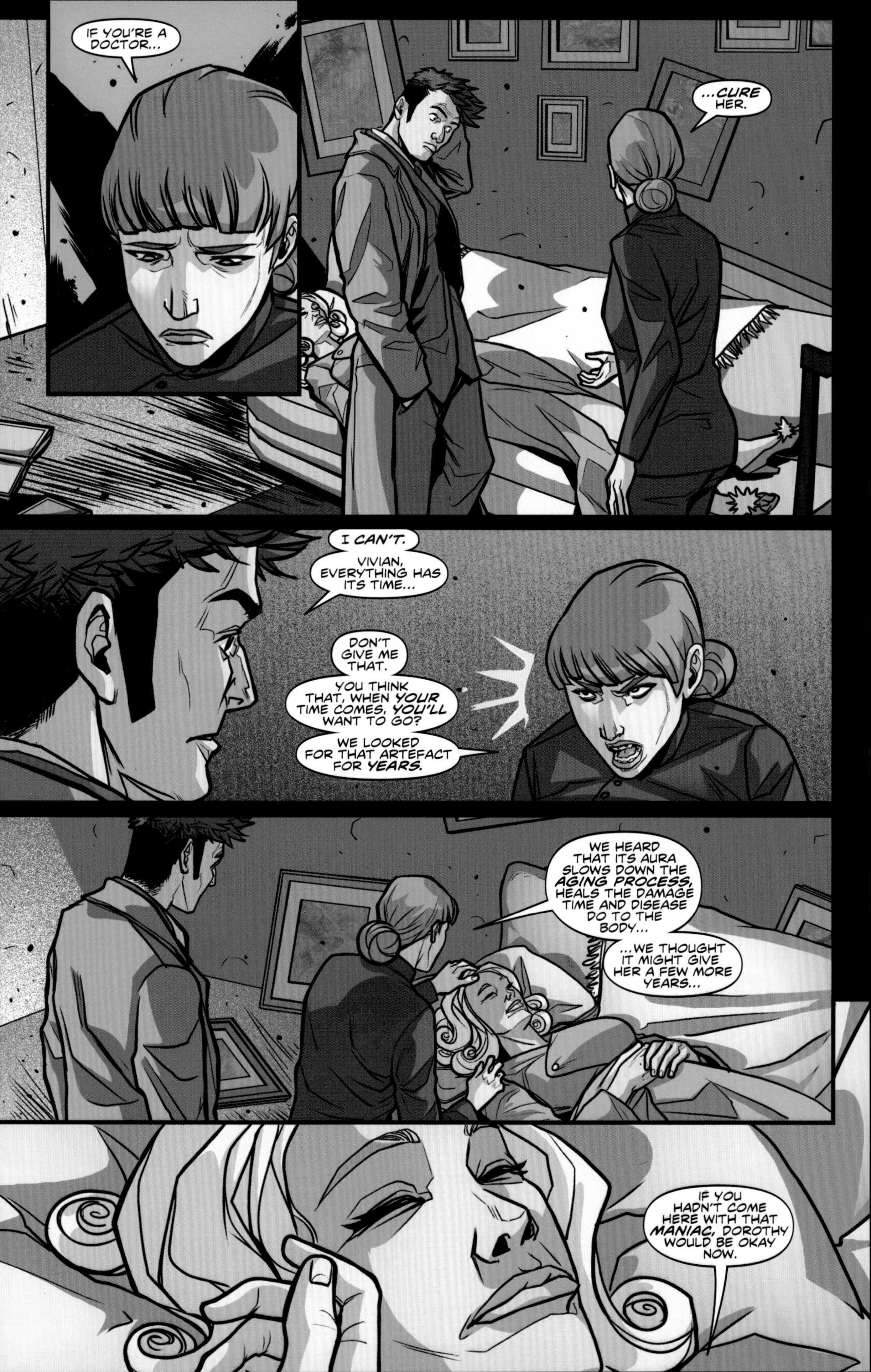
IF YOU'RE A DOCTOR...
...CURE HER.
I CAN'T.
VIVIAN, EVERYTHING HAS ITS TIME...
DON'T GIVE ME THAT.
YOU THINK THAT, WHEN YOUR TIME COMES, YOU'LL WANT TO GO?
WE LOOKED FOR THAT ARTEFACT FOR YEARS.
WE HEARD THAT ITS AURA SLOWS DOWN THE AGING PROCESS, HEALS THE DAMAGE TIME AND DISEASE DO TO THE BODY...
...WE THOUGHT IT MIGHT GIVE HER A FEW MORE YEARS...
IF YOU HADN'T COME HERE WITH THAT MANIAC, DOROTHY WOULD BE OKAY NOW.

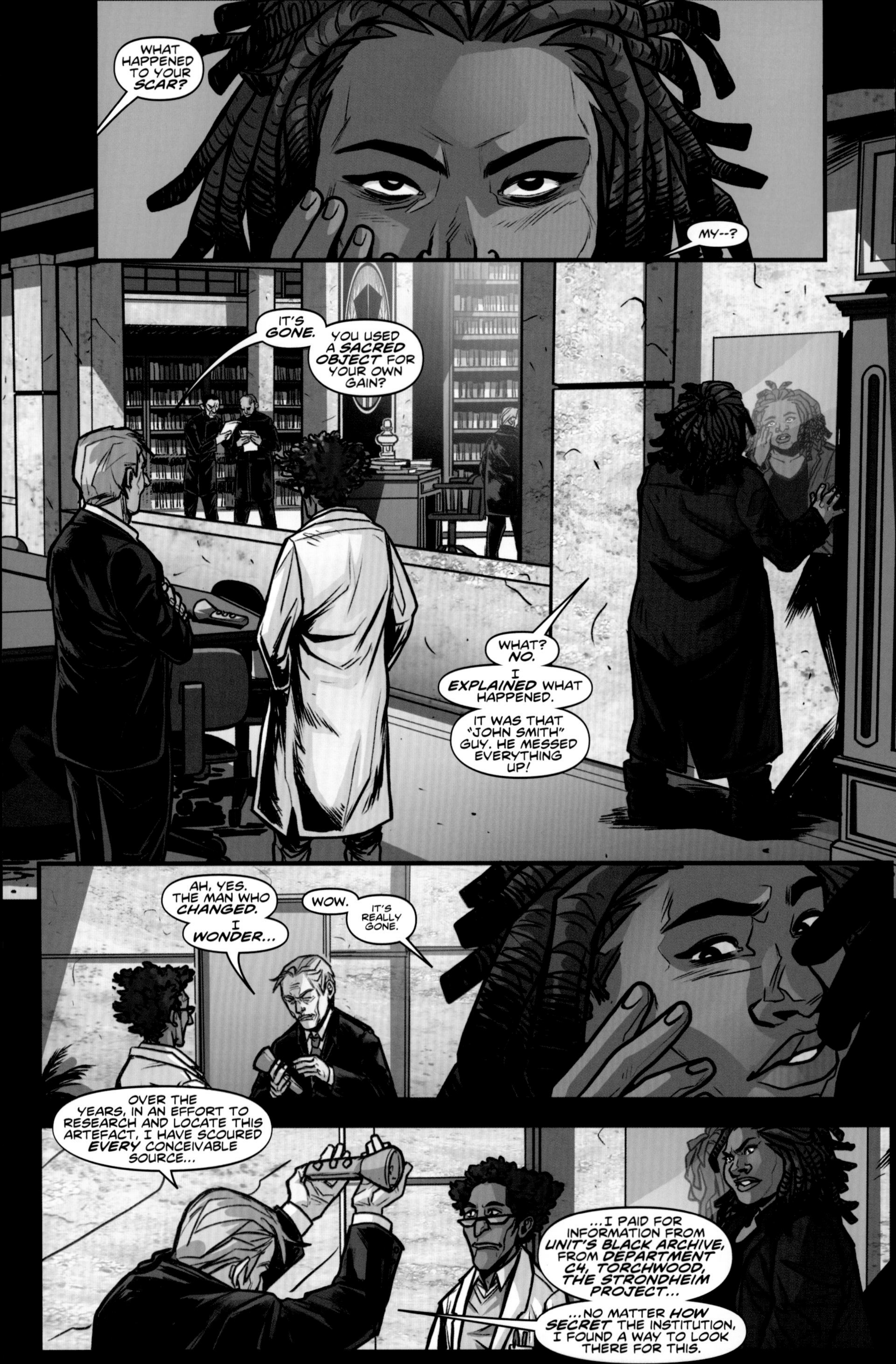
WHAT HAPPENED TO YOUR SCAR?
MY--?
IT'S GONE.
YOU USED A SACRED OBJECT FOR YOUR OWN GAIN?
WHAT? NO.
I EXPLAINED WHAT HAPPENED.
IT WAS THAT "JOHN SMITH" GUY. HE MESSED EVERYTHING UP!
AH, YES. THE MAN WHO CHANGED. I WONDER...
WOW.
IT'S REALLY GONE.
OVER THE YEARS, IN AN EFFORT TO RESEARCH AND LOCATE THIS ARTEFACT, I HAVE SCOURED EVERY CONCEIVABLE SOURCE...
...I PAID FOR INFORMATION FROM UNIT'S BLACK ARCHIVE, FROM DEPARTMENT C4, TORCHWOOD, THE STRONDHEIM PROJECT...
...NO MATTER HOW SECRET THE INSTITUTION, I FOUND A WAY TO LOOK THERE FOR THIS.

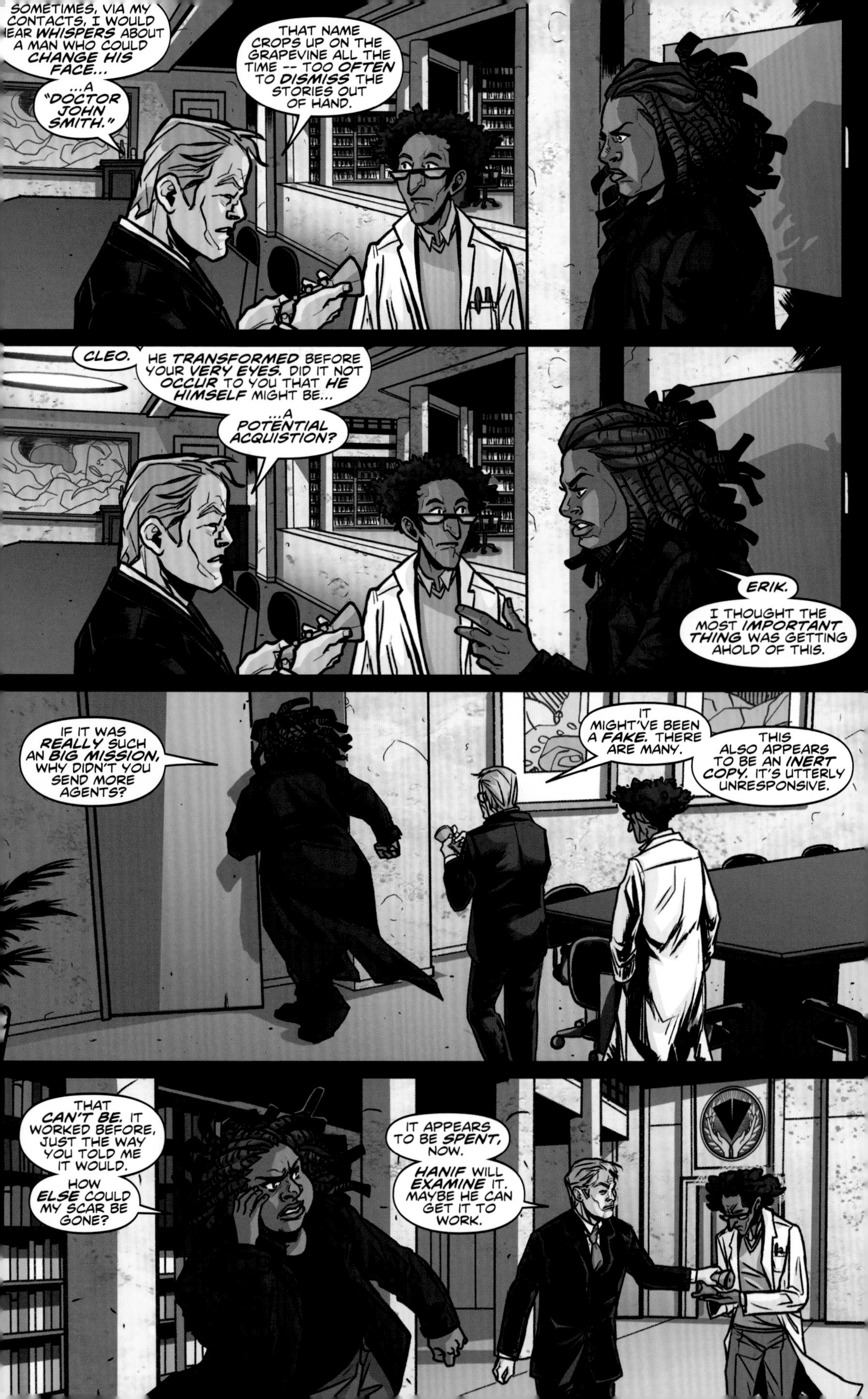

SOMETIMES, VIA MY CONTACTS, I WOULD HEAR WHISPERS ABOUT A MAN WHO COULD CHANGE HIS FACE...
...A "DOCTOR JOHN SMITH."
THAT NAME CROPS UP ON THE GRAPEVINE ALL THE TIME -- TOO OFTEN TO DISMISS THE STORIES OUT OF HAND.
CLEO.
HE TRANSFORMED BEFORE YOUR VERY EYES. DID IT NOT OCCUR TO YOU THAT HE HIMSELF MIGHT BE...
...A POTENTIAL ACQUISTION?
ERIK.
I THOUGHT THE MOST IMPORTANT THING WAS GETTING AHOLD OF THIS.
IF IT WAS REALLY SUCH AN BIG MISSION, WHY DIDN'T YOU SEND MORE AGENTS?
IT MIGHT'VE BEEN A FAKE. THERE ARE MANY.
THIS ALSO APPEARS TO BE AN INERT COPY. IT'S UTTERLY UNRESPONSIVE.
THAT CAN'T BE. IT WORKED BEFORE, JUST THE WAY YOU TOLD ME IT WOULD.
HOW ELSE COULD MY SCAR BE GONE?
IT APPEARS TO BE SPENT, NOW.
HANIF WILL EXAMINE IT. MAYBE HE CAN GET IT TO WORK.

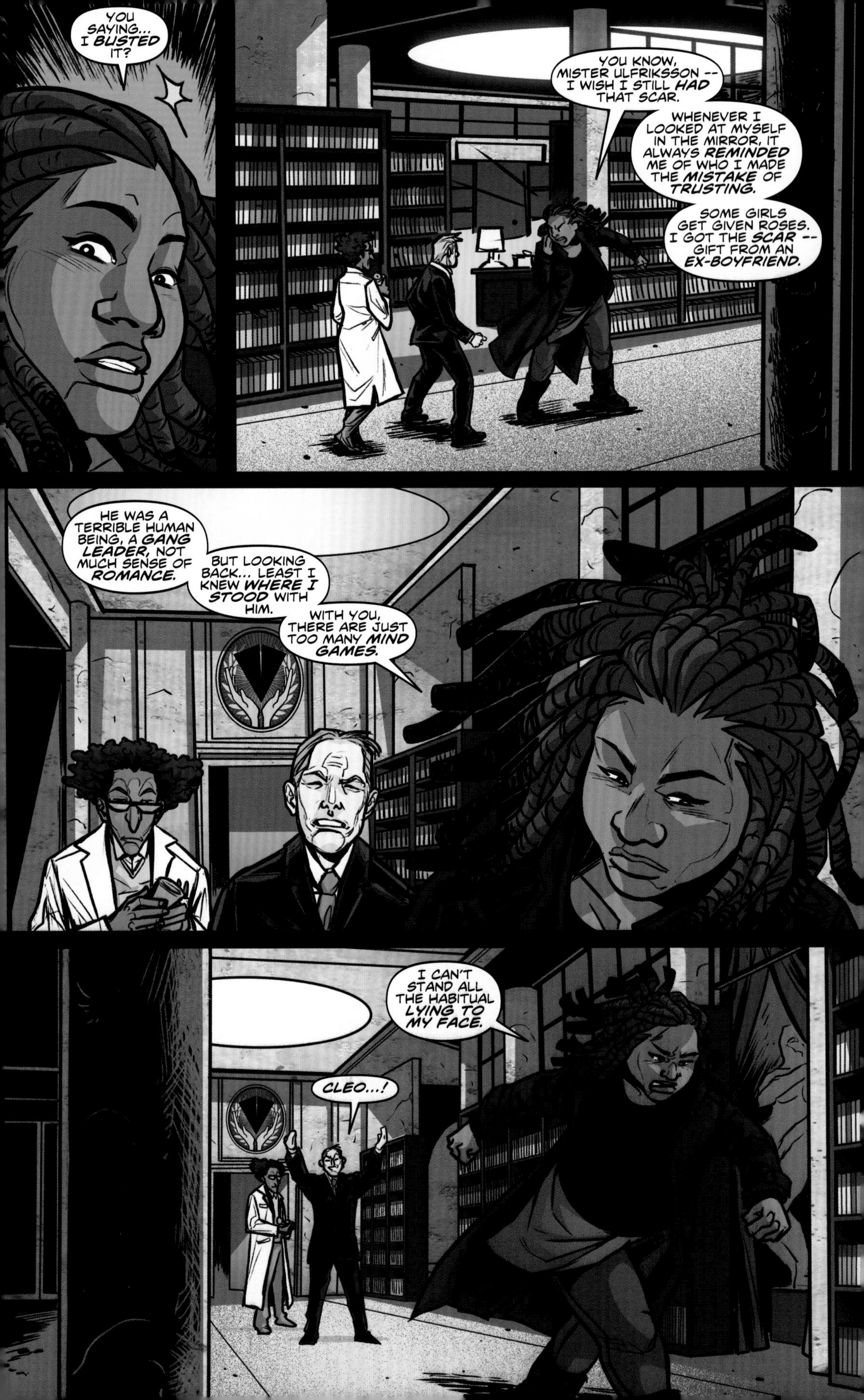
YOU SAYING... I BUSTED IT?
YOU KNOW, MISTER ULFRIKSSON -- I WISH I STILL HAD THAT SCAR.
WHENEVER I LOOKED AT MYSELF IN THE MIRROR, IT ALWAYS REMINDED ME OF WHO I MADE THE MISTAKE OF TRUSTING.
SOME GIRLS GET GIVEN ROSES. I GOT THE SCAR -- GIFT FROM AN EX-BOYFRIEND.
HE WAS A TERRIBLE HUMAN BEING, A GANG LEADER, NOT MUCH SENSE OF ROMANCE.
BUT LOOKING BACK... LEAST I KNEW WHERE I STOOD WITH HIM.
WITH YOU, THERE ARE JUST TOO MANY MIND GAMES.
I CAN'T STAND ALL THE HABITUAL LYING TO MY FACE.
CLEO...!

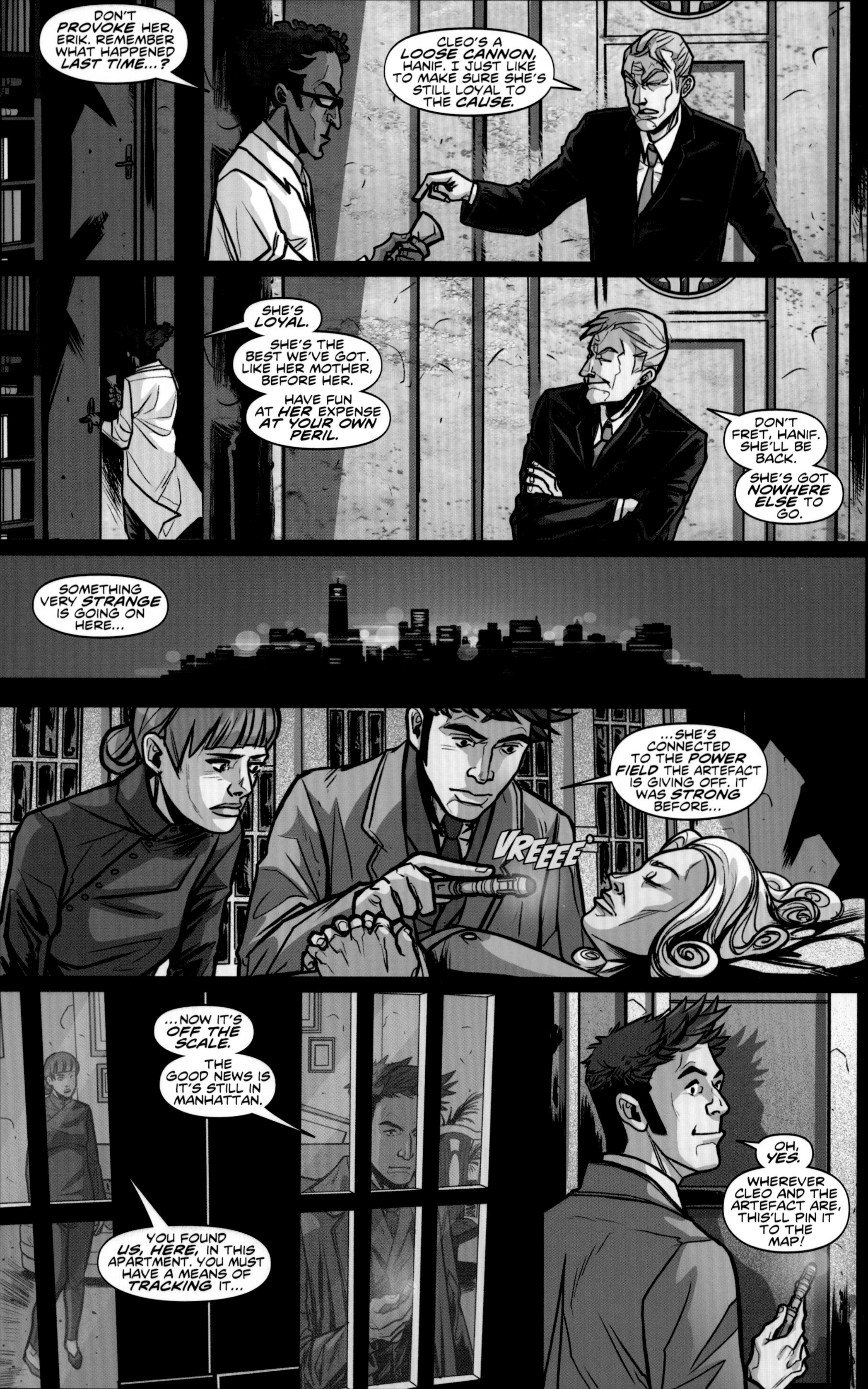
DON'T PROVOKE HER, ERIK. REMEMBER WHAT HAPPENED LAST TIME...?
CLEO'S A LOOSE CANNON, HANIF. I JUST LIKE TO MAKE SURE SHE'S STILL LOYAL TO THE CAUSE.
SHE'S LOYAL.
SHE'S THE BEST WE'VE GOT. LIKE HER MOTHER, BEFORE HER.
HAVE FUN AT HER EXPENSE AT YOUR OWN PERIL.
DON'T FRET, HANIF. SHE'LL BE BACK.
SHE'S GOT NOWHERE ELSE TO GO.
SOMETHING VERY STRANGE IS GOING ON HERE...
...SHE'S CONNECTED TO THE POWER FIELD THE ARTEFACT IS GIVING OFF. IT WAS STRONG BEFORE...
VREEEE
...NOW IT'S OFF THE SCALE.
THE GOOD NEWS IS IT'S STILL IN MANHATTAN.
YOU FOUND US, HERE, IN THIS APARTMENT. YOU MUST HAVE A MEANS OF TRACKING IT...
OH, YES.
WHEREVER CLEO AND THE ARTEFACT ARE, THIS'LL PIN IT TO THE MAP!

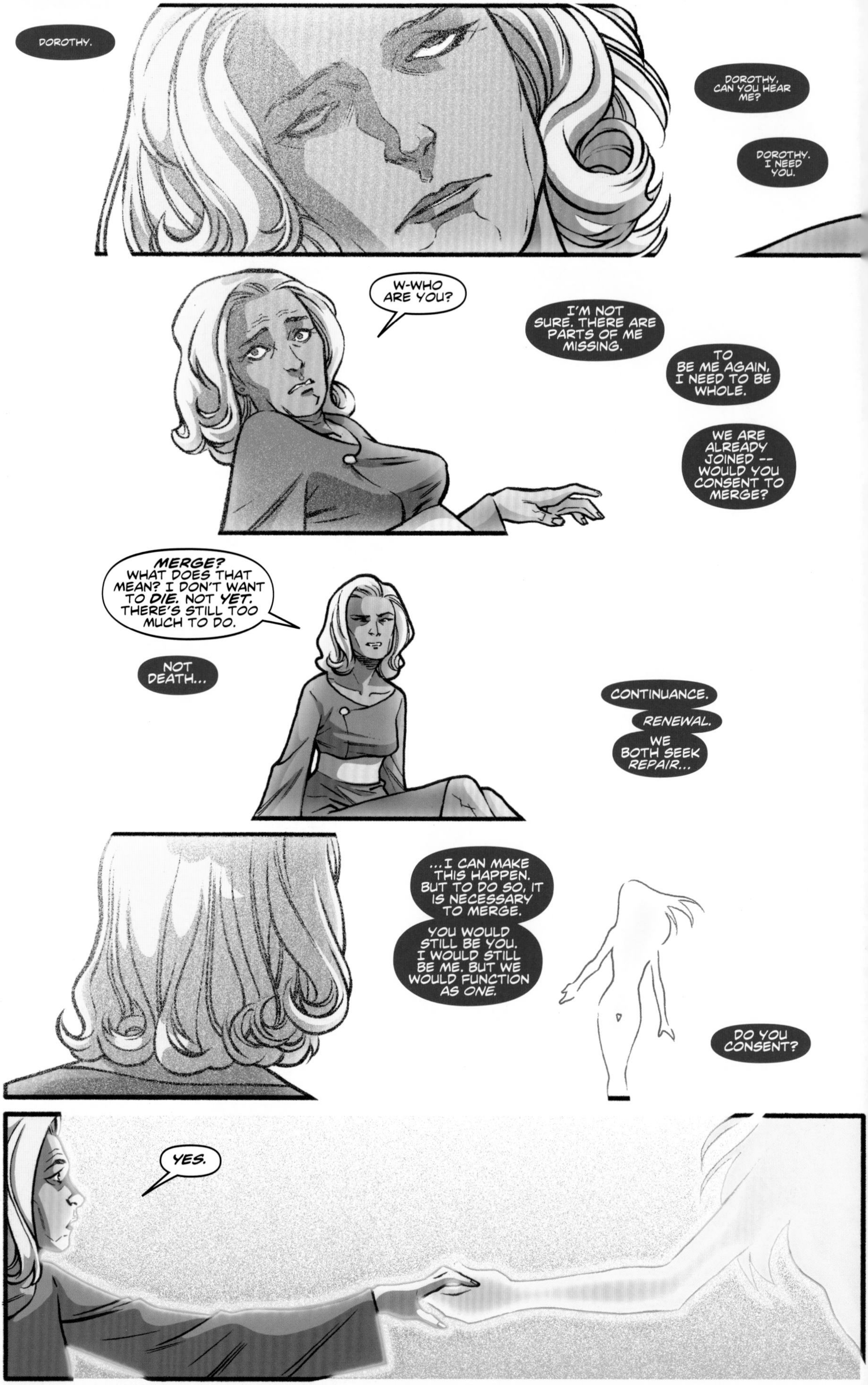

DOROTHY.
DOROTHY, CAN YOU HEAR ME?
DOROTHY. I NEED YOU.
W-WHO ARE YOU?
I'M NOT SURE. THERE ARE PARTS OF ME MISSING.
TO BE ME AGAIN, I NEED TO BE WHOLE.
WE ARE ALREADY JOINED -- WOULD YOU CONSENT TO MERGE?
MERGE? WHAT DOES THAT MEAN? I DON'T WANT TO DIE. NOT YET. THERE'S STILL TOO MUCH TO DO.
NOT DEATH...
CONTINUANCE.
RENEWAL.
WE BOTH SEEK REPAIR...
...I CAN MAKE THIS HAPPEN. BUT TO DO SO, IT IS NECESSARY TO MERGE.
YOU WOULD STILL BE YOU. I WOULD STILL BE ME. BUT WE WOULD FUNCTION AS ONE.
DO YOU CONSENT?
YES.

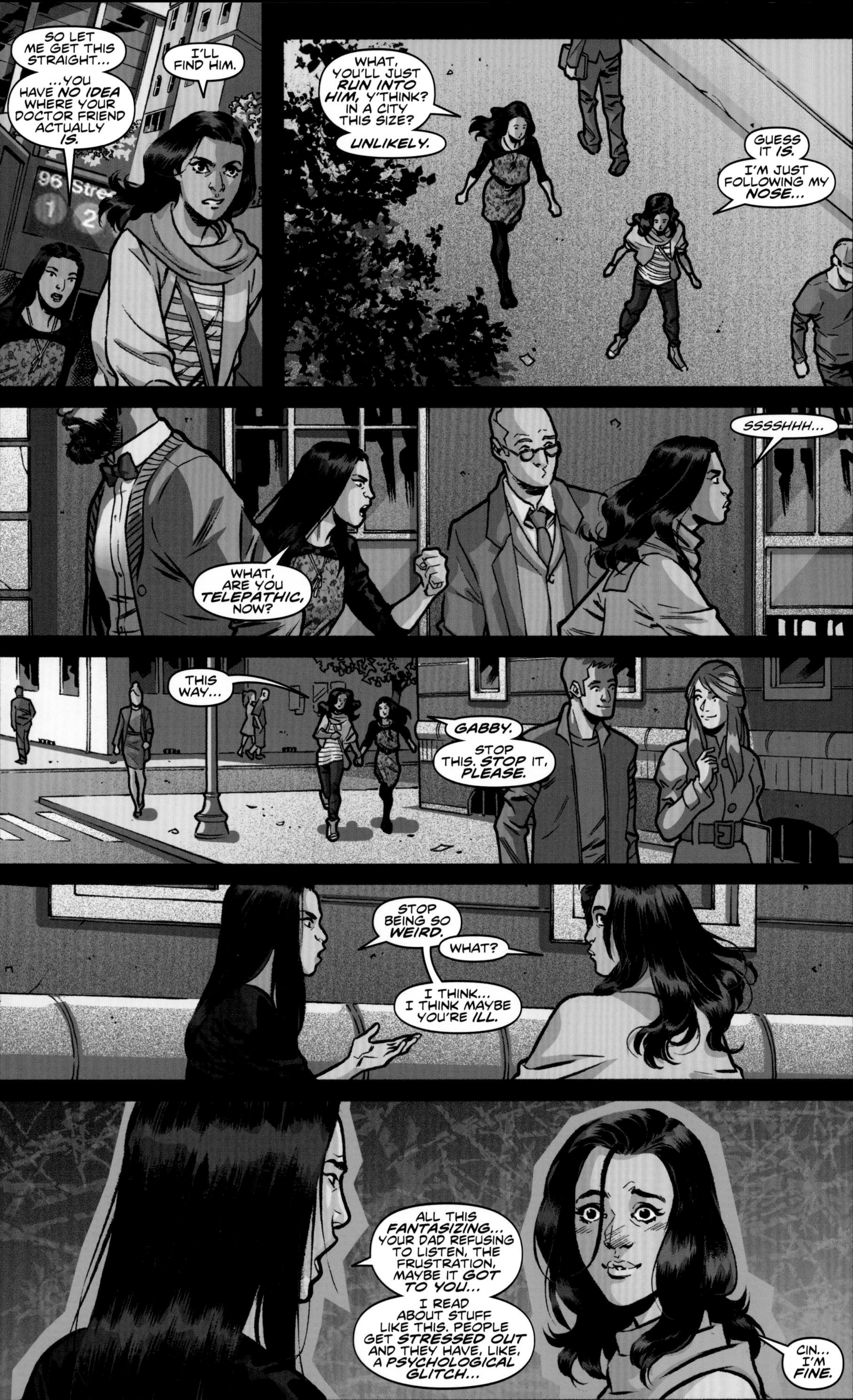

SO LET ME GET THIS STRAIGHT...
...YOU HAVE NO IDEA WHERE YOUR DOCTOR FRIEND ACTUALLY IS.
I'LL FIND HIM.
96 Stre
1
2
WHAT, YOU'LL JUST RUN INTO HIM, Y'THINK? IN A CITY THIS SIZE?
UNLIKELY.
GUESS IT IS.
I'M JUST FOLLOWING MY NOSE...
SSSSHHH...
WHAT, ARE YOU TELEPATHIC, NOW?
THIS WAY...
GABBY.
STOP THIS. STOP IT, PLEASE.
STOP BEING SO WEIRD.
WHAT?
I THINK... I THINK MAYBE YOU'RE ILL.
ALL THIS FANTASIZING... YOUR DAD REFUSING TO LISTEN, THE FRUSTRATION, MAYBE IT GOT TO YOU...
I READ ABOUT STUFF LIKE THIS. PEOPLE GET STRESSED OUT AND THEY HAVE, LIKE, A PSYCHOLOGICAL GLITCH...
CIN... I'M FINE.

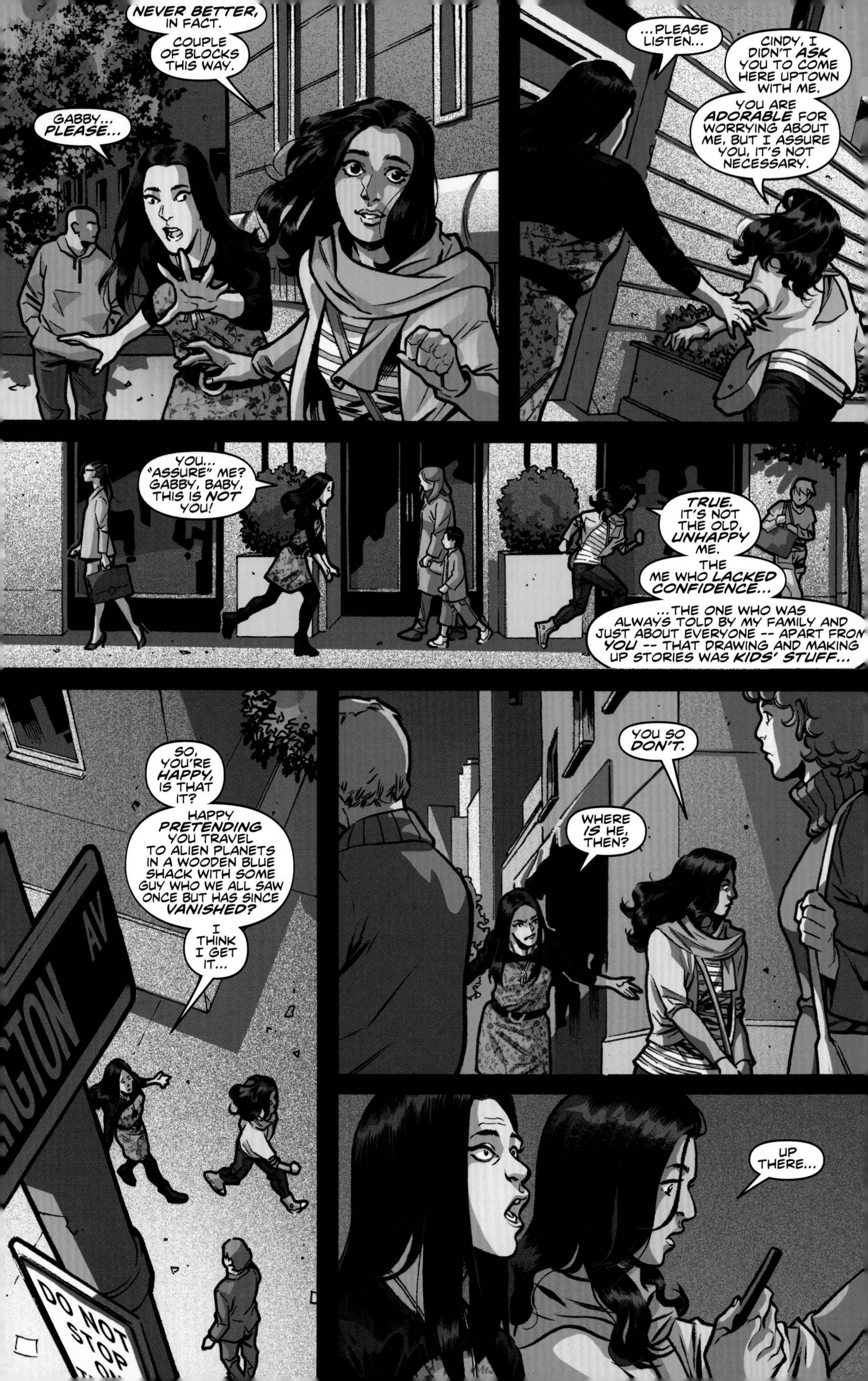

NEVER BETTER, IN FACT.
COUPLE OF BLOCKS THIS WAY.
GABBY... PLEASE...
...PLEASE LISTEN...
CINDY, I DIDN'T ASK YOU TO COME HERE UPTOWN WITH ME.
YOU ARE ADORABLE FOR WORRYING ABOUT ME, BUT I ASSURE YOU, IT'S NOT NECESSARY.
YOU... "ASSURE" ME? GABBY, BABY, THIS IS NOT YOU!
TRUE. IT'S NOT THE OLD, UNHAPPY ME.
THE ME WHO LACKED CONFIDENCE...
...THE ONE WHO WAS ALWAYS TOLD BY MY FAMILY AND JUST ABOUT EVERYONE -- APART FROM YOU -- THAT DRAWING AND MAKING UP STORIES WAS KIDS' STUFF...
SO, YOU'RE HAPPY, IS THAT IT?
HAPPY PRETENDING YOU TRAVEL TO ALIEN PLANETS IN A WOODEN BLUE SHACK WITH SOME GUY WHO WE ALL SAW ONCE BUT HAS SINCE VANISHED?
I THINK I GET IT...
AV
GTON
DO NOT STOP
YOU SO DON'T.
WHERE IS HE, THEN?
UP THERE...

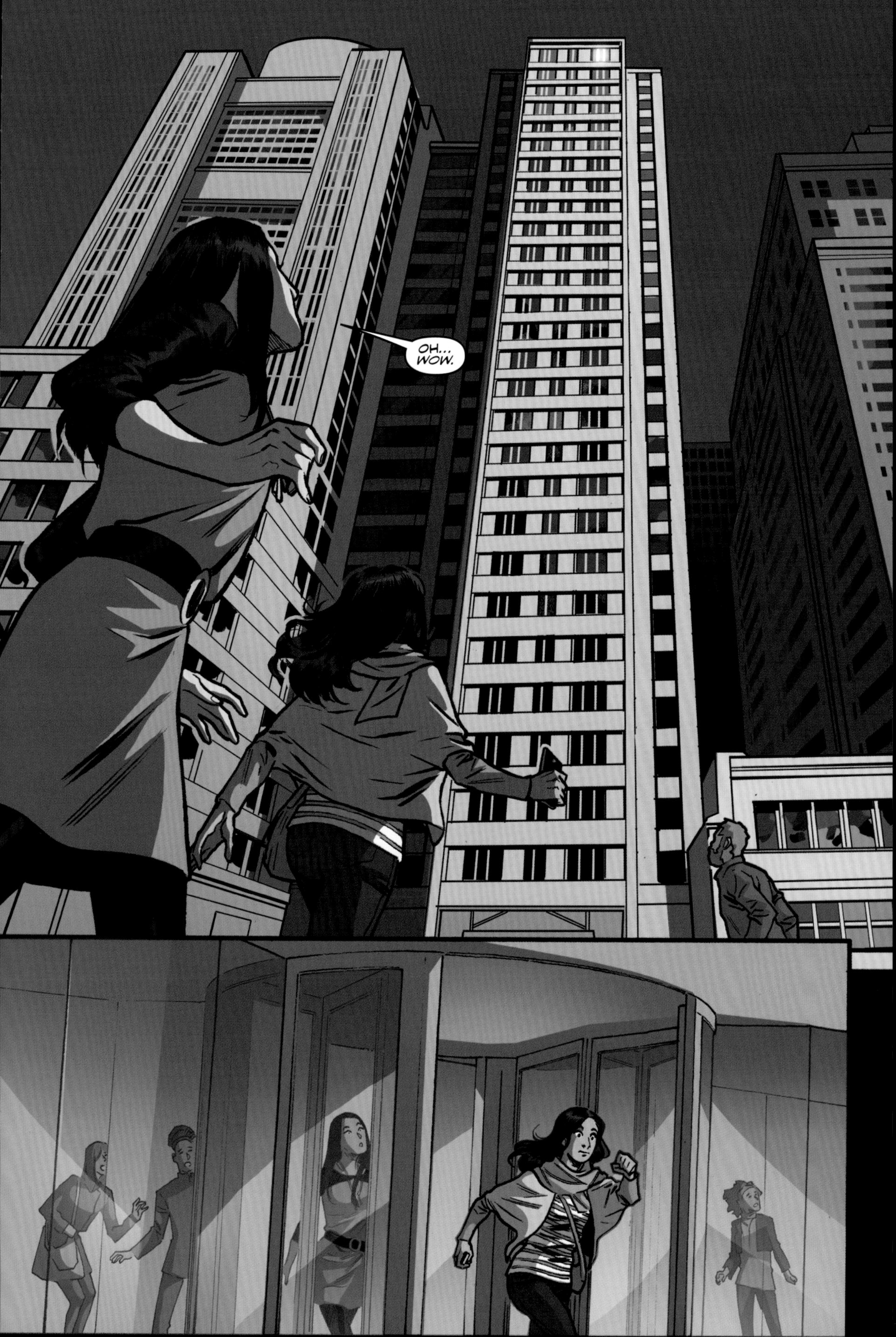
OH... WOW.

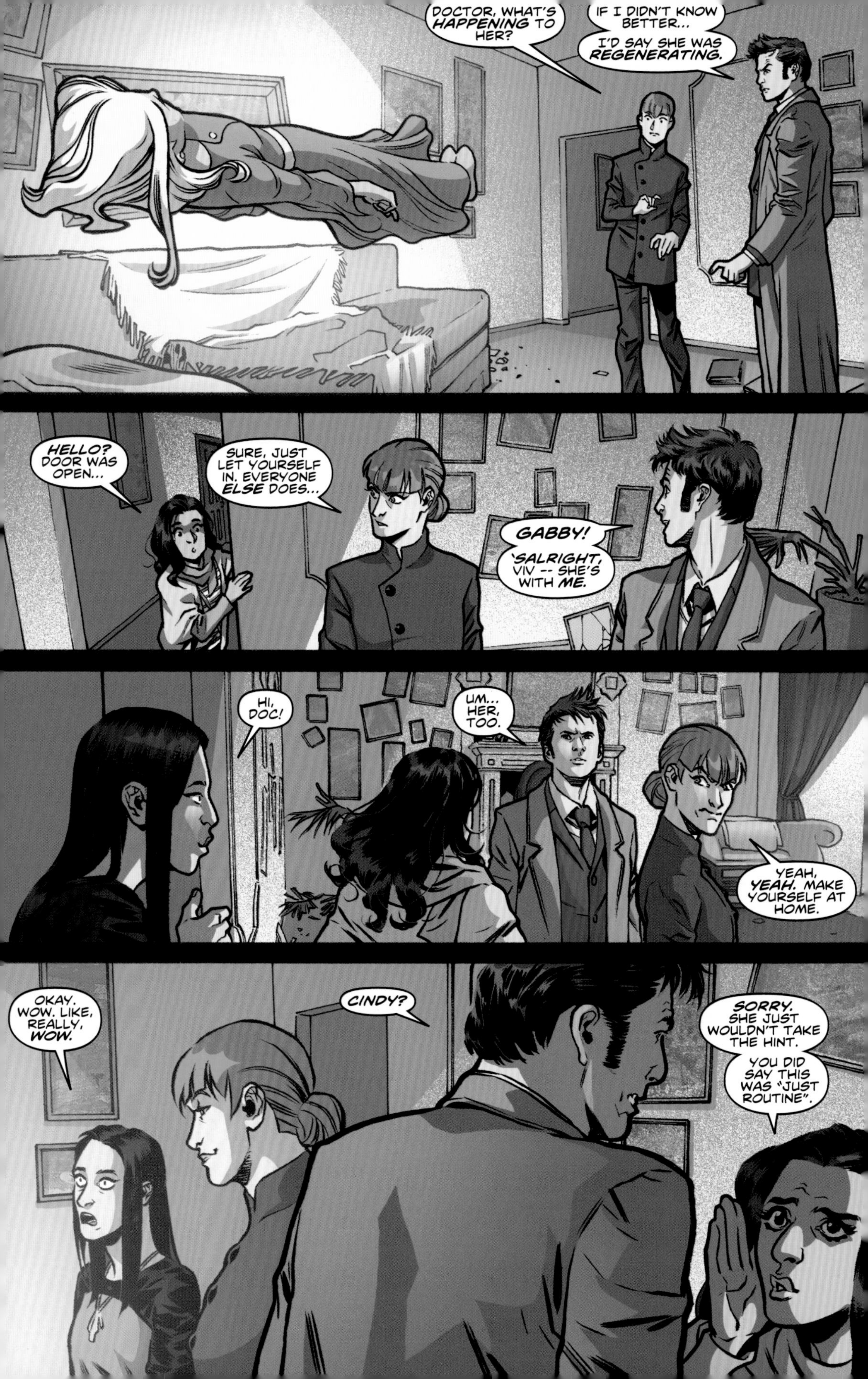
DOCTOR, WHAT'S HAPPENING TO HER?
IF I DIDN'T KNOW BETTER...
I'D SAY SHE WAS REGENERATING.
HELLO? DOOR WAS OPEN...
SURE, JUST LET YOURSELF IN. EVERYONE ELSE DOES...
GABBY!
'SALRIGHT, VIV -- SHE'S WITH ME.
HI, DOC!
UM... HER, TOO.
YEAH, YEAH. MAKE YOURSELF AT HOME.
OKAY. WOW. LIKE, REALLY, WOW.
CINDY?
SORRY. SHE JUST WOULDN'T TAKE THE HINT.
YOU DID SAY THIS WAS "JUST ROUTINE".

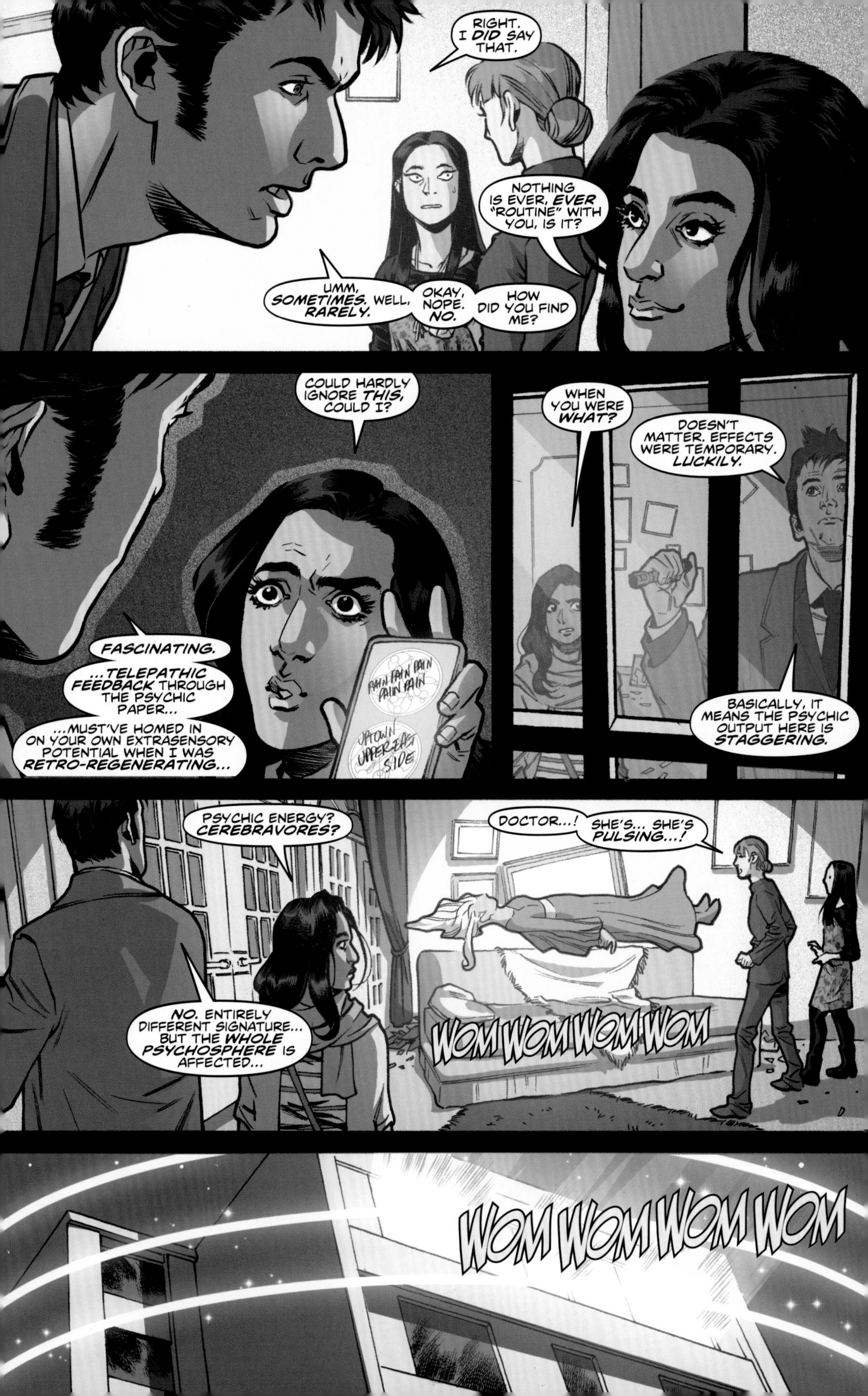
RIGHT. I DID SAY THAT.
NOTHING IS EVER, EVER "ROUTINE" WITH YOU, IS IT?
UMM, SOMETIMES. WELL, RARELY.
OKAY, NOPE. NO.
HOW DID YOU FIND ME?
COULD HARDLY IGNORE THIS, COULD I?
FASCINATING.
...TELEPATHIC FEEDBACK THROUGH THE PSYCHIC PAPER...
...MUST'VE HOMED IN ON YOUR OWN EXTRASENSORY POTENTIAL WHEN I WAS RETRO-REGENERATING...
PAIN PAIN PAIN PAIN PAIN
UPTOWN UPPER EAST SIDE
WHEN YOU WERE WHAT?
DOESN'T MATTER. EFFECTS WERE TEMPORARY. LUCKILY.
BASICALLY, IT MEANS THE PSYCHIC OUTPUT HERE IS STAGGERING.
PSYCHIC ENERGY? CEREBRAVORES?
NO. ENTIRELY DIFFERENT SIGNATURE... BUT THE WHOLE PSYCHOSPHERE IS AFFECTED...
DOCTOR...!
SHE'S... SHE'S PULSING...!
WOM WOM WOM WOM
WOM WOM WOM WOM

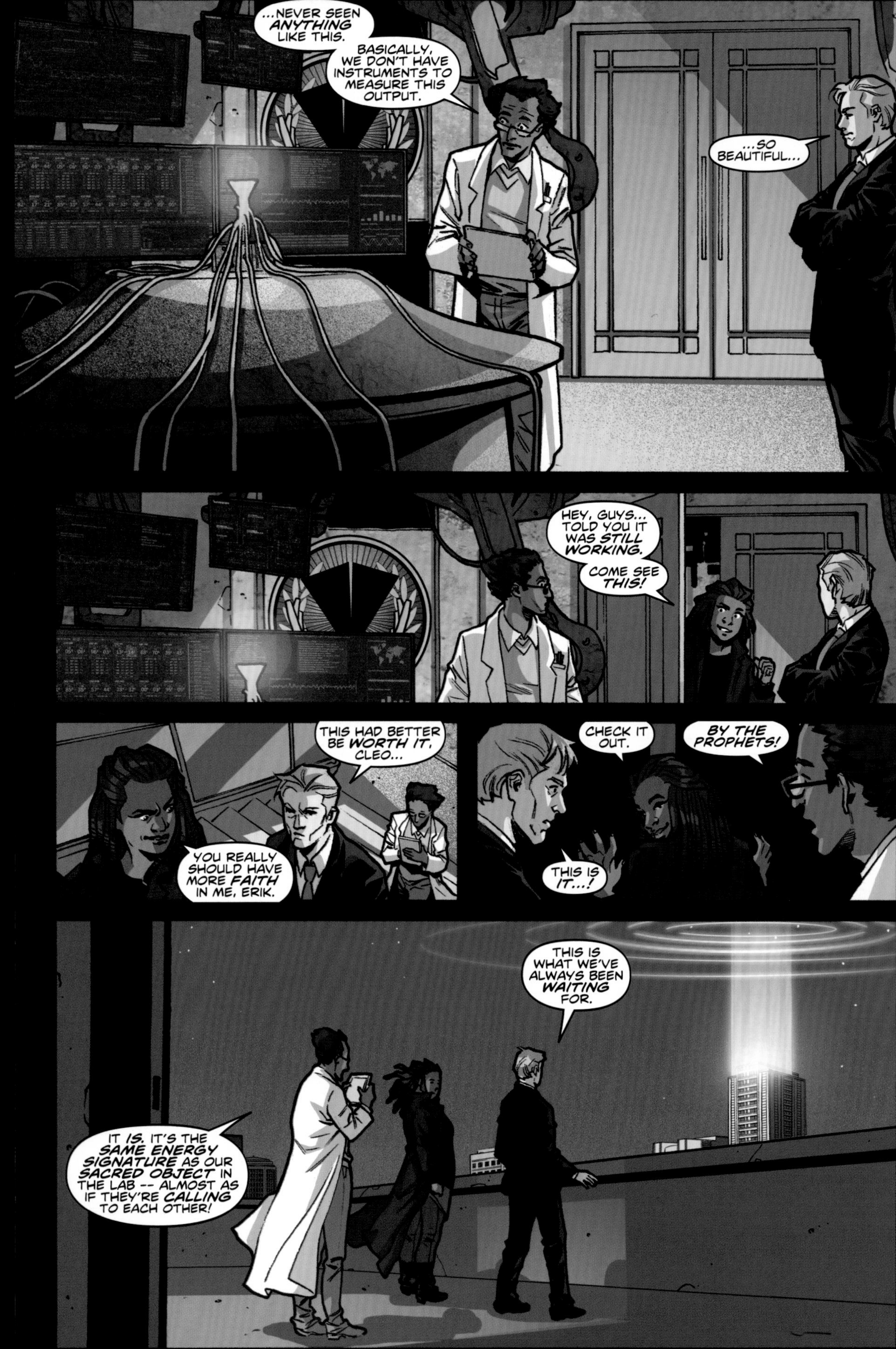
...NEVER SEEN ANYTHING LIKE THIS.
BASICALLY, WE DON'T HAVE INSTRUMENTS TO MEASURE THIS OUTPUT.
...SO BEAUTIFUL...
HEY, GUYS... TOLD YOU IT WAS STILL WORKING.
COME SEE THIS!
THIS HAD BETTER BE WORTH IT, CLEO...
YOU REALLY SHOULD HAVE MORE FAITH IN ME, ERIK.
CHECK IT OUT.
BY THE PROPHETS!
THIS IS IT...!
THIS IS WHAT WE'VE ALWAYS BEEN WAITING FOR.
IT IS. IT'S THE SAME ENERGY SIGNATURE AS OUR SACRED OBJECT IN THE LAB -- ALMOST AS IF THEY'RE CALLING TO EACH OTHER!

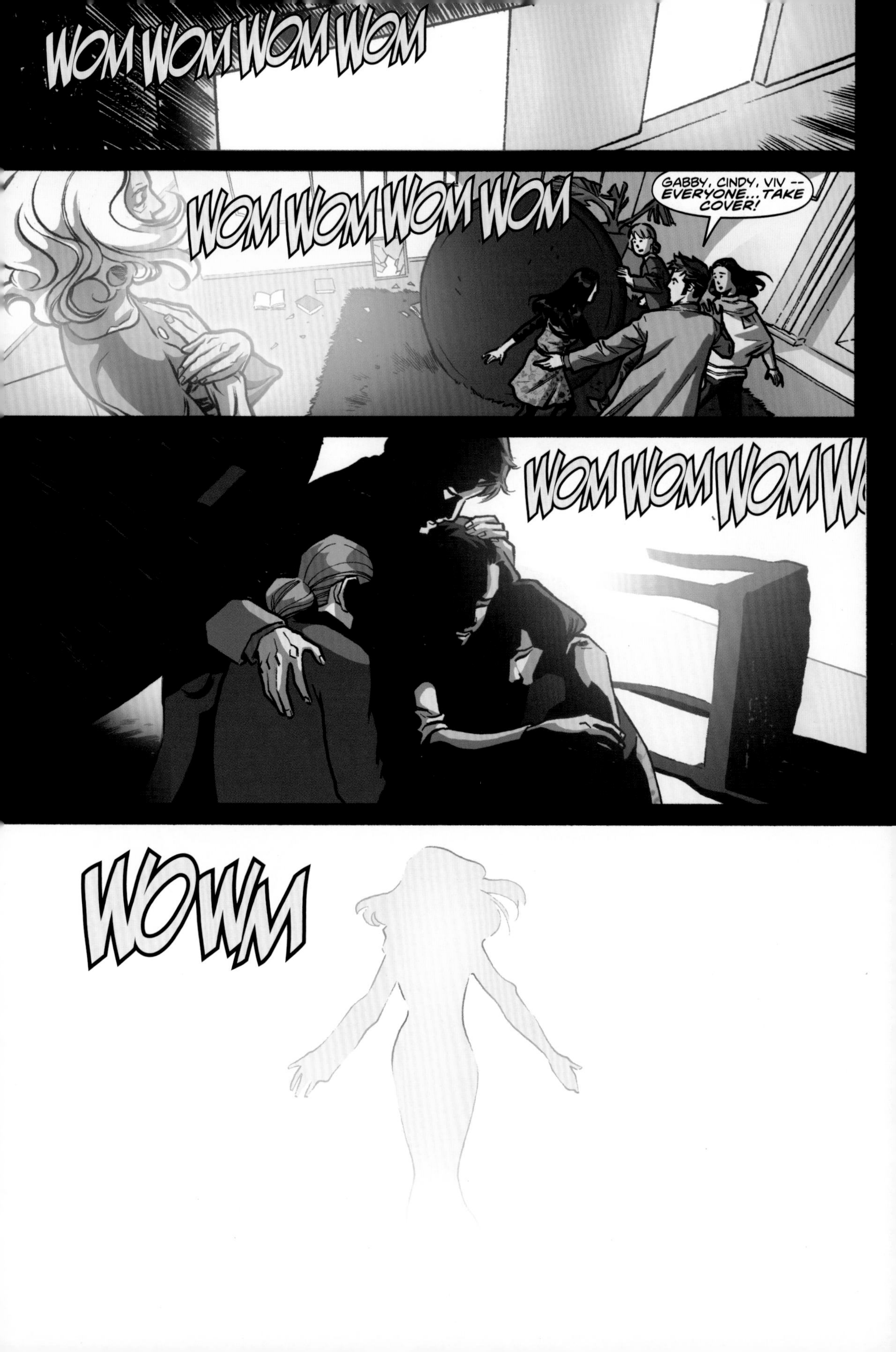
WOM WOM WOM WOM
WOM WOM WOM WOM
GABBY, CINDY, VIV -- EVERYONE... TAKE COVER!
WOM WOM WOM W
WOWM

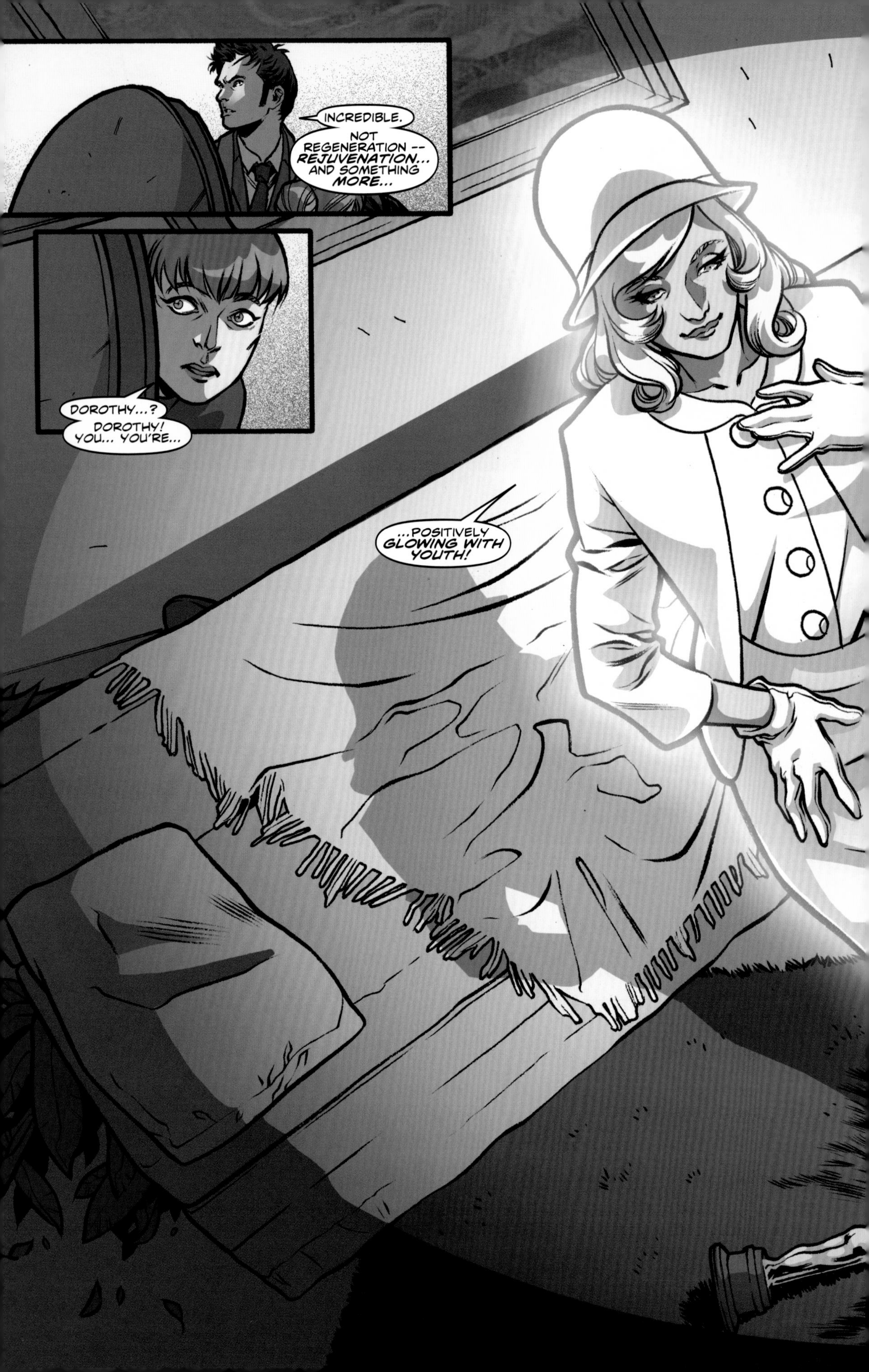
INCREDIBLE.
NOT REGENERATION -- REJUVENATION... AND SOMETHING MORE...
DOROTHY...?
DOROTHY! YOU... YOU'RE...
...POSITIVELY GLOWING WITH YOUTH!

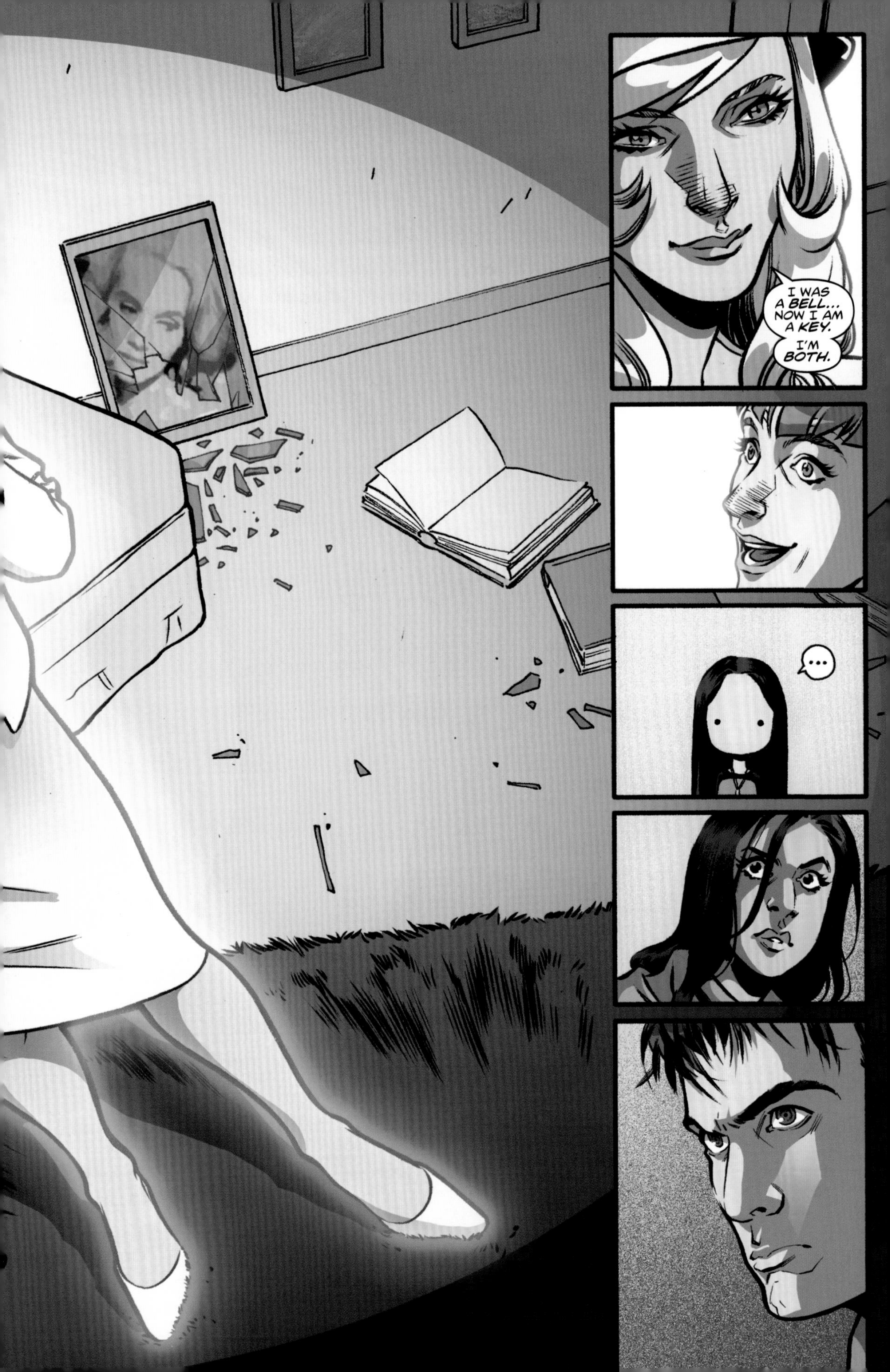

I WAS A BELL... NOW I AM A KEY. I'M BOTH.
...

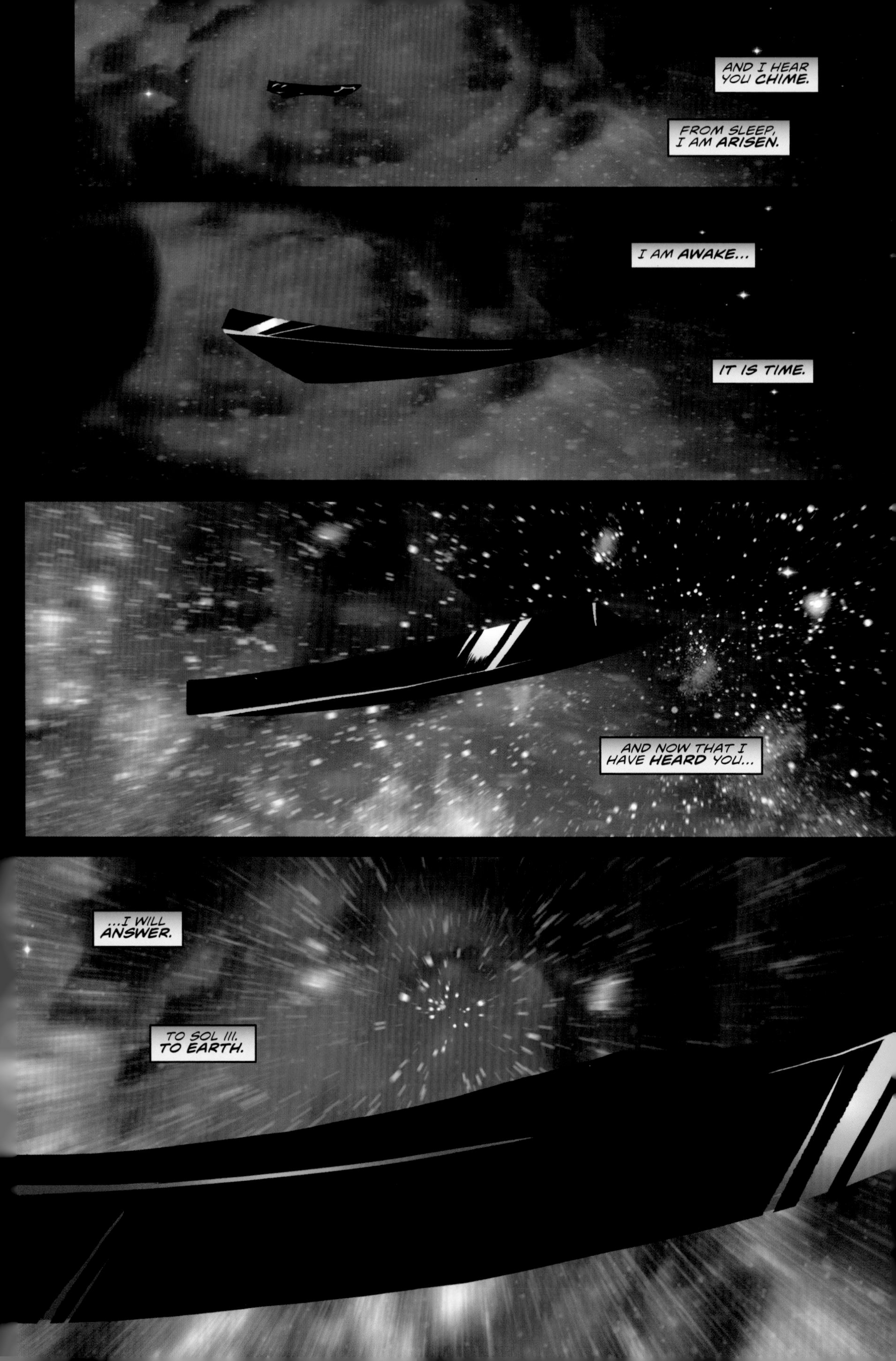
AND I HEAR YOU CHIME.
FROM SLEEP, I AM ARISEN.
I AM AWAKE...
IT IS TIME.
AND NOW THAT I HAVE HEARD YOU...
...I WILL ANSWER.
TO SOL III. TO EARTH.

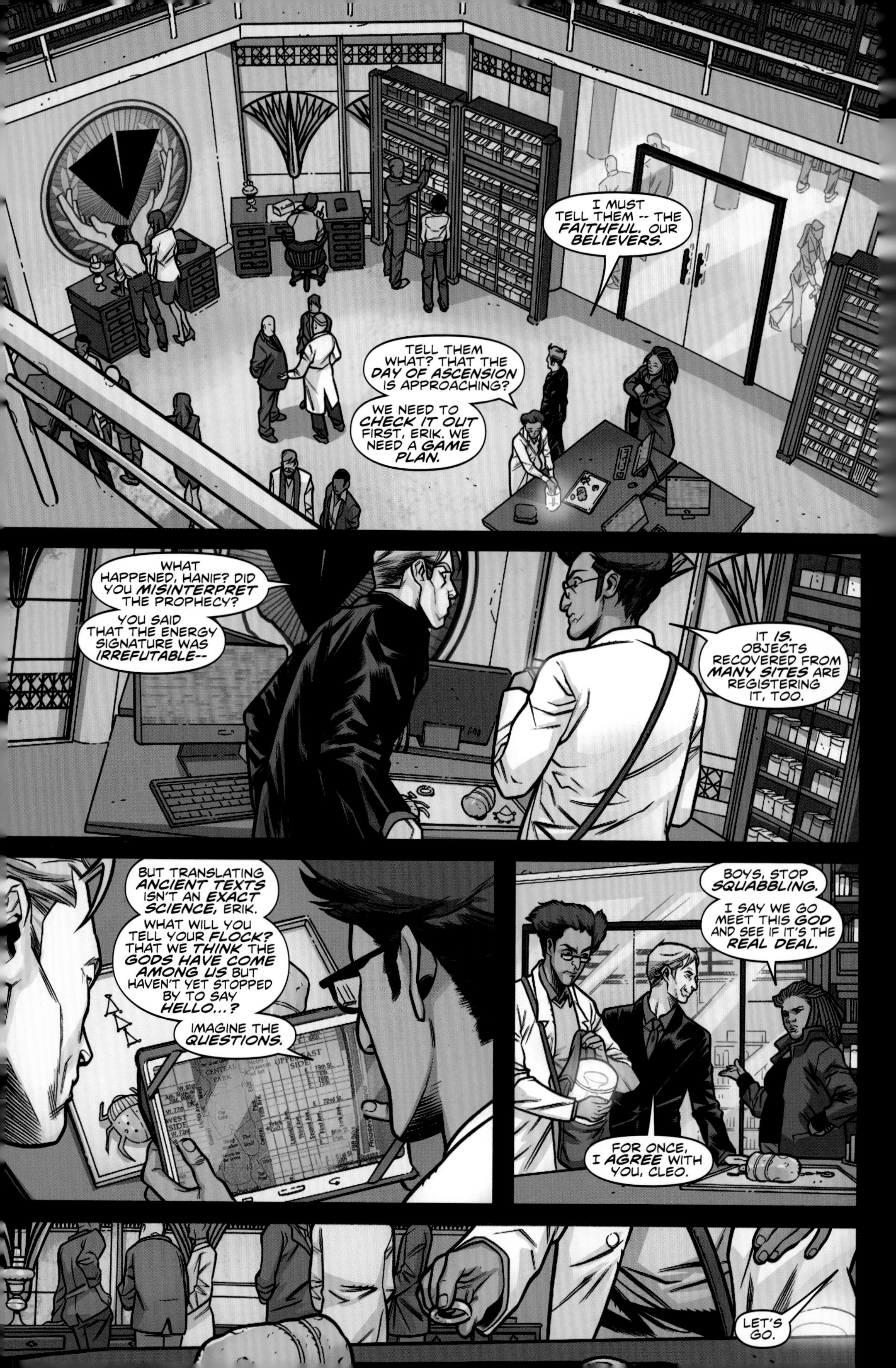
I MUST TELL THEM -- THE FAITHFUL. OUR BELIEVERS.
TELL THEM WHAT? THAT THE DAY OF ASCENSION IS APPROACHING?
WE NEED TO CHECK IT OUT FIRST, ERIK. WE NEED A GAME PLAN.
WHAT HAPPENED, HANIF? DID YOU MISINTERPRET THE PROPHECY?
YOU SAID THAT THE ENERGY SIGNATURE WAS IRREFUTABLE--
IT IS. OBJECTS RECOVERED FROM MANY SITES ARE REGISTERING IT, TOO.
BUT TRANSLATING ANCIENT TEXTS ISN'T AN EXACT SCIENCE, ERIK.
WHAT WILL YOU TELL YOUR FLOCK? THAT WE THINK THE GODS HAVE COME AMONG US BUT HAVEN'T YET STOPPED BY TO SAY HELLO...?
IMAGINE THE QUESTIONS.
CENTRAL PARK
UPPER EAST SIDE
WEST SIDE
BOYS, STOP SQUABBLING.
I SAY WE GO MEET THIS GOD AND SEE IF IT'S THE REAL DEAL.
FOR ONCE, I AGREE WITH YOU, CLEO.
LET'S GO.

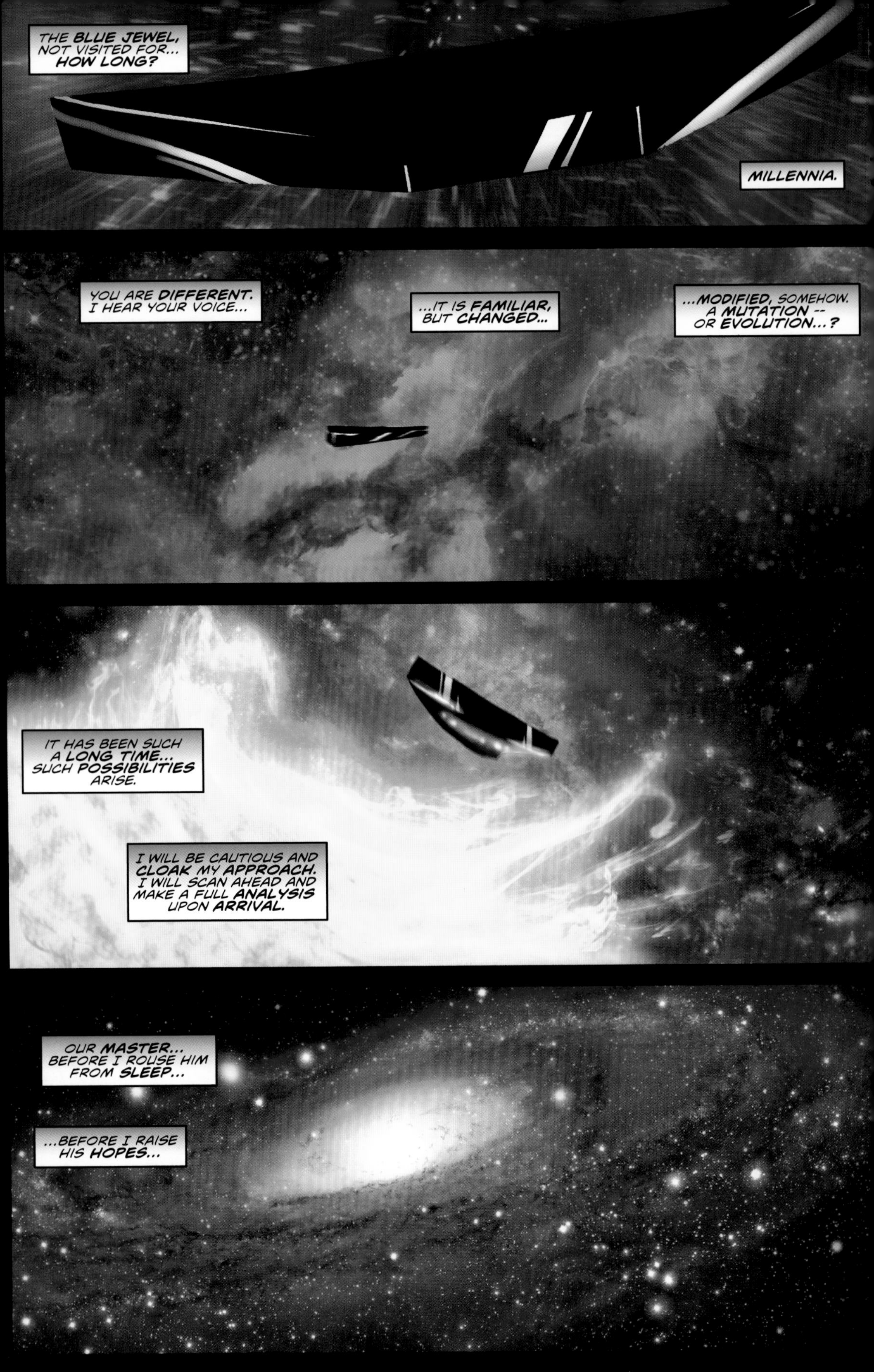
THE BLUE JEWEL, NOT VISITED FOR... HOW LONG?
MILLENNIA.
YOU ARE DIFFERENT. I HEAR YOUR VOICE...
...IT IS FAMILIAR, BUT CHANGED...
...MODIFIED, SOMEHOW. A MUTATION -- OR EVOLUTION...?
IT HAS BEEN SUCH A LONG TIME... SUCH POSSIBILITIES ARISE.
I WILL BE CAUTIOUS AND CLOAK MY APPROACH. I WILL SCAN AHEAD AND MAKE A FULL ANALYSIS UPON ARRIVAL.
OUR MASTER... BEFORE I ROUSE HIM FROM SLEEP...
...BEFORE I RAISE HIS HOPES...

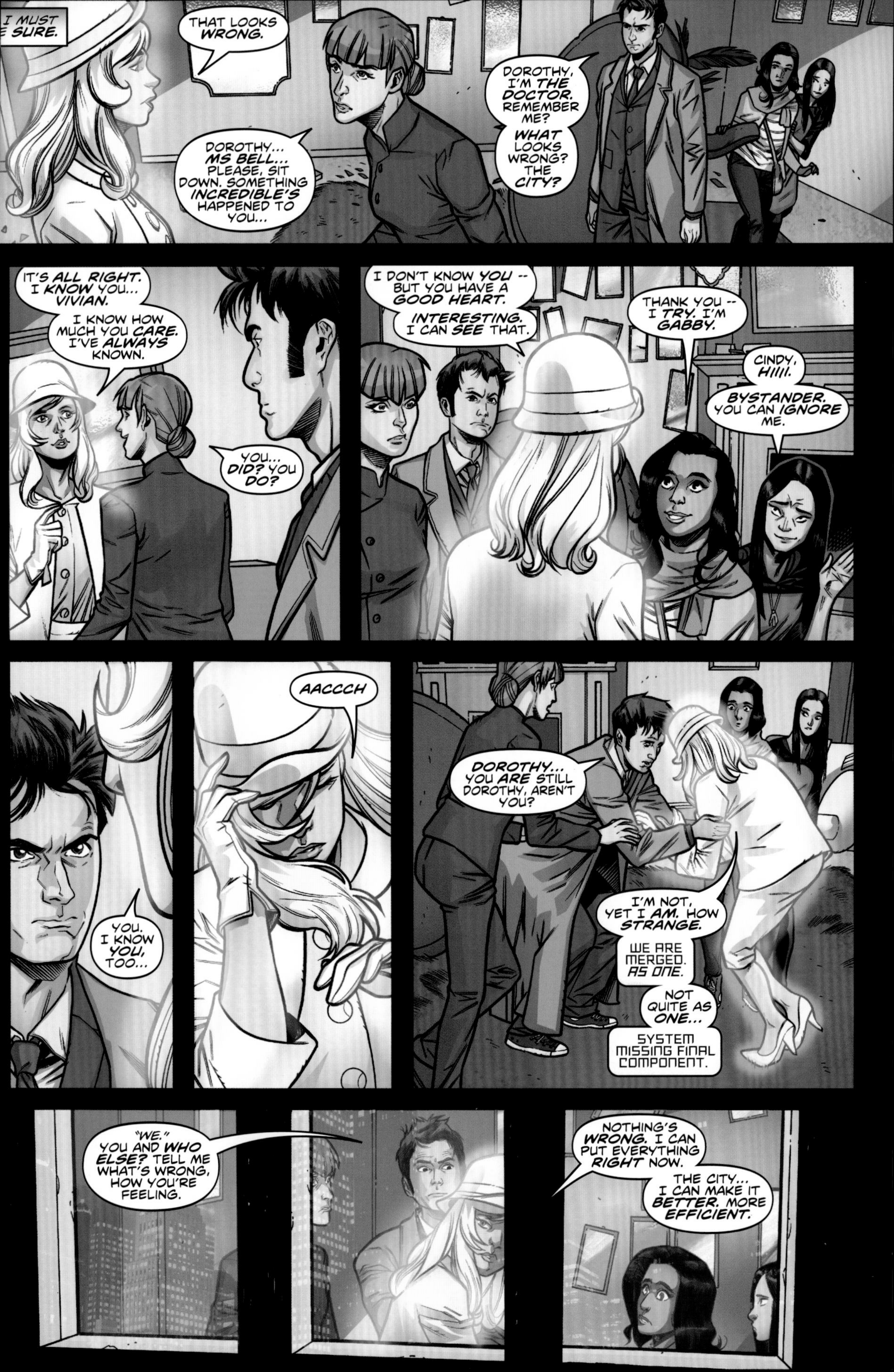
I MUST
E SURE.
THAT LOOKS WRONG.
DOROTHY... MS BELL... PLEASE, SIT DOWN. SOMETHING INCREDIBLE'S HAPPENED TO YOU...
DOROTHY, I'M THE DOCTOR. REMEMBER ME? WHAT LOOKS WRONG? THE CITY?
IT'S ALL RIGHT. I KNOW YOU... VIVIAN.
I KNOW HOW MUCH YOU CARE. I'VE ALWAYS KNOWN.
YOU... DID? YOU DO?
I DON'T KNOW YOU -- BUT YOU HAVE A GOOD HEART.
INTERESTING. I CAN SEE THAT.
THANK YOU -- I TRY. I'M GABBY.
CINDY, HIIII.
BYSTANDER. YOU CAN IGNORE ME.
YOU. I KNOW YOU, TOO...
AACCCH
DOROTHY... YOU ARE STILL DOROTHY, AREN'T YOU?
I'M NOT, YET I AM. HOW STRANGE.
WE ARE MERGED. AS ONE.
NOT QUITE AS ONE...
SYSTEM MISSING FINAL COMPONENT.
"WE." YOU AND WHO ELSE? TELL ME WHAT'S WRONG, HOW YOU'RE FEELING.
NOTHING'S WRONG. I CAN PUT EVERYTHING RIGHT NOW.
THE CITY... I CAN MAKE IT BETTER. MORE EFFICIENT.

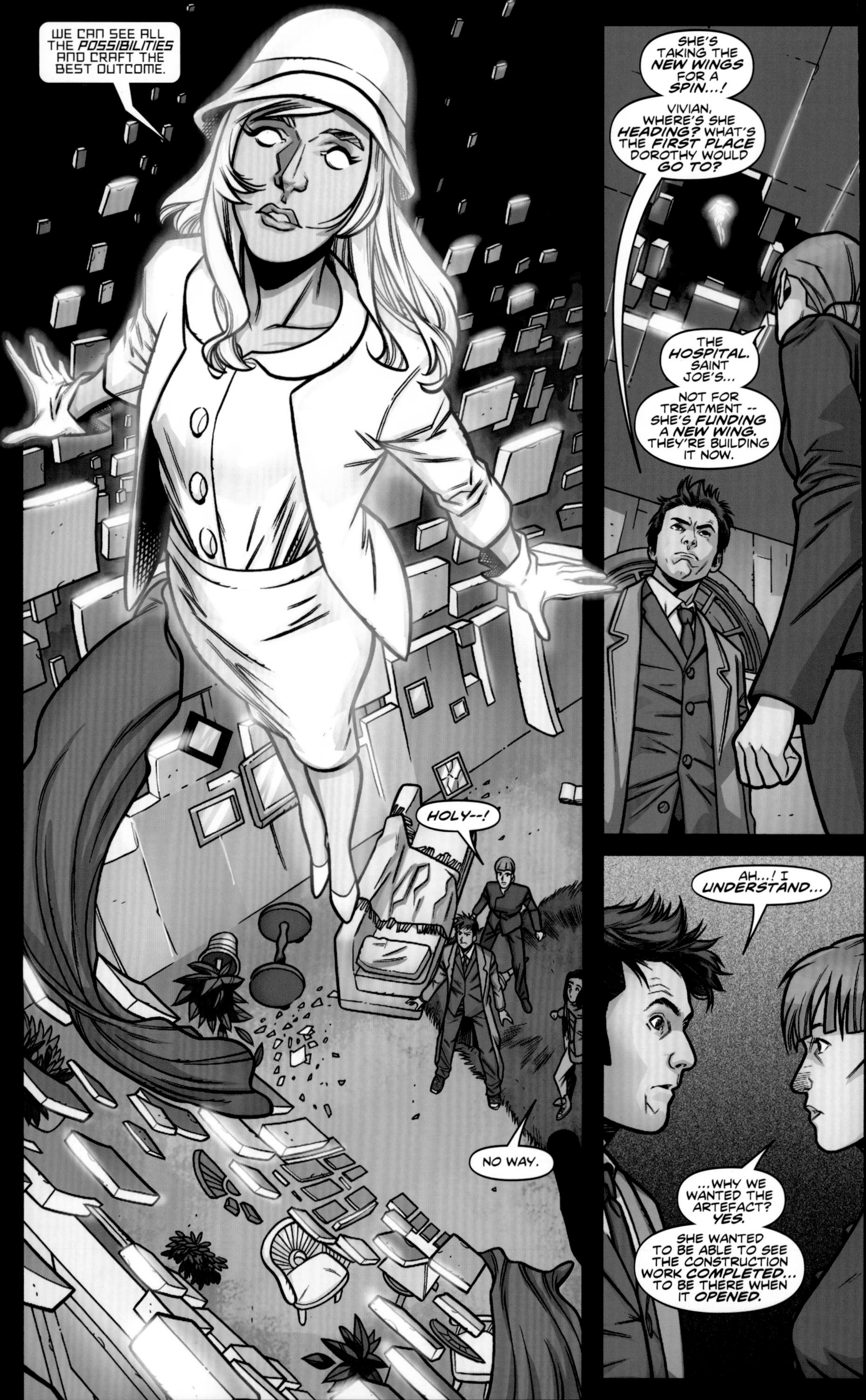
WE CAN SEE ALL THE POSSIBILITIES AND CRAFT THE BEST OUTCOME.
HOLY--!
NO WAY.
SHE'S TAKING THE NEW WINGS FOR A SPIN...!
VIVIAN, WHERE'S SHE HEADING? WHAT'S THE FIRST PLACE DOROTHY WOULD GO TO?
THE HOSPITAL. SAINT JOE'S...
NOT FOR TREATMENT -- SHE'S FUNDING A NEW WING. THEY'RE BUILDING IT NOW.
AH...! I UNDERSTAND...
...WHY WE WANTED THE ARTEFACT? YES.
SHE WANTED TO BE ABLE TO SEE THE CONSTRUCTION WORK COMPLETED... TO BE THERE WHEN IT OPENED.

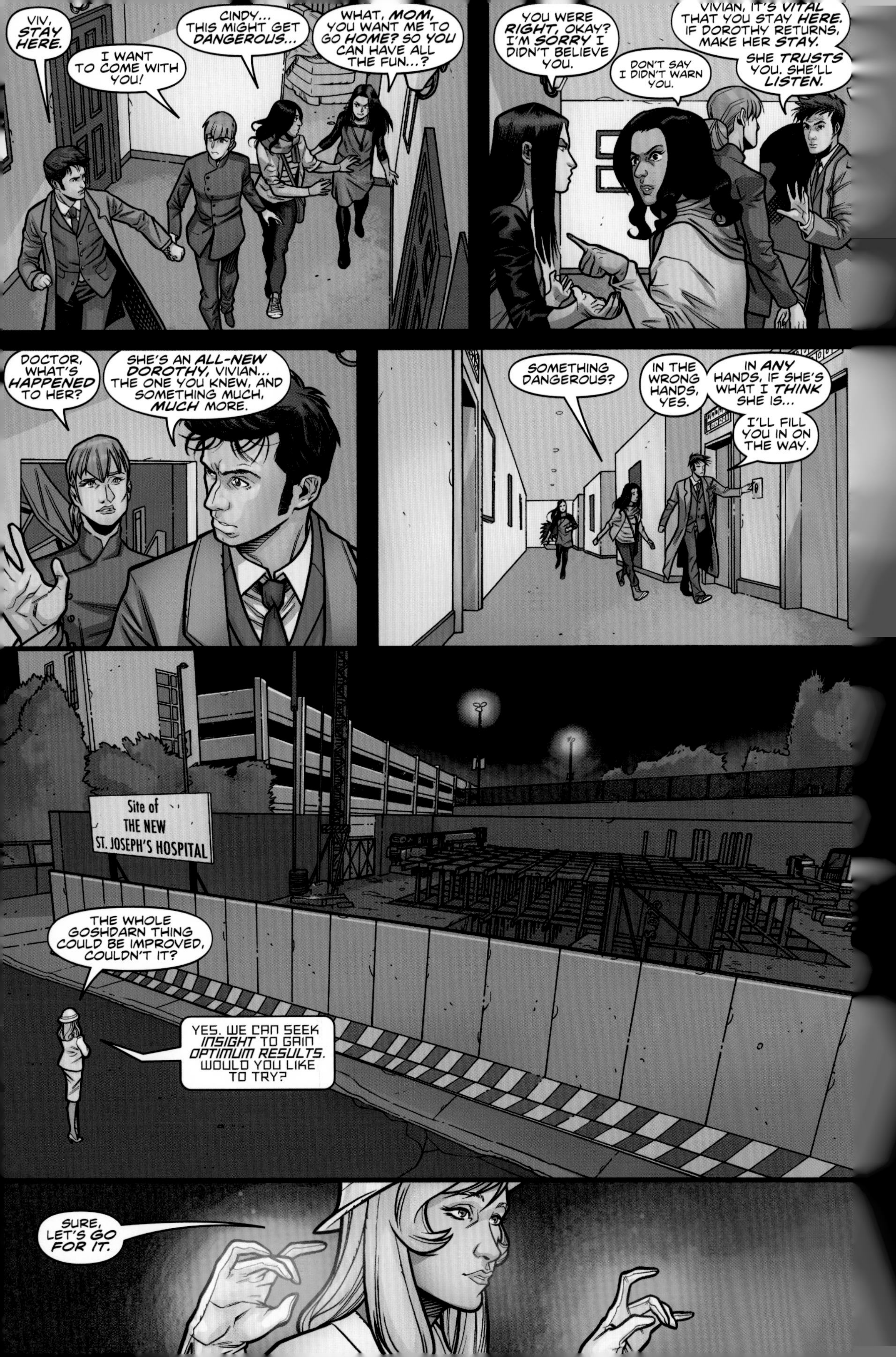
VIV, STAY HERE.
I WANT TO COME WITH YOU!
CINDY... THIS MIGHT GET DANGEROUS...
WHAT, MOM, YOU WANT ME TO GO HOME? SO YOU CAN HAVE ALL THE FUN...?
YOU WERE RIGHT, OKAY? I'M SORRY I DIDN'T BELIEVE YOU.
DON'T SAY I DIDN'T WARN YOU.
VIVIAN, IT'S VITAL THAT YOU STAY HERE. IF DOROTHY RETURNS, MAKE HER STAY.
SHE TRUSTS YOU. SHE'LL LISTEN.
DOCTOR, WHAT'S HAPPENED TO HER?
SHE'S AN ALL-NEW DOROTHY, VIVIAN... THE ONE YOU KNEW, AND SOMETHING MUCH, MUCH MORE.
SOMETHING DANGEROUS?
IN THE WRONG HANDS, YES.
IN ANY HANDS, IF SHE'S WHAT I THINK SHE IS...
I'LL FILL YOU IN ON THE WAY.
Site of THE NEW ST. JOSEPH'S HOSPITAL
THE WHOLE GOSHDARN THING COULD BE IMPROVED, COULDN'T IT?
YES. WE CAN SEEK INSIGHT TO GAIN OPTIMUM RESULTS. WOULD YOU LIKE TO TRY?
SURE, LET'S GO FOR IT.

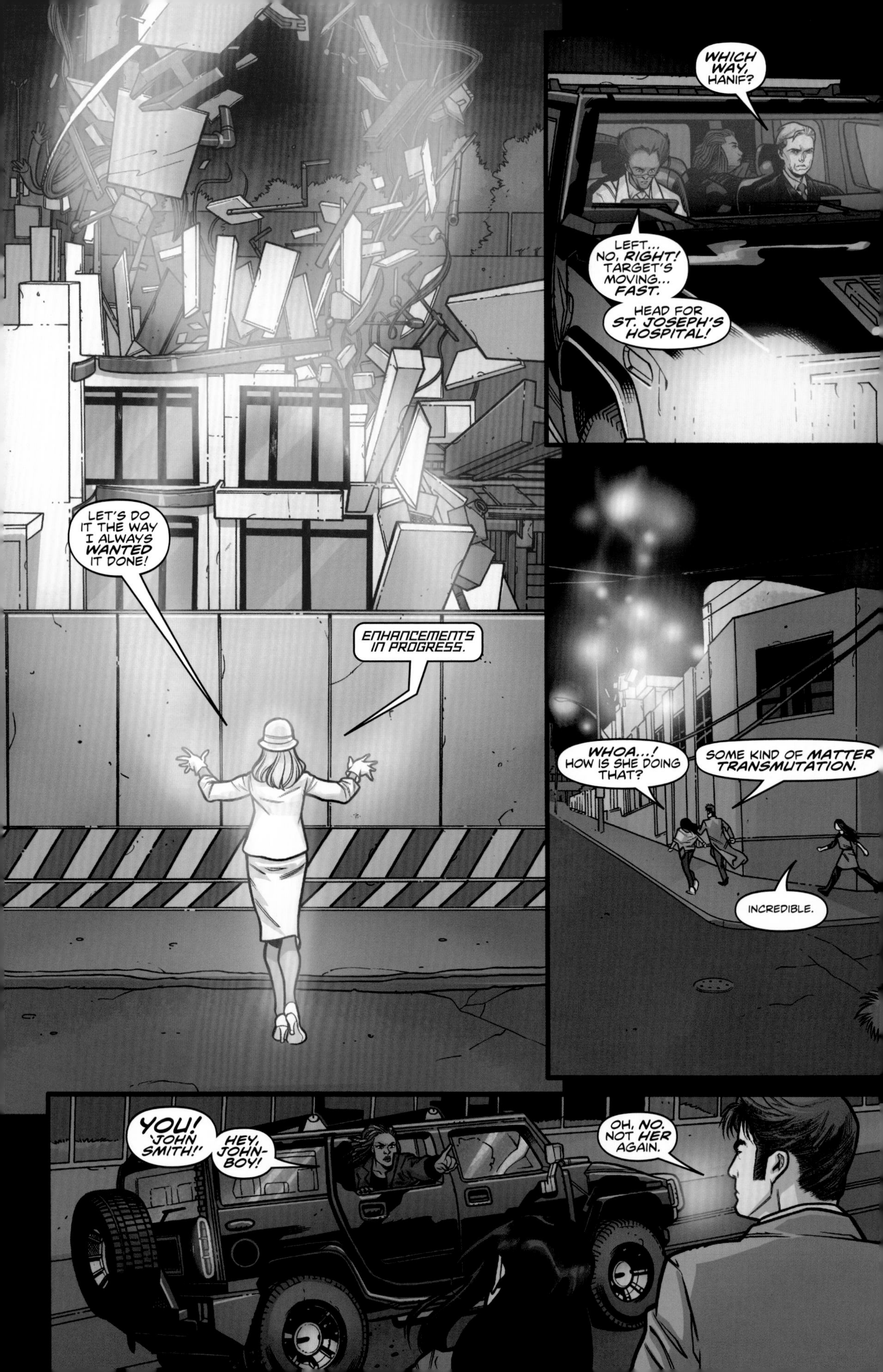
LET'S DO IT THE WAY I ALWAYS WANTED IT DONE!
ENHANCEMENTS IN PROGRESS.
WHICH WAY, HANIF?
LEFT... NO, RIGHT! TARGET'S MOVING... FAST.
HEAD FOR ST. JOSEPH'S HOSPITAL!
WHOA...! HOW IS SHE DOING THAT?
SOME KIND OF MATTER TRANSMUTATION.
INCREDIBLE.
YOU! 'JOHN SMITH!'
HEY, JOHN-BOY!
OH, NO. NOT HER AGAIN.

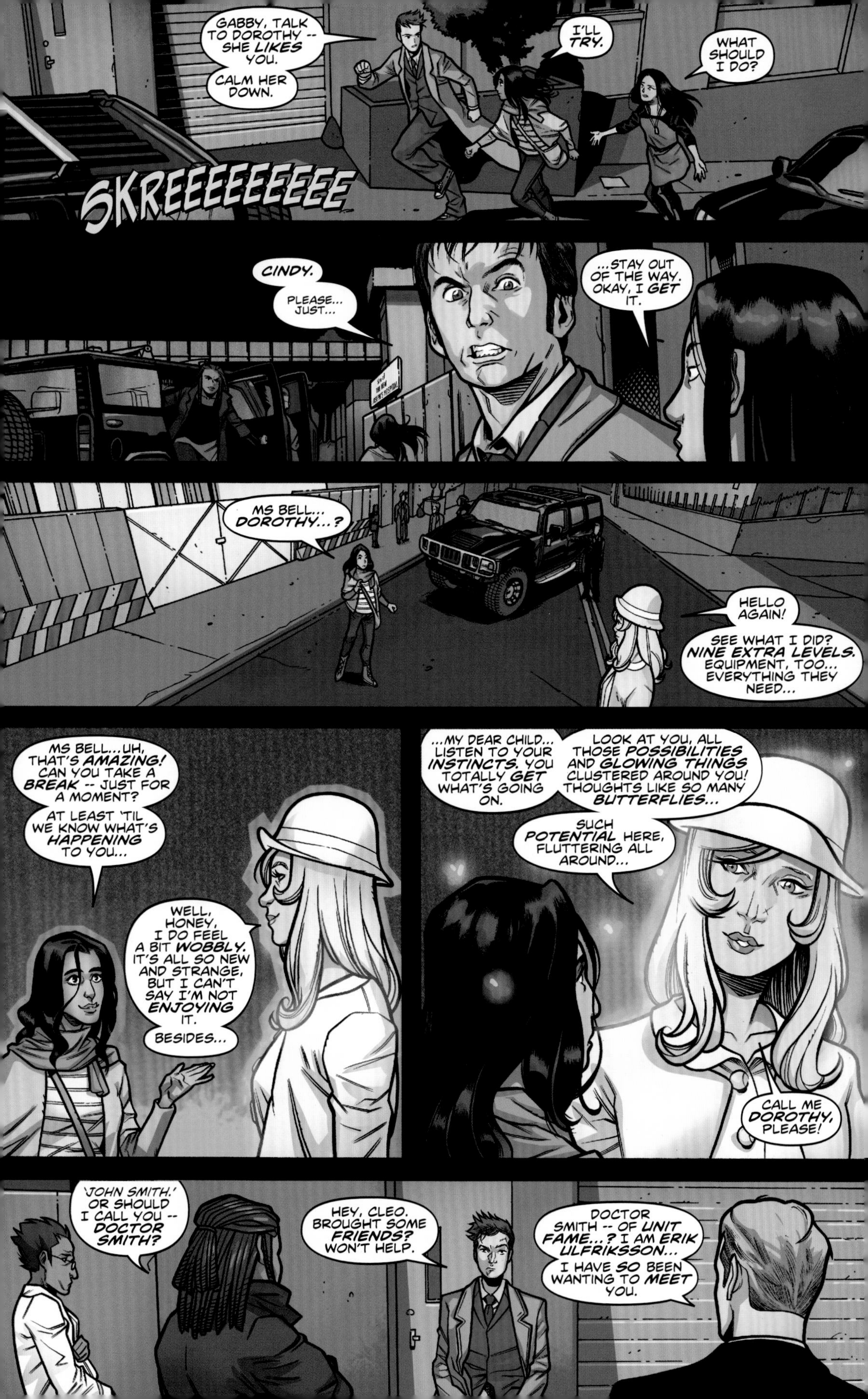
GABBY, TALK TO DOROTHY -- SHE LIKES YOU.
CALM HER DOWN.
I'LL TRY.
WHAT SHOULD I DO?
SKREEEEEEEEEE
CINDY.
PLEASE... JUST...
...STAY OUT OF THE WAY. OKAY, I GET IT.
MS BELL... DOROTHY...?
HELLO AGAIN!
SEE WHAT I DID? NINE EXTRA LEVELS. EQUIPMENT, TOO... EVERYTHING THEY NEED...
MS BELL...UH, THAT'S AMAZING! CAN YOU TAKE A BREAK -- JUST FOR A MOMENT?
AT LEAST 'TIL WE KNOW WHAT'S HAPPENING TO YOU...
WELL, HONEY, I DO FEEL A BIT WOBBLY. IT'S ALL SO NEW AND STRANGE, BUT I CAN'T SAY I'M NOT ENJOYING IT.
BESIDES...
...MY DEAR CHILD... LISTEN TO YOUR INSTINCTS. YOU TOTALLY GET WHAT'S GOING ON.
LOOK AT YOU, ALL THOSE POSSIBILITIES AND GLOWING THINGS CLUSTERED AROUND YOU! THOUGHTS LIKE SO MANY BUTTERFLIES...
SUCH POTENTIAL HERE, FLUTTERING ALL AROUND...
CALL ME DOROTHY, PLEASE!
'JOHN SMITH.' OR SHOULD I CALL YOU -- DOCTOR SMITH?
HEY, CLEO. BROUGHT SOME FRIENDS? WON'T HELP.
DOCTOR SMITH -- OF UNIT FAME...? I AM ERIK ULFRIKSSON...
I HAVE SO BEEN WANTING TO MEET YOU.

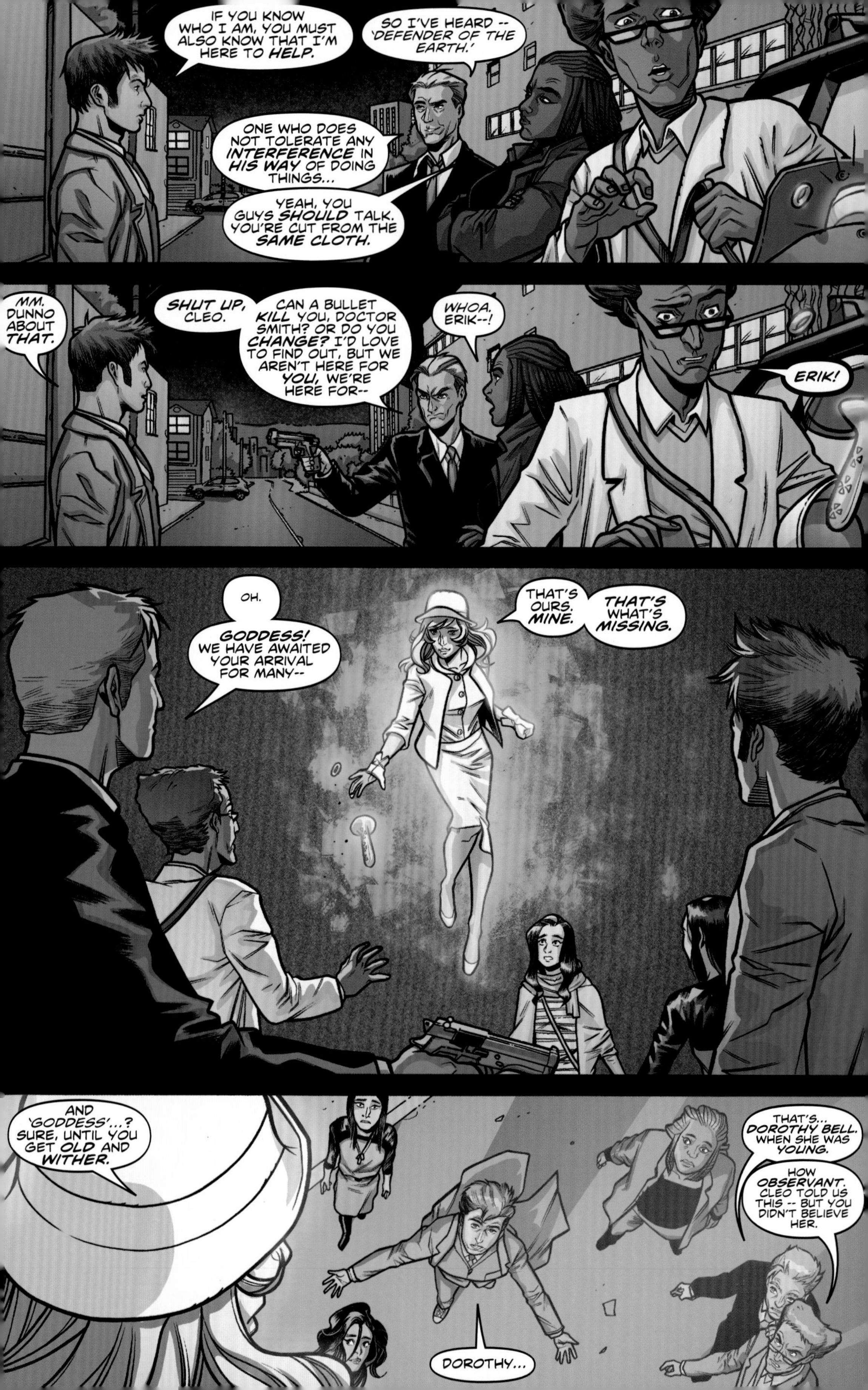
IF YOU KNOW WHO I AM, YOU MUST ALSO KNOW THAT I'M HERE TO HELP.
SO I'VE HEARD -- 'DEFENDER OF THE EARTH.'
ONE WHO DOES NOT TOLERATE ANY INTERFERENCE IN HIS WAY OF DOING THINGS...
YEAH, YOU GUYS SHOULD TALK. YOU'RE CUT FROM THE SAME CLOTH.
MM. DUNNO ABOUT THAT.
SHUT UP, CLEO.
CAN A BULLET KILL YOU, DOCTOR SMITH? OR DO YOU CHANGE? I'D LOVE TO FIND OUT, BUT WE AREN'T HERE FOR YOU, WE'RE HERE FOR--
WHOA. ERIK--!
ERIK!
OH.
GODDESS! WE HAVE AWAITED YOUR ARRIVAL FOR MANY--
THAT'S OURS. MINE.
THAT'S WHAT'S MISSING.
AND 'GODDESS'...? SURE, UNTIL YOU GET OLD AND WITHER.
THAT'S... DOROTHY BELL. WHEN SHE WAS YOUNG.
HOW OBSERVANT. CLEO TOLD US THIS -- BUT YOU DIDN'T BELIEVE HER.
DOROTHY...

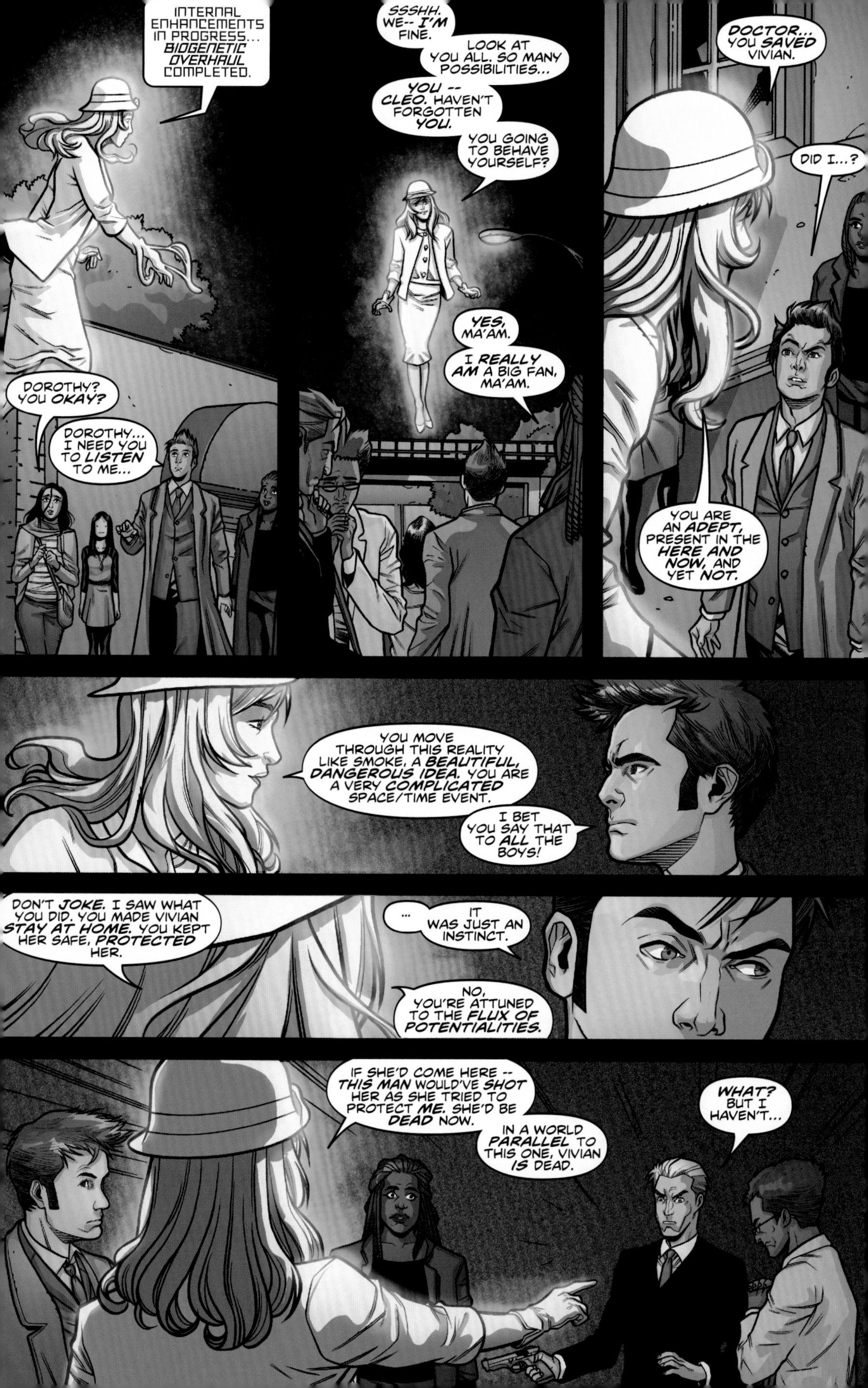
INTERNAL ENHANCEMENTS IN PROGRESS... BIOGENETIC OVERHAUL COMPLETED.
DOROTHY? YOU OKAY?
DOROTHY... I NEED YOU TO LISTEN TO ME...
SSSHH. WE-- I'M FINE.
LOOK AT YOU ALL. SO MANY POSSIBILITIES...
YOU -- CLEO. HAVEN'T FORGOTTEN YOU.
YOU GOING TO BEHAVE YOURSELF?
YES, MA'AM.
I REALLY AM A BIG FAN, MA'AM.
DOCTOR... YOU SAVED VIVIAN.
DID I...?
YOU ARE AN ADEPT, PRESENT IN THE HERE AND NOW, AND YET NOT.
YOU MOVE THROUGH THIS REALITY LIKE SMOKE, A BEAUTIFUL, DANGEROUS IDEA. YOU ARE A VERY COMPLICATED SPACE/TIME EVENT.
I BET YOU SAY THAT TO ALL THE BOYS!
DON'T JOKE. I SAW WHAT YOU DID. YOU MADE VIVIAN STAY AT HOME. YOU KEPT HER SAFE, PROTECTED HER.
... IT WAS JUST AN INSTINCT.
NO, YOU'RE ATTUNED TO THE FLUX OF POTENTIALITIES.
IF SHE'D COME HERE -- THIS MAN WOULD'VE SHOT HER AS SHE TRIED TO PROTECT ME. SHE'D BE DEAD NOW.
IN A WORLD PARALLEL TO THIS ONE, VIVIAN IS DEAD.
WHAT? BUT I HAVEN'T...

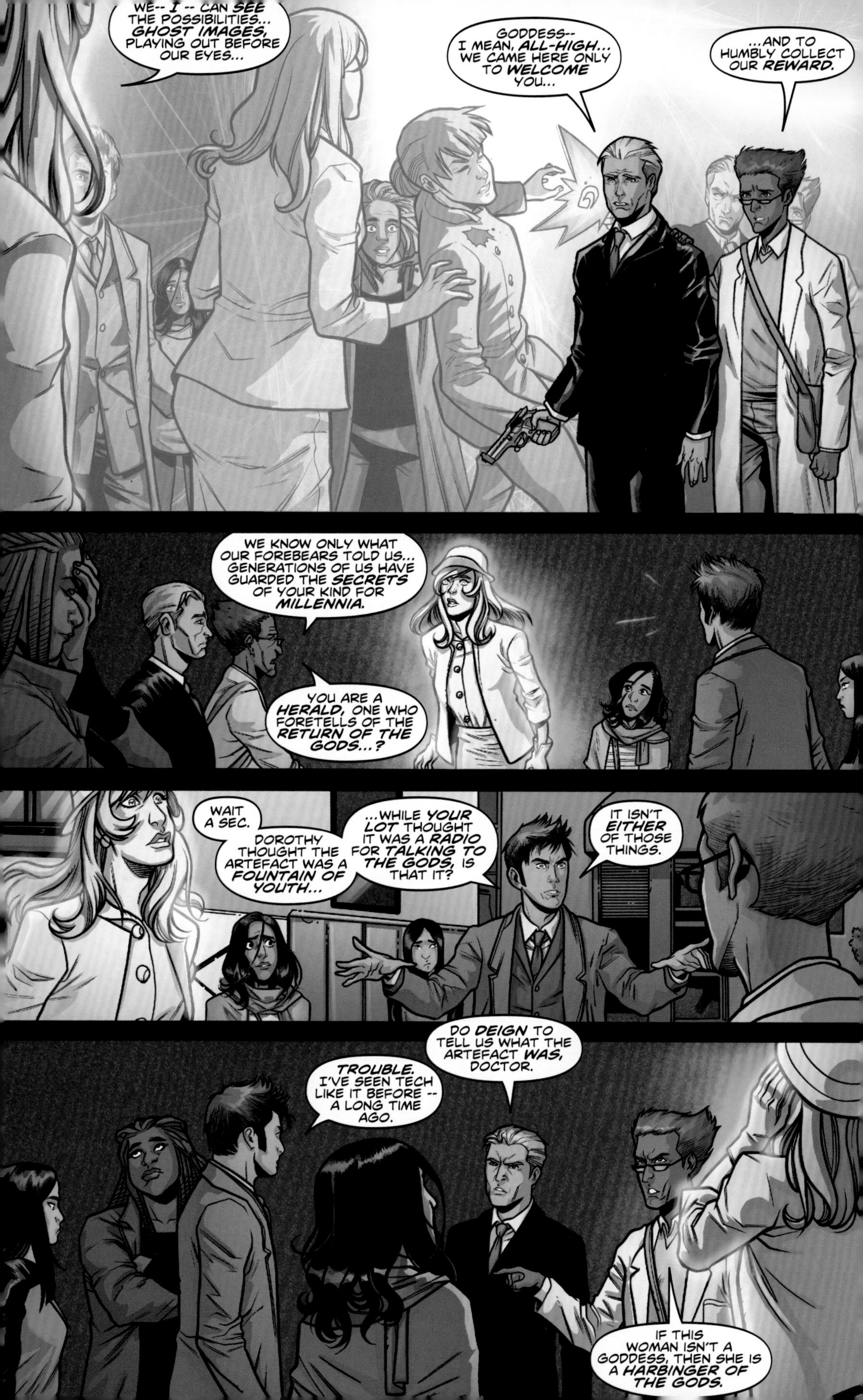

WE-- I -- CAN SEE THE POSSIBILITIES... GHOST IMAGES, PLAYING OUT BEFORE OUR EYES...
GODDESS-- I MEAN, ALL-HIGH... WE CAME HERE ONLY TO WELCOME YOU...
...AND TO HUMBLY COLLECT OUR REWARD.
WE KNOW ONLY WHAT OUR FOREBEARS TOLD US... GENERATIONS OF US HAVE GUARDED THE SECRETS OF YOUR KIND FOR MILLENNIA.
YOU ARE A HERALD, ONE WHO FORETELLS OF THE RETURN OF THE GODS...?
WAIT A SEC.
DOROTHY THOUGHT THE ARTEFACT WAS A FOUNTAIN OF YOUTH...
...WHILE YOUR LOT THOUGHT IT WAS A RADIO FOR TALKING TO THE GODS, IS THAT IT?
IT ISN'T EITHER OF THOSE THINGS.
TROUBLE. I'VE SEEN TECH LIKE IT BEFORE -- A LONG TIME AGO.
DO DEIGN TO TELL US WHAT THE ARTEFACT WAS, DOCTOR.
IF THIS WOMAN ISN'T A GODDESS, THEN SHE IS A HARBINGER OF THE GODS.

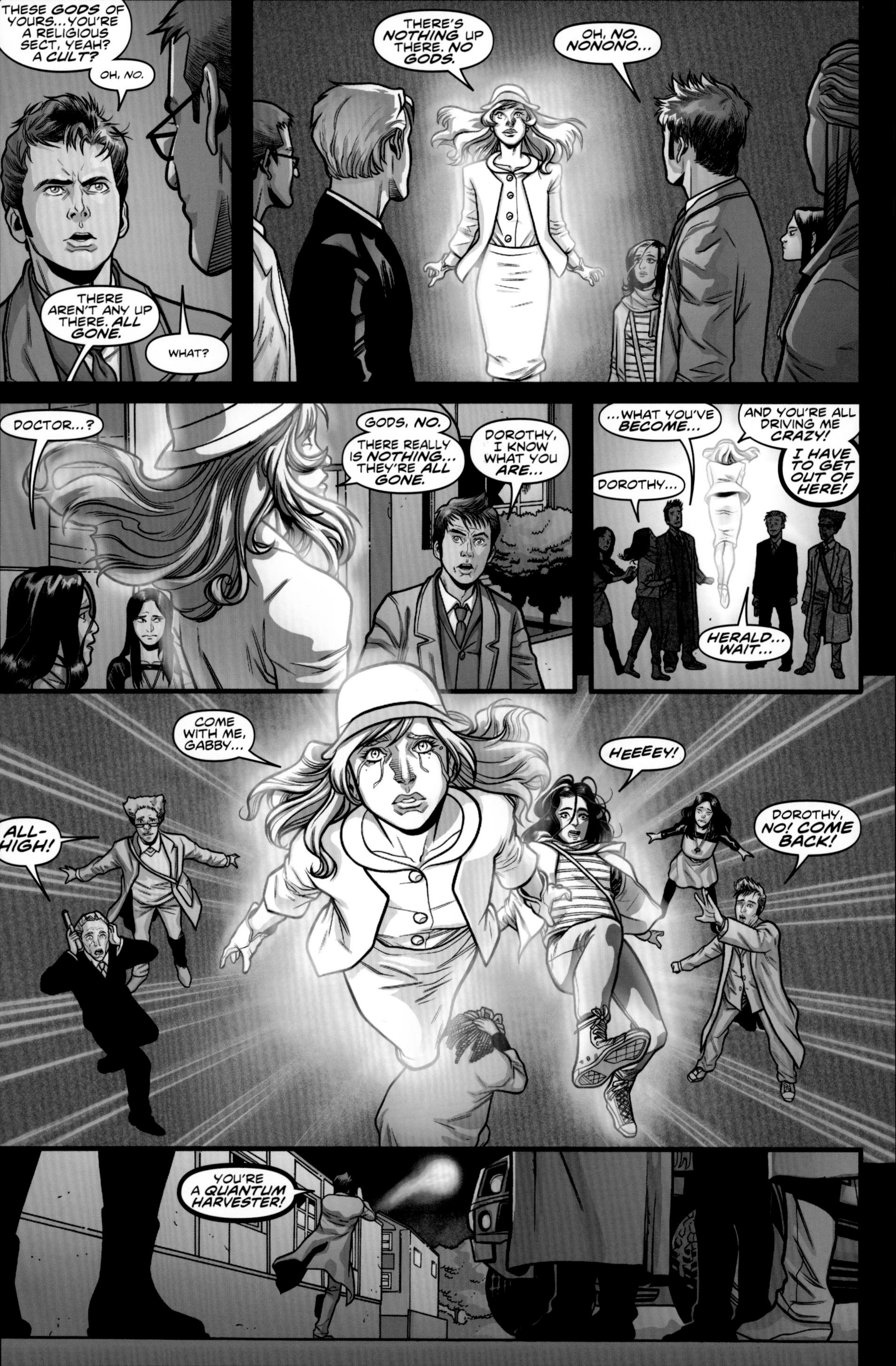
THESE GODS OF YOURS...YOU'RE A RELIGIOUS SECT, YEAH? A CULT?
OH, NO.
THERE AREN'T ANY UP THERE. ALL GONE.
WHAT?
THERE'S NOTHING UP THERE. NO GODS.
OH, NO. NONONO...
DOCTOR...?
GODS, NO.
THERE REALLY IS NOTHING... THEY'RE ALL GONE.
DOROTHY, I KNOW WHAT YOU ARE...
...WHAT YOU'VE BECOME...
DOROTHY...
AND YOU'RE ALL DRIVING ME CRAZY!
I HAVE TO GET OUT OF HERE!
HERALD... WAIT...
COME WITH ME, GABBY...
HEEEEY!
ALL-HIGH!
DOROTHY, NO! COME BACK!
YOU'RE A QUANTUM HARVESTER!

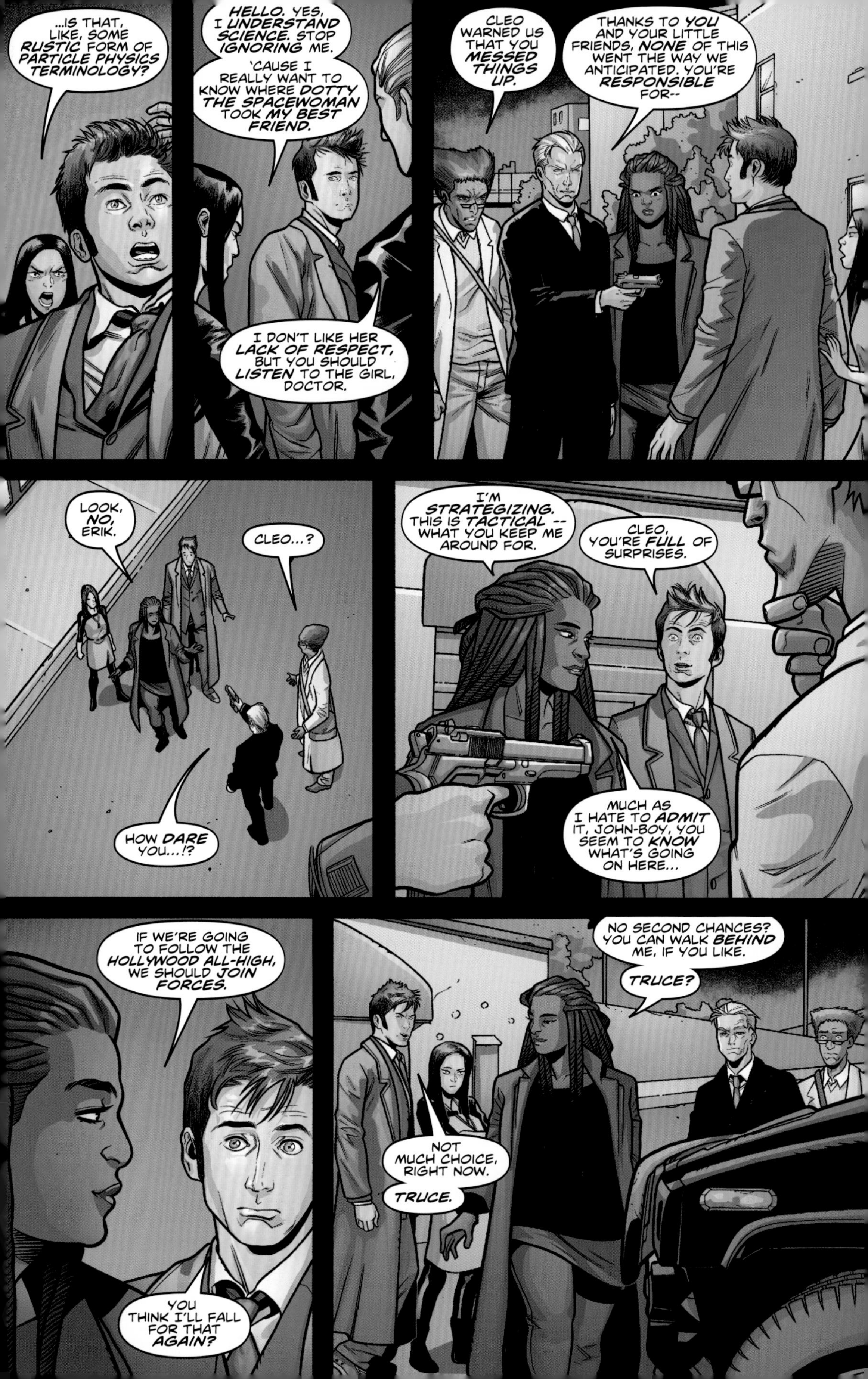
...IS THAT, LIKE, SOME RUSTIC FORM OF PARTICLE PHYSICS TERMINOLOGY?
HELLO. YES, I UNDERSTAND SCIENCE. STOP IGNORING ME.
'CAUSE I REALLY WANT TO KNOW WHERE DOTTY THE SPACEWOMAN TOOK MY BEST FRIEND.
I DON'T LIKE HER LACK OF RESPECT, BUT YOU SHOULD LISTEN TO THE GIRL, DOCTOR.
CLEO WARNED US THAT YOU MESSED THINGS UP.
THANKS TO YOU AND YOUR LITTLE FRIENDS, NONE OF THIS WENT THE WAY WE ANTICIPATED. YOU'RE RESPONSIBLE FOR--
LOOK, NO, ERIK.
CLEO...?
HOW DARE YOU...!?
I'M STRATEGIZING. THIS IS TACTICAL -- WHAT YOU KEEP ME AROUND FOR.
CLEO, YOU'RE FULL OF SURPRISES.
MUCH AS I HATE TO ADMIT IT, JOHN-BOY, YOU SEEM TO KNOW WHAT'S GOING ON HERE...
IF WE'RE GOING TO FOLLOW THE HOLLYWOOD ALL-HIGH, WE SHOULD JOIN FORCES.
YOU THINK I'LL FALL FOR THAT AGAIN?
NO SECOND CHANCES? YOU CAN WALK BEHIND ME, IF YOU LIKE.
TRUCE?
NOT MUCH CHOICE, RIGHT NOW.
TRUCE.

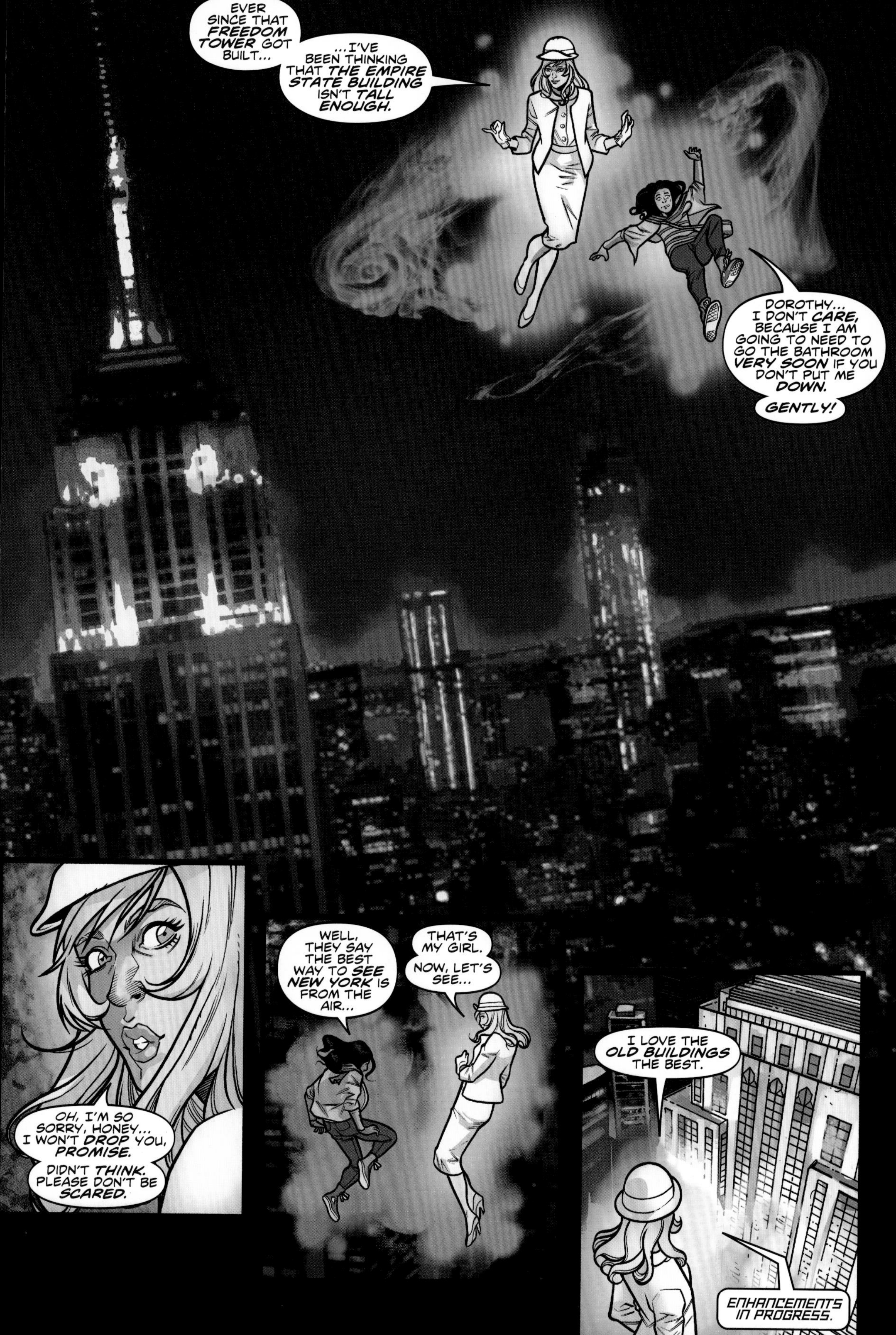
EVER SINCE THAT FREEDOM TOWER GOT BUILT...
...I'VE BEEN THINKING THAT THE EMPIRE STATE BUILDING ISN'T TALL ENOUGH.
DOROTHY... I DON'T CARE, BECAUSE I AM GOING TO NEED TO GO THE BATHROOM VERY SOON IF YOU DON'T PUT ME DOWN.
GENTLY!
OH, I'M SO SORRY, HONEY... I WON'T DROP YOU, PROMISE.
DIDN'T THINK. PLEASE DON'T BE SCARED.
WELL, THEY SAY THE BEST WAY TO SEE NEW YORK IS FROM THE AIR...
THAT'S MY GIRL.
NOW, LET'S SEE...
I LOVE THE OLD BUILDINGS THE BEST.
ENHANCEMENTS IN PROGRESS.

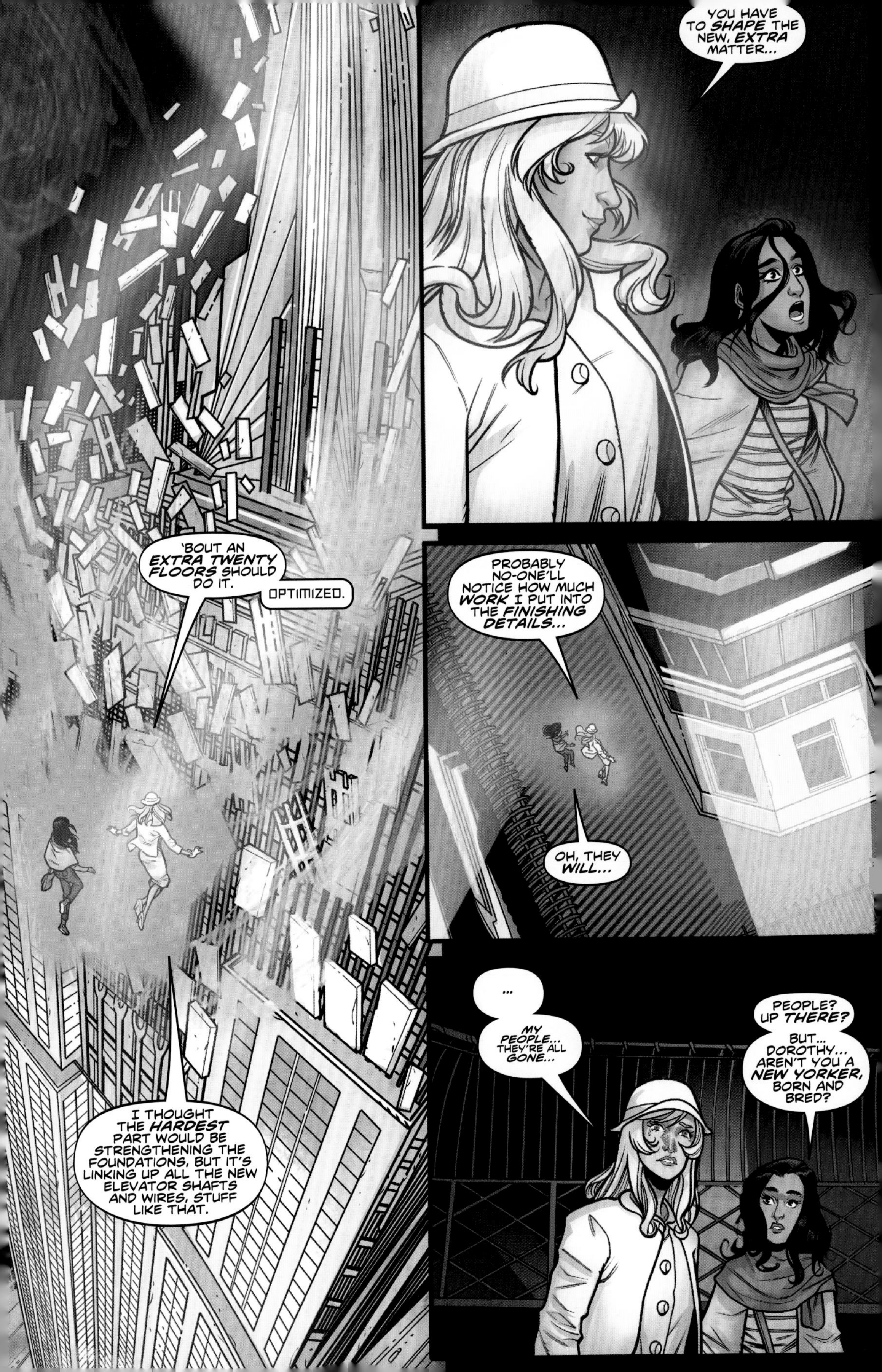

'BOUT AN EXTRA TWENTY FLOORS SHOULD DO IT.
OPTIMIZED.
I THOUGHT THE HARDEST PART WOULD BE STRENGTHENING THE FOUNDATIONS, BUT IT'S LINKING UP ALL THE NEW ELEVATOR SHAFTS AND WIRES, STUFF LIKE THAT.
YOU HAVE TO SHAPE THE NEW, EXTRA MATTER...
PROBABLY NO-ONE'LL NOTICE HOW MUCH WORK I PUT INTO THE FINISHING DETAILS...
OH, THEY WILL...
...
MY PEOPLE... THEY'RE ALL GONE...
PEOPLE? UP THERE?
BUT... DOROTHY... AREN'T YOU A NEW YORKER, BORN AND BRED?

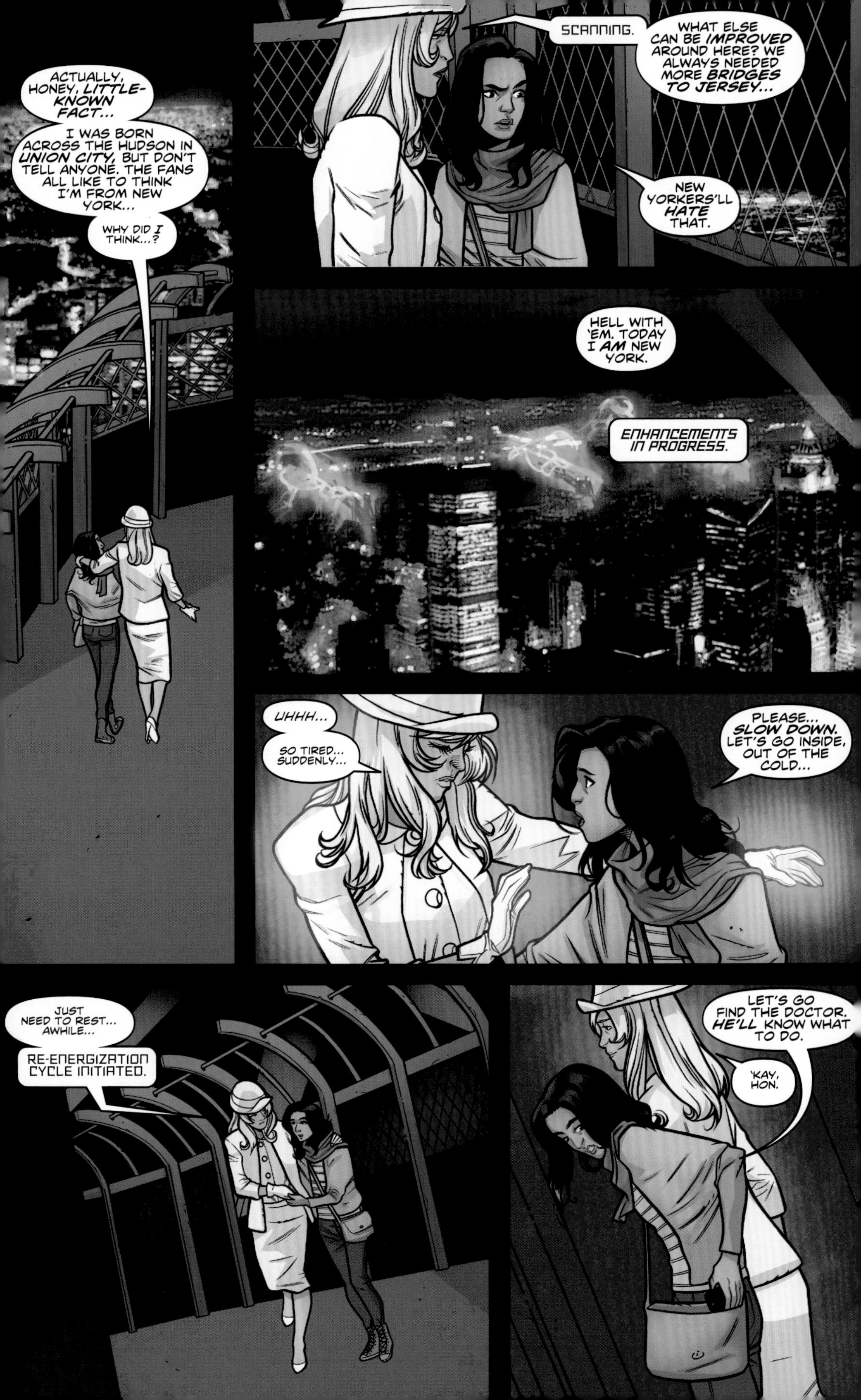

ACTUALLY, HONEY, LITTLE-KNOWN FACT...
I WAS BORN ACROSS THE HUDSON IN UNION CITY, BUT DON'T TELL ANYONE. THE FANS ALL LIKE TO THINK I'M FROM NEW YORK...
WHY DID I THINK...?
SCANNING.
WHAT ELSE CAN BE IMPROVED AROUND HERE? WE ALWAYS NEEDED MORE BRIDGES TO JERSEY...
NEW YORKERS'LL HATE THAT.
HELL WITH 'EM. TODAY I AM NEW YORK.
ENHANCEMENTS IN PROGRESS.
UHHH...
SO TIRED... SUDDENLY...
PLEASE... SLOW DOWN. LET'S GO INSIDE, OUT OF THE COLD...
JUST NEED TO REST... AWHILE...
RE-ENERGIZATION CYCLE INITIATED.
LET'S GO FIND THE DOCTOR. HE'LL KNOW WHAT TO DO.
'KAY, HON.

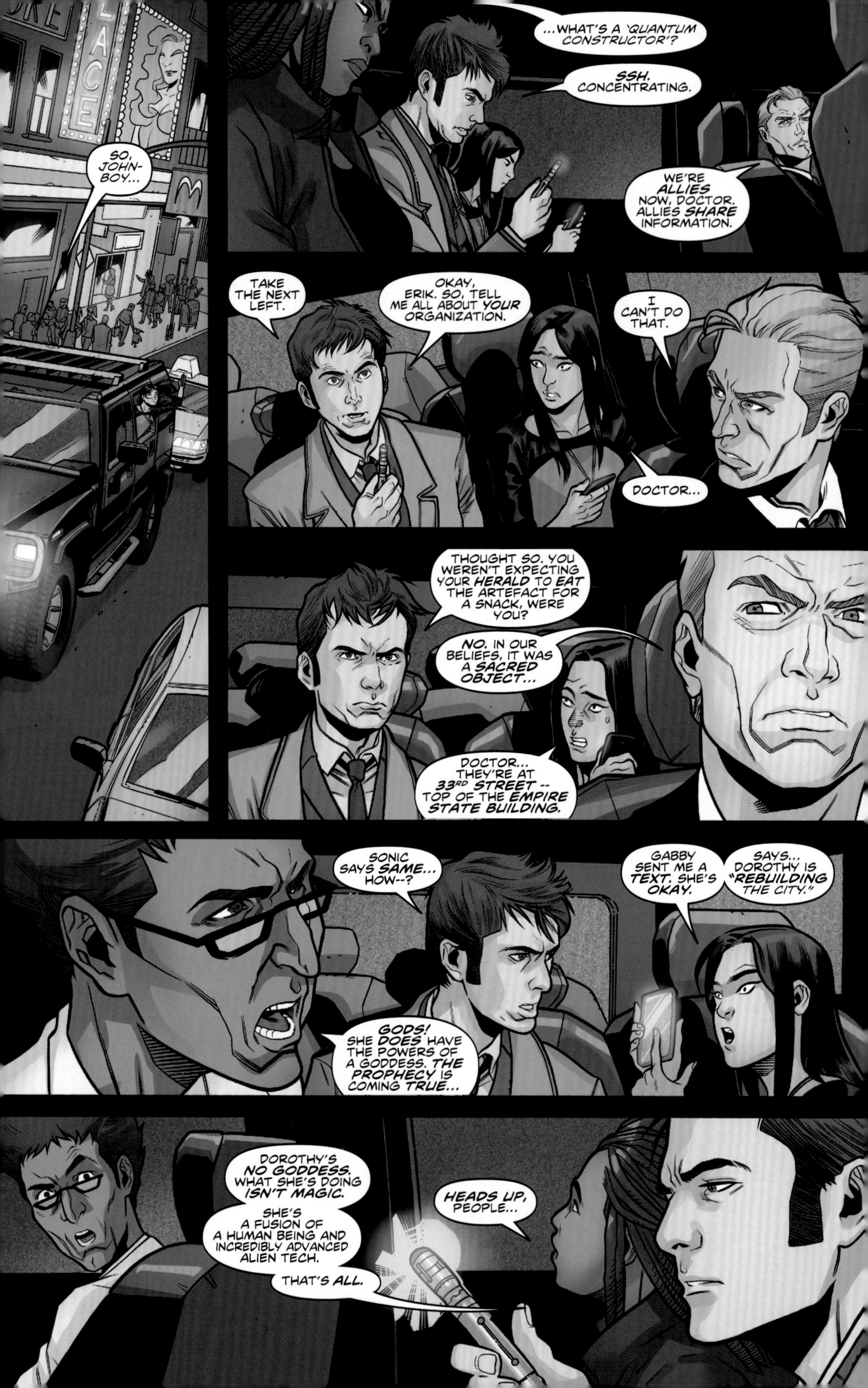

SO, JOHN-BOY...
...WHAT'S A 'QUANTUM CONSTRUCTOR'?
SSH. CONCENTRATING.
WE'RE ALLIES NOW, DOCTOR. ALLIES SHARE INFORMATION.
TAKE THE NEXT LEFT.
OKAY, ERIK. SO, TELL ME ALL ABOUT YOUR ORGANIZATION.
I CAN'T DO THAT.
DOCTOR...
THOUGHT SO. YOU WEREN'T EXPECTING YOUR HERALD TO EAT THE ARTEFACT FOR A SNACK, WERE YOU?
NO. IN OUR BELIEFS, IT WAS A SACRED OBJECT...
DOCTOR... THEY'RE AT 33RD STREET -- TOP OF THE EMPIRE STATE BUILDING.
SONIC SAYS SAME... HOW--?
GABBY SENT ME A TEXT. SHE'S OKAY.
SAYS... DOROTHY IS "REBUILDING THE CITY."
GODS! SHE DOES HAVE THE POWERS OF A GODDESS. THE PROPHECY IS COMING TRUE...
DOROTHY'S NO GODDESS. WHAT SHE'S DOING ISN'T MAGIC.
SHE'S A FUSION OF A HUMAN BEING AND INCREDIBLY ADVANCED ALIEN TECH.
THAT'S ALL.
HEADS UP, PEOPLE...

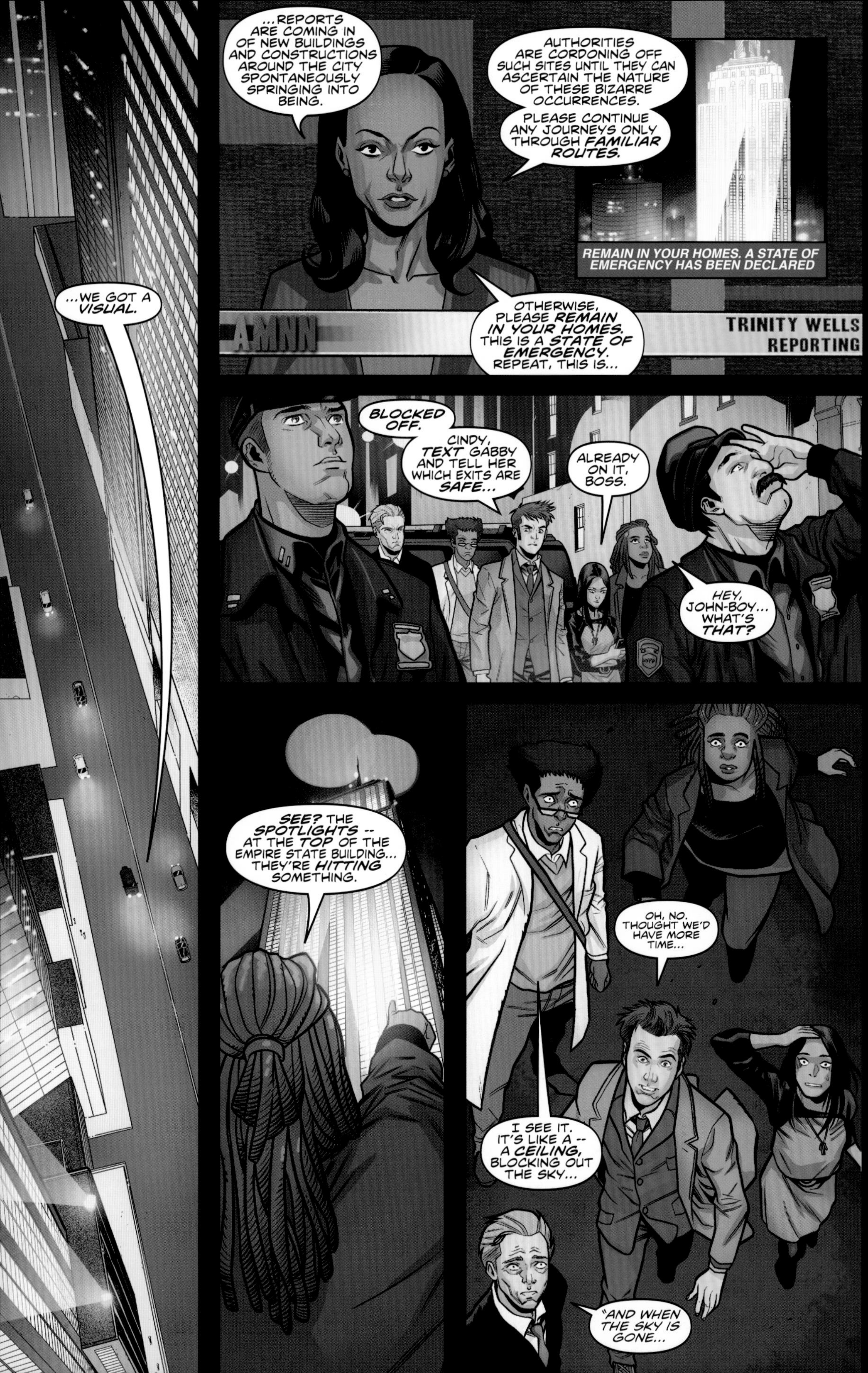

...REPORTS ARE COMING IN OF NEW BUILDINGS AND CONSTRUCTIONS AROUND THE CITY SPONTANEOUSLY SPRINGING INTO BEING.
AUTHORITIES ARE CORDONING OFF SUCH SITES UNTIL THEY CAN ASCERTAIN THE NATURE OF THESE BIZARRE OCCURRENCES.
PLEASE CONTINUE ANY JOURNEYS ONLY THROUGH FAMILIAR ROUTES.
REMAIN IN YOUR HOMES. A STATE OF EMERGENCY HAS BEEN DECLARED
OTHERWISE, PLEASE REMAIN IN YOUR HOMES. THIS IS A STATE OF EMERGENCY. REPEAT, THIS IS...
AMNN
TRINITY WELLS REPORTING
...WE GOT A VISUAL.
BLOCKED OFF.
CINDY, TEXT GABBY AND TELL HER WHICH EXITS ARE SAFE...
ALREADY ON IT, BOSS.
HEY, JOHN-BOY... WHAT'S THAT?
SEE? THE SPOTLIGHTS -- AT THE TOP OF THE EMPIRE STATE BUILDING... THEY'RE HITTING SOMETHING.
OH, NO. THOUGHT WE'D HAVE MORE TIME...
I SEE IT. IT'S LIKE A -- A CEILING, BLOCKING OUT THE SKY...
"AND WHEN THE SKY IS GONE...

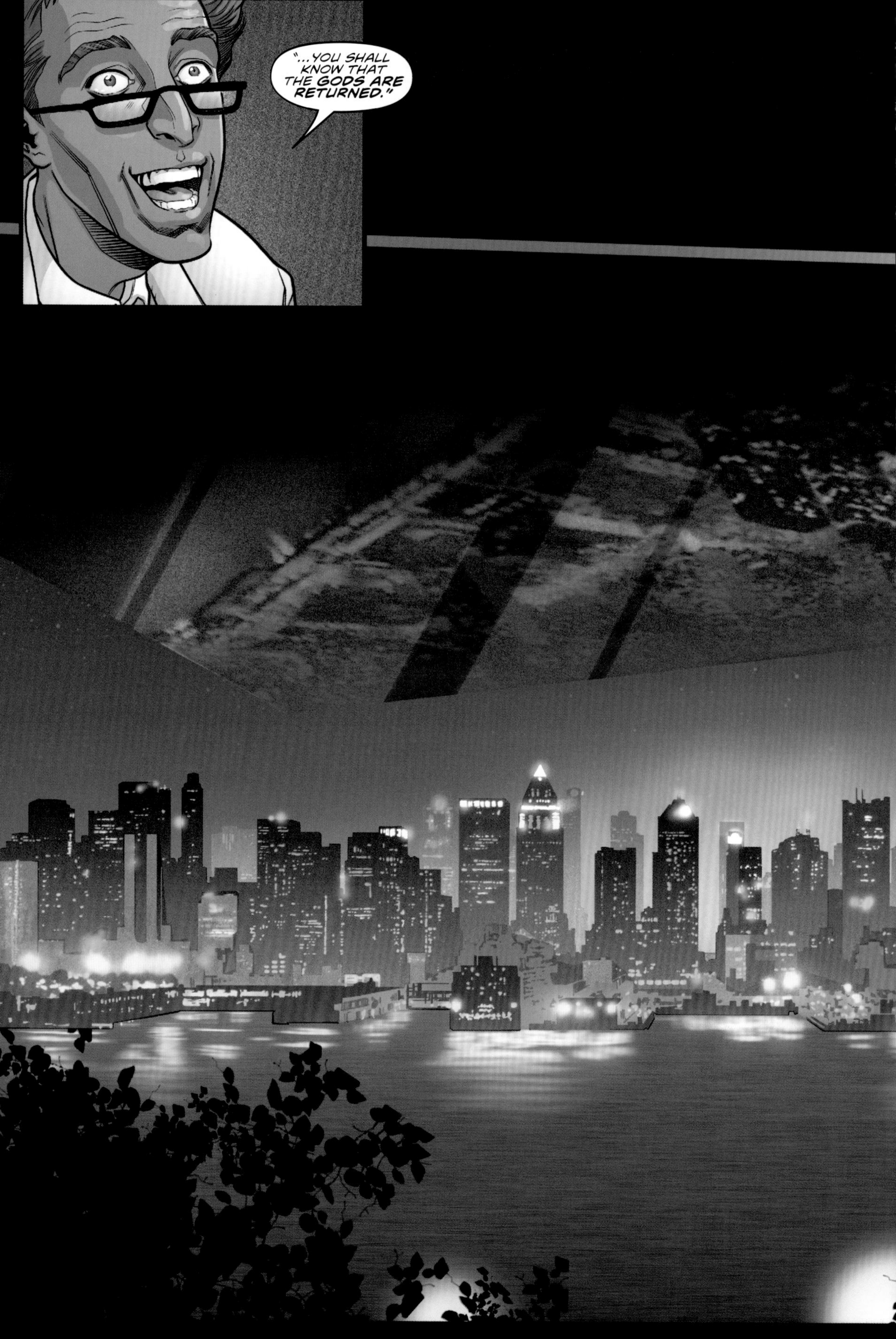
"...YOU SHALL KNOW THAT THE GODS ARE RETURNED."

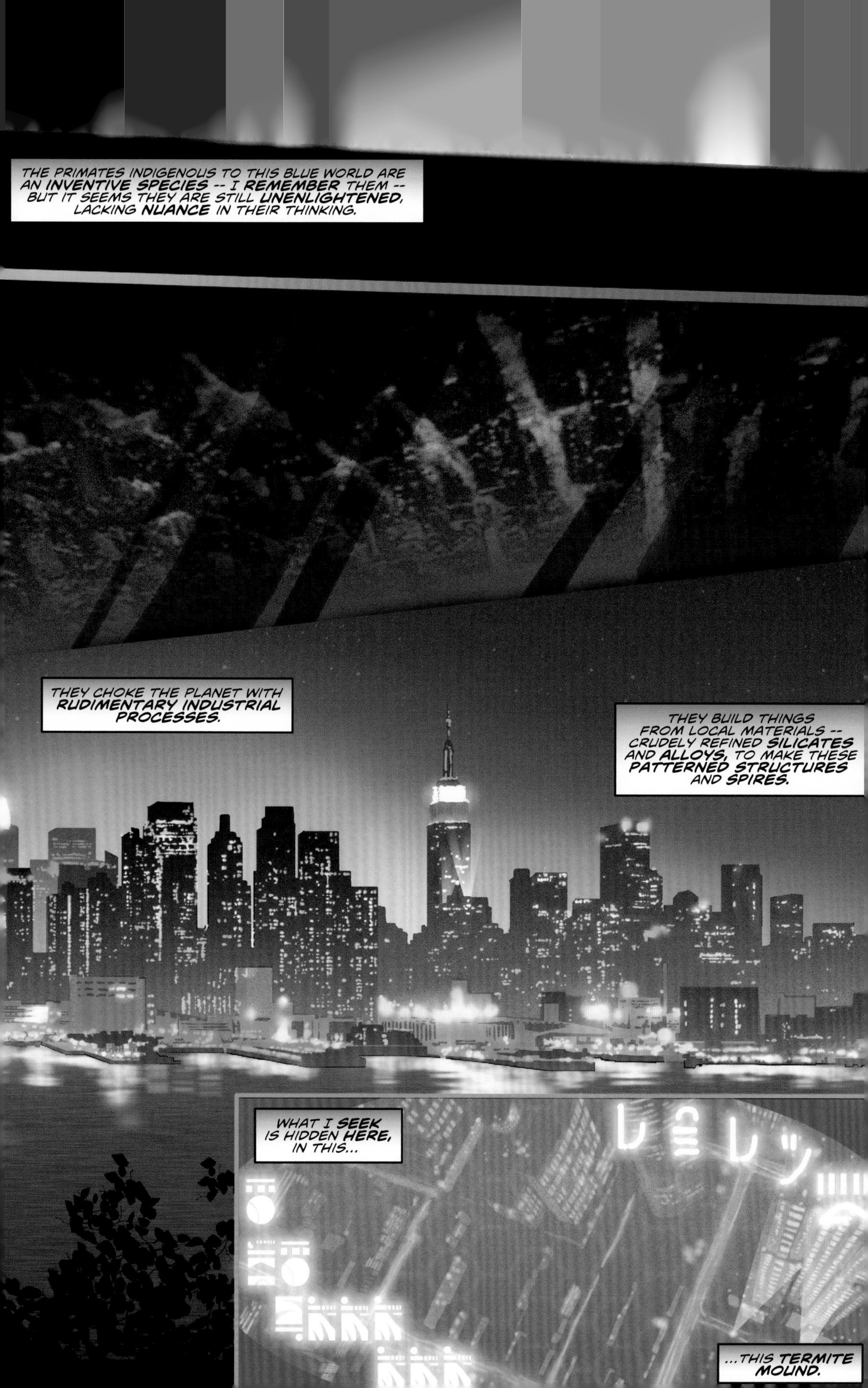
THE PRIMATES INDIGENOUS TO THIS BLUE WORLD ARE AN INVENTIVE SPECIES -- I REMEMBER THEM -- BUT IT SEEMS THEY ARE STILL UNENLIGHTENED, LACKING NUANCE IN THEIR THINKING.
THEY CHOKE THE PLANET WITH RUDIMENTARY INDUSTRIAL PROCESSES.
THEY BUILD THINGS FROM LOCAL MATERIALS -- CRUDELY REFINED SILICATES AND ALLOYS, TO MAKE THESE PATTERNED STRUCTURES AND SPIRES.
WHAT I SEEK IS HIDDEN HERE, IN THIS...
...THIS TERMITE MOUND.

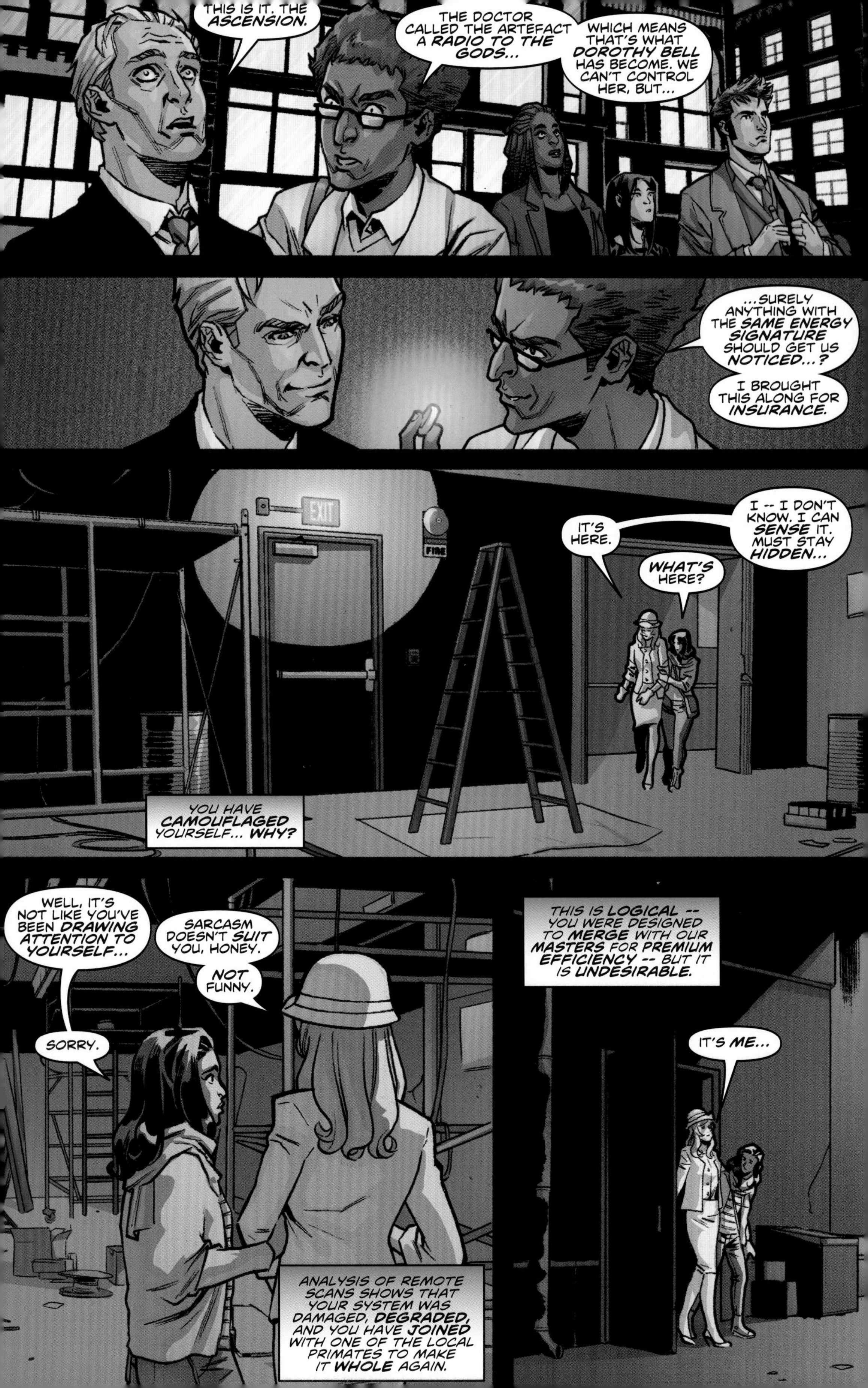
THIS IS IT. THE ASCENSION.
THE DOCTOR CALLED THE ARTEFACT A RADIO TO THE GODS...
WHICH MEANS THAT'S WHAT DOROTHY BELL HAS BECOME. WE CAN'T CONTROL HER, BUT...
...SURELY ANYTHING WITH THE SAME ENERGY SIGNATURE SHOULD GET US NOTICED...?
I BROUGHT THIS ALONG FOR INSURANCE.
EXIT
FIRE
IT'S HERE.
WHAT'S HERE?
I -- I DON'T KNOW. I CAN SENSE IT. MUST STAY HIDDEN...
YOU HAVE CAMOUFLAGED YOURSELF... WHY?
WELL, IT'S NOT LIKE YOU'VE BEEN DRAWING ATTENTION TO YOURSELF...
SARCASM DOESN'T SUIT YOU, HONEY.
NOT FUNNY.
SORRY.
ANALYSIS OF REMOTE SCANS SHOWS THAT YOUR SYSTEM WAS DAMAGED, DEGRADED, AND YOU HAVE JOINED WITH ONE OF THE LOCAL PRIMATES TO MAKE IT WHOLE AGAIN.
THIS IS LOGICAL -- YOU WERE DESIGNED TO MERGE WITH OUR MASTERS FOR PREMIUM EFFICIENCY -- BUT IT IS UNDESIRABLE.
IT'S ME...

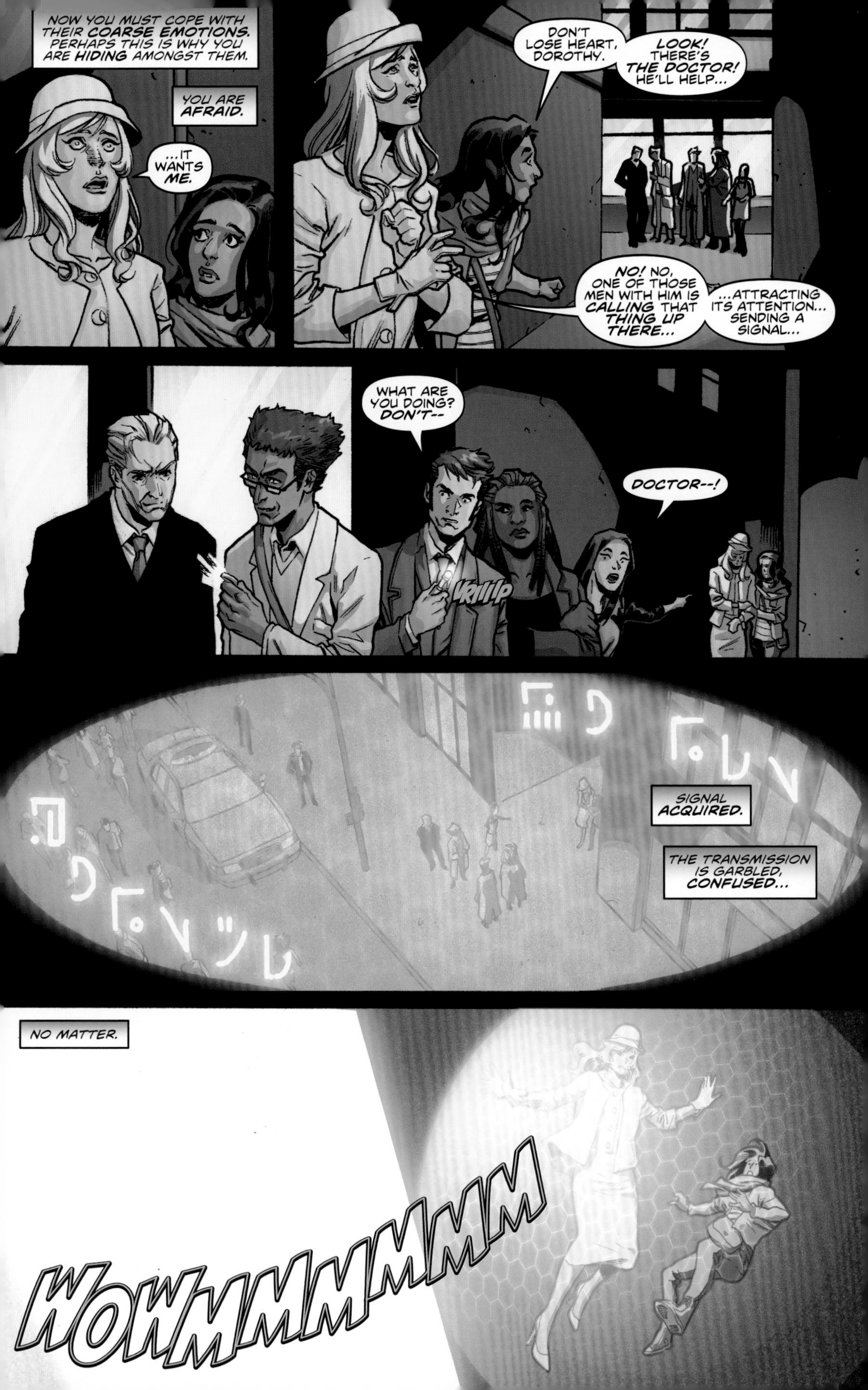
NOW YOU MUST COPE WITH THEIR COARSE EMOTIONS. PERHAPS THIS IS WHY YOU ARE HIDING AMONGST THEM.
YOU ARE AFRAID.
...IT WANTS ME.
DON'T LOSE HEART, DOROTHY.
LOOK! THERE'S THE DOCTOR! HE'LL HELP...
NO! NO, ONE OF THOSE MEN WITH HIM IS CALLING THAT THING UP THERE...
...ATTRACTING ITS ATTENTION... SENDING A SIGNAL...
WHAT ARE YOU DOING? DON'T--
VRIIIP
DOCTOR--!
SIGNAL ACQUIRED.
THE TRANSMISSION IS GARBLED, CONFUSED...
NO MATTER.
WOWMMMMMMM

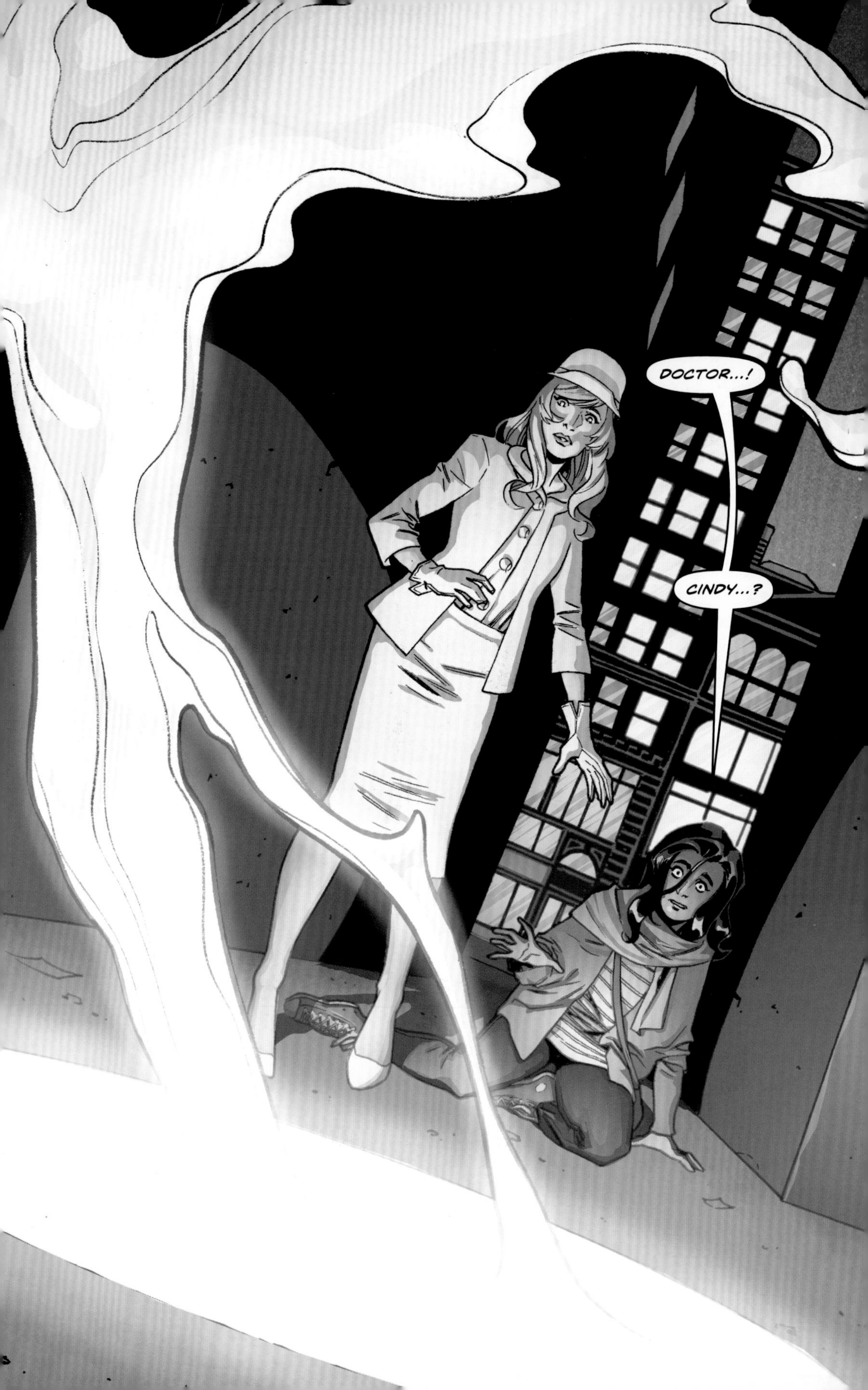
DOCTOR...!
CINDY...?

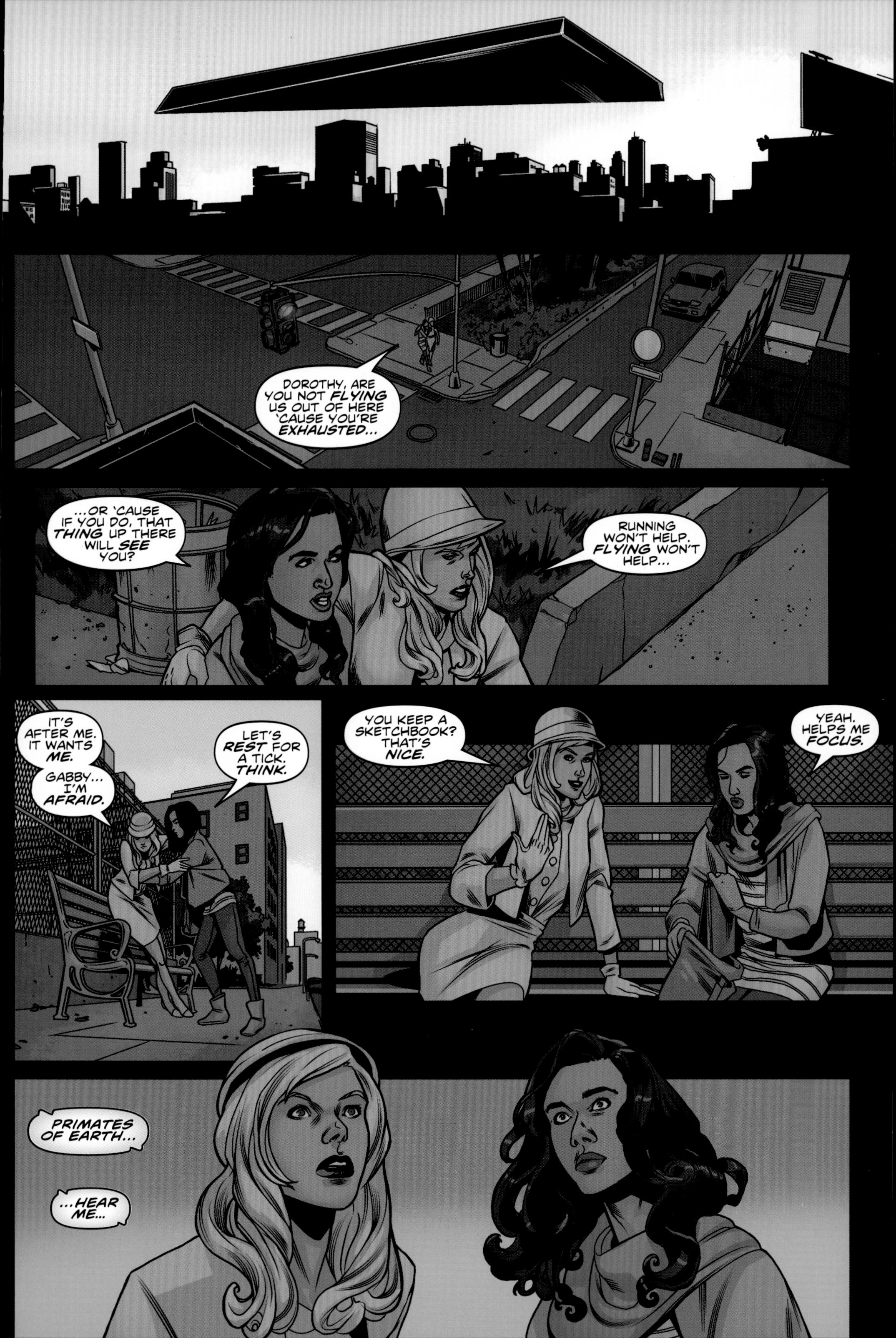
DOROTHY, ARE YOU NOT FLYING US OUT OF HERE 'CAUSE YOU'RE EXHAUSTED...
...OR 'CAUSE IF YOU DO, THAT THING UP THERE WILL SEE YOU?
RUNNING WON'T HELP. FLYING WON'T HELP...
IT'S AFTER ME. IT WANTS ME.
GABBY... I'M AFRAID.
LET'S REST FOR A TICK. THINK.
YOU KEEP A SKETCHBOOK? THAT'S NICE.
YEAH. HELPS ME FOCUS.
PRIMATES OF EARTH...
...HEAR ME...

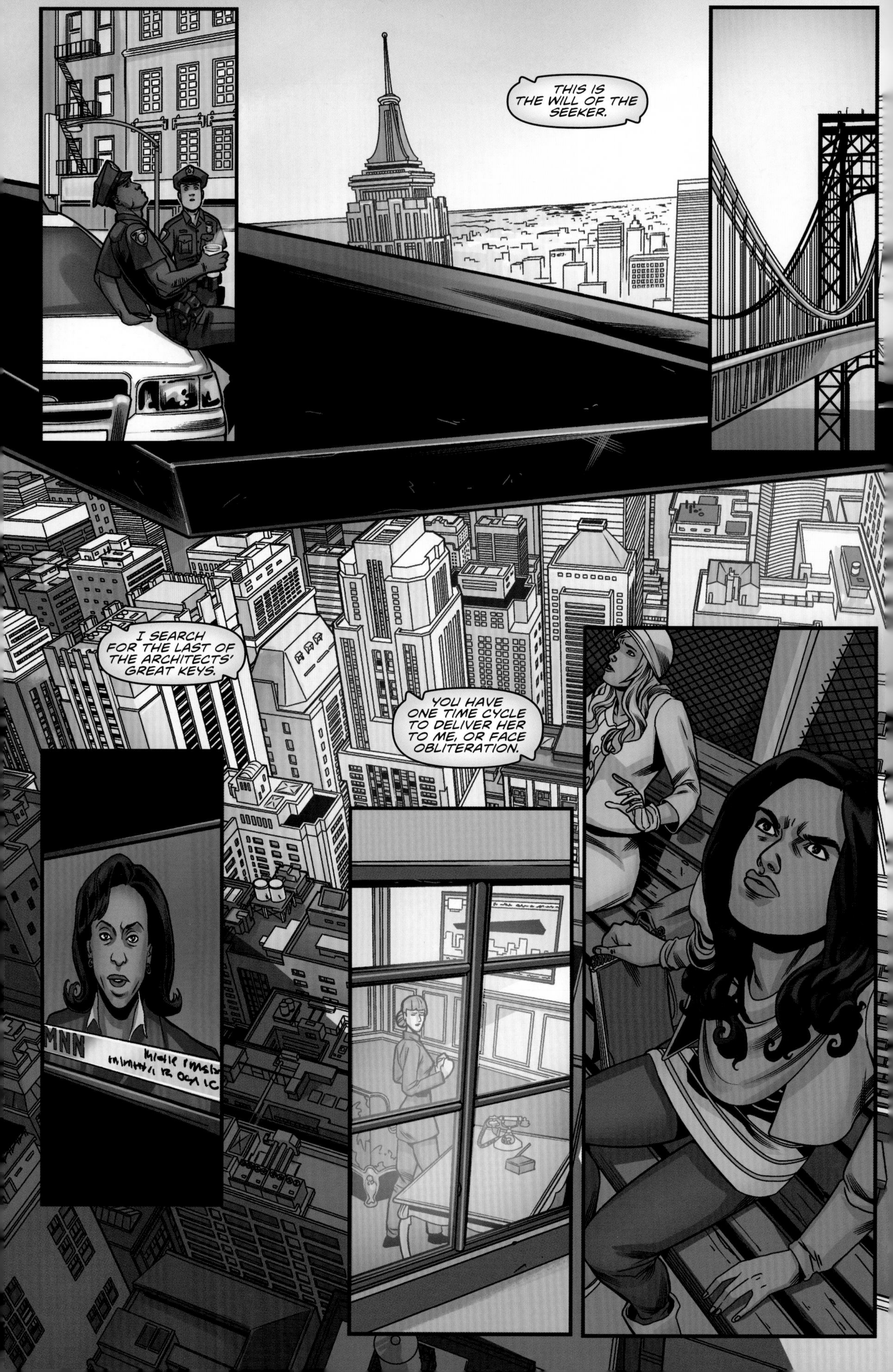
THIS IS THE WILL OF THE SEEKER.
I SEARCH FOR THE LAST OF THE ARCHITECTS' GREAT KEYS.
YOU HAVE ONE TIME CYCLE TO DELIVER HER TO ME, OR FACE OBLITERATION.
MNN

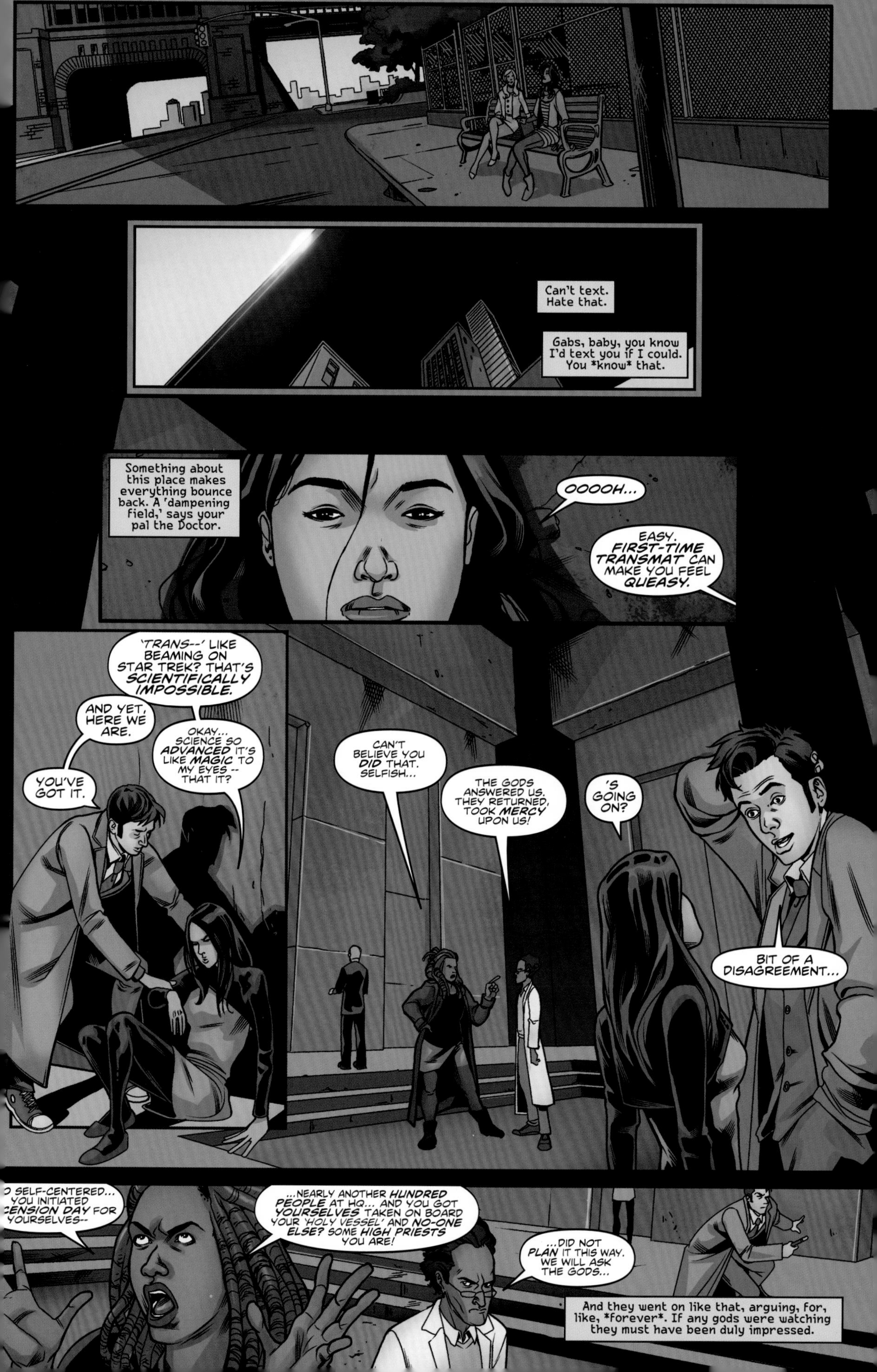
Can't text. Hate that.
Gabs, baby, you know I'd text you if I could. You *know* that.
Something about this place makes everything bounce back. A 'dampening field,' says your pal the Doctor.
OOOOH...
EASY. FIRST-TIME TRANSMAT CAN MAKE YOU FEEL QUEASY.
'TRANS--' LIKE BEAMING ON STAR TREK? THAT'S SCIENTIFICALLY IMPOSSIBLE.
AND YET, HERE WE ARE.
OKAY... SCIENCE SO ADVANCED IT'S LIKE MAGIC TO MY EYES -- THAT IT?
YOU'VE GOT IT.
CAN'T BELIEVE YOU DID THAT. SELFISH...
THE GODS ANSWERED US. THEY RETURNED, TOOK MERCY UPON US!
'S GOING ON?
BIT OF A DISAGREEMENT...
O SELF-CENTERED... YOU INITIATED CENSION DAY FOR YOURSELVES--
...NEARLY ANOTHER HUNDRED PEOPLE AT HQ... AND YOU GOT YOURSELVES TAKEN ON BOARD YOUR 'HOLY VESSEL' AND NO-ONE ELSE? SOME HIGH PRIESTS YOU ARE!
...DID NOT PLAN IT THIS WAY. WE WILL ASK THE GODS...
And they went on like that, arguing, for, like, *forever*. If any gods were watching they must have been duly impressed.

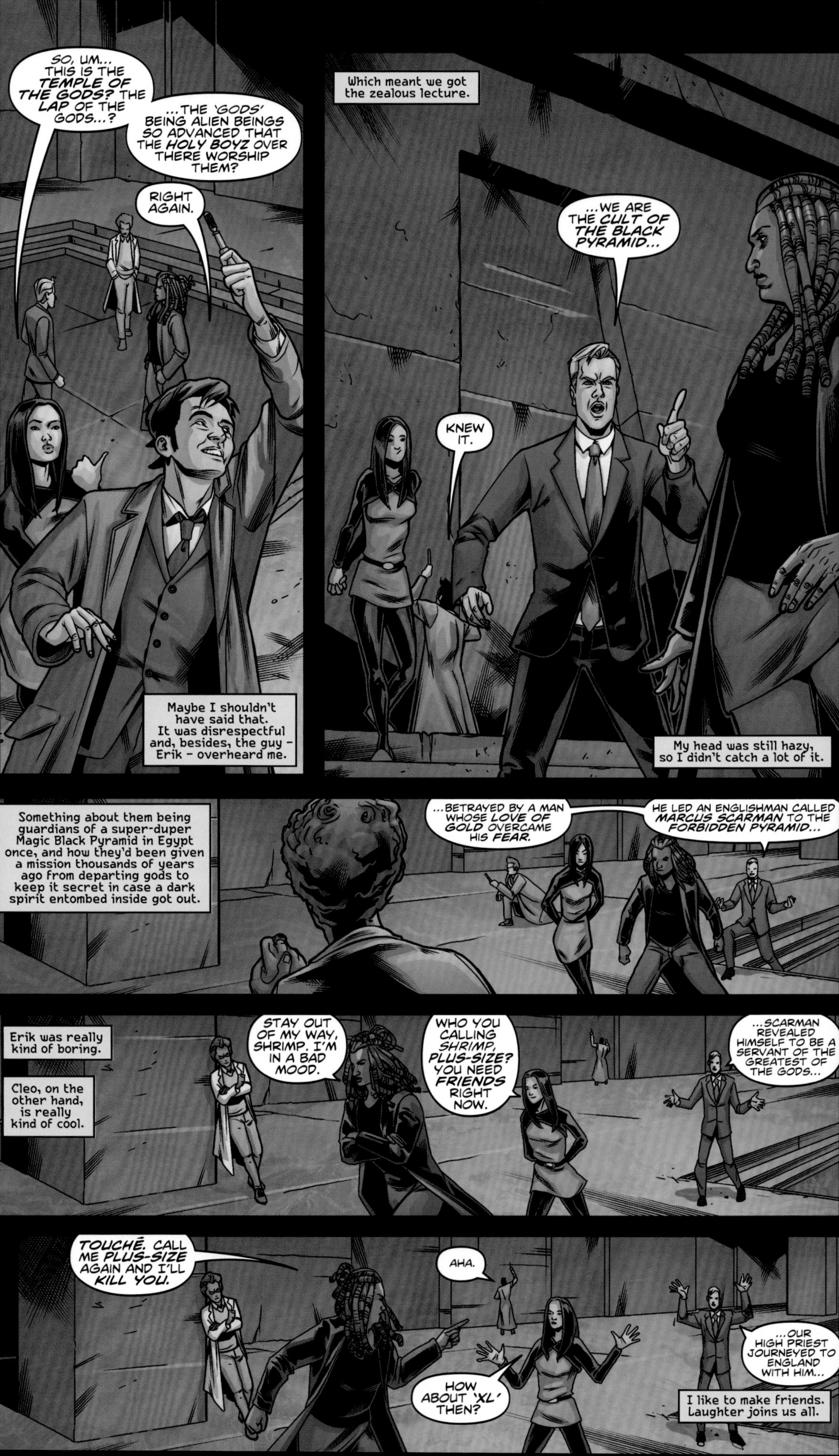
SO, UM... THIS IS THE TEMPLE OF THE GODS? THE LAP OF THE GODS...?
...THE 'GODS' BEING ALIEN BEINGS SO ADVANCED THAT THE HOLY BOYZ OVER THERE WORSHIP THEM?
RIGHT AGAIN.
Maybe I shouldn't have said that. It was disrespectful and, besides, the guy – Erik – overheard me.
Which meant we got the zealous lecture.
...WE ARE THE CULT OF THE BLACK PYRAMID...
KNEW IT.
My head was still hazy, so I didn't catch a lot of it.
Something about them being guardians of a super-duper Magic Black Pyramid in Egypt once, and how they'd been given a mission thousands of years ago from departing gods to keep it secret in case a dark spirit entombed inside got out.
...BETRAYED BY A MAN WHOSE LOVE OF GOLD OVERCAME HIS FEAR.
HE LED AN ENGLISHMAN CALLED MARCUS SCARMAN TO THE FORBIDDEN PYRAMID...
Erik was really kind of boring.
Cleo, on the other hand, is really kind of cool.
STAY OUT OF MY WAY, SHRIMP. I'M IN A BAD MOOD.
WHO YOU CALLING SHRIMP, PLUS-SIZE? YOU NEED FRIENDS RIGHT NOW.
...SCARMAN REVEALED HIMSELF TO BE A SERVANT OF THE GREATEST OF THE GODS...
TOUCHÉ. CALL ME PLUS-SIZE AGAIN AND I'LL KILL YOU.
AHA.
HOW ABOUT 'XL' THEN?
...OUR HIGH PRIEST JOURNEYED TO ENGLAND WITH HIM...
I like to make friends. Laughter joins us all.

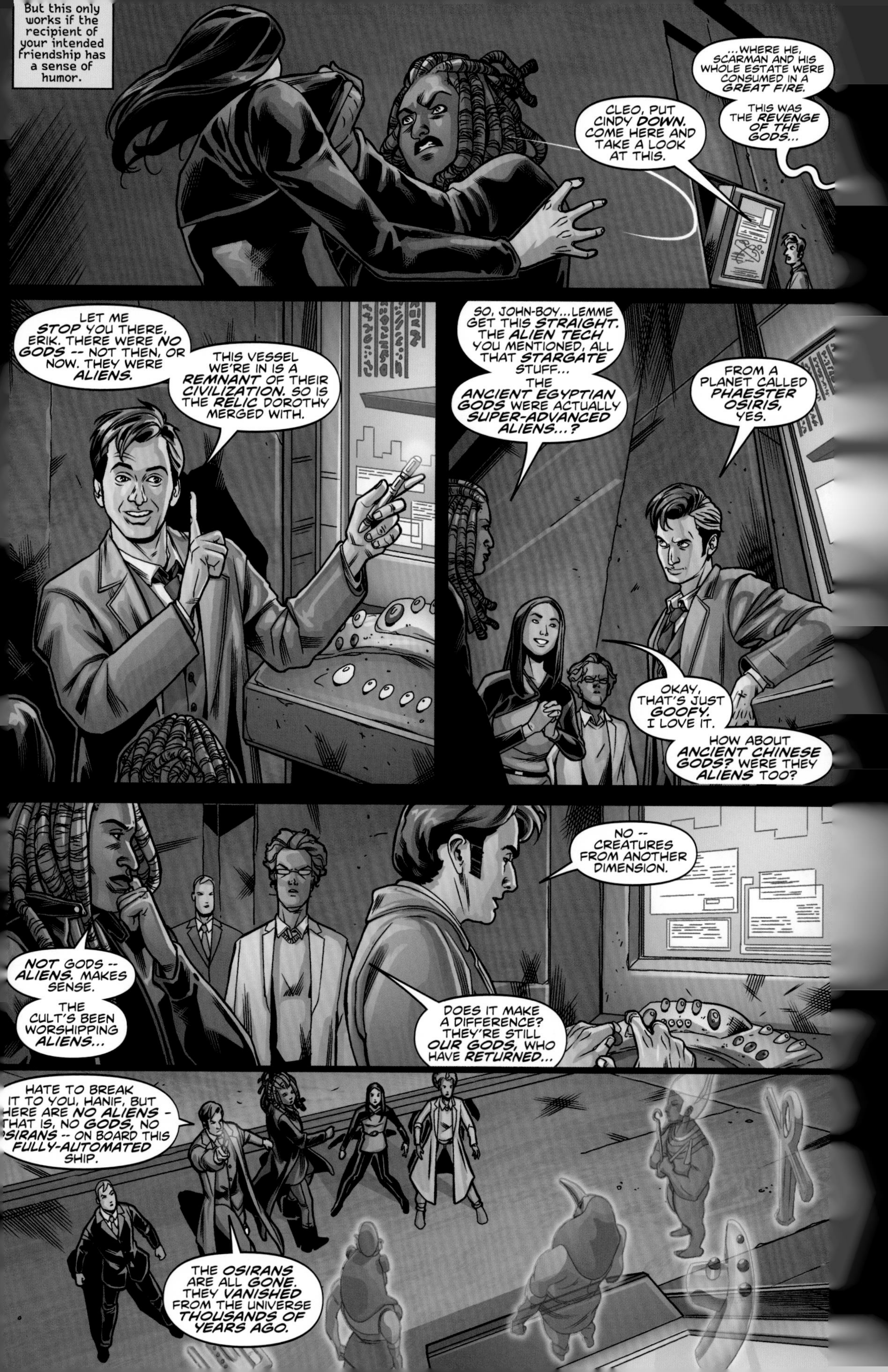
But this only works if the recipient of your intended friendship has a sense of humor.
CLEO, PUT CINDY DOWN. COME HERE AND TAKE A LOOK AT THIS.
...WHERE HE, SCARMAN AND HIS WHOLE ESTATE WERE CONSUMED IN A GREAT FIRE.
THIS WAS THE REVENGE OF THE GODS...
LET ME STOP YOU THERE, ERIK. THERE WERE NO GODS -- NOT THEN, OR NOW. THEY WERE ALIENS.
THIS VESSEL WE'RE IN IS A REMNANT OF THEIR CIVILIZATION. SO IS THE RELIC DOROTHY MERGED WITH.
SO, JOHN-BOY...LEMME GET THIS STRAIGHT. THE ALIEN TECH YOU MENTIONED, ALL THAT STARGATE STUFF... THE ANCIENT EGYPTIAN GODS WERE ACTUALLY SUPER-ADVANCED ALIENS...?
FROM A PLANET CALLED PHAESTER OSIRIS, YES.
OKAY, THAT'S JUST GOOFY. I LOVE IT.
HOW ABOUT ANCIENT CHINESE GODS? WERE THEY ALIENS TOO?
NO -- CREATURES FROM ANOTHER DIMENSION.
NOT GODS -- ALIENS. MAKES SENSE.
THE CULT'S BEEN WORSHIPPING ALIENS...
DOES IT MAKE A DIFFERENCE? THEY'RE STILL OUR GODS, WHO HAVE RETURNED...
HATE TO BREAK IT TO YOU, HANIF, BUT HERE ARE NO ALIENS - THAT IS, NO GODS, NO OSIRANS -- ON BOARD THIS FULLY-AUTOMATED SHIP.
THE OSIRANS ARE ALL GONE. THEY VANISHED FROM THE UNIVERSE THOUSANDS OF YEARS AGO.

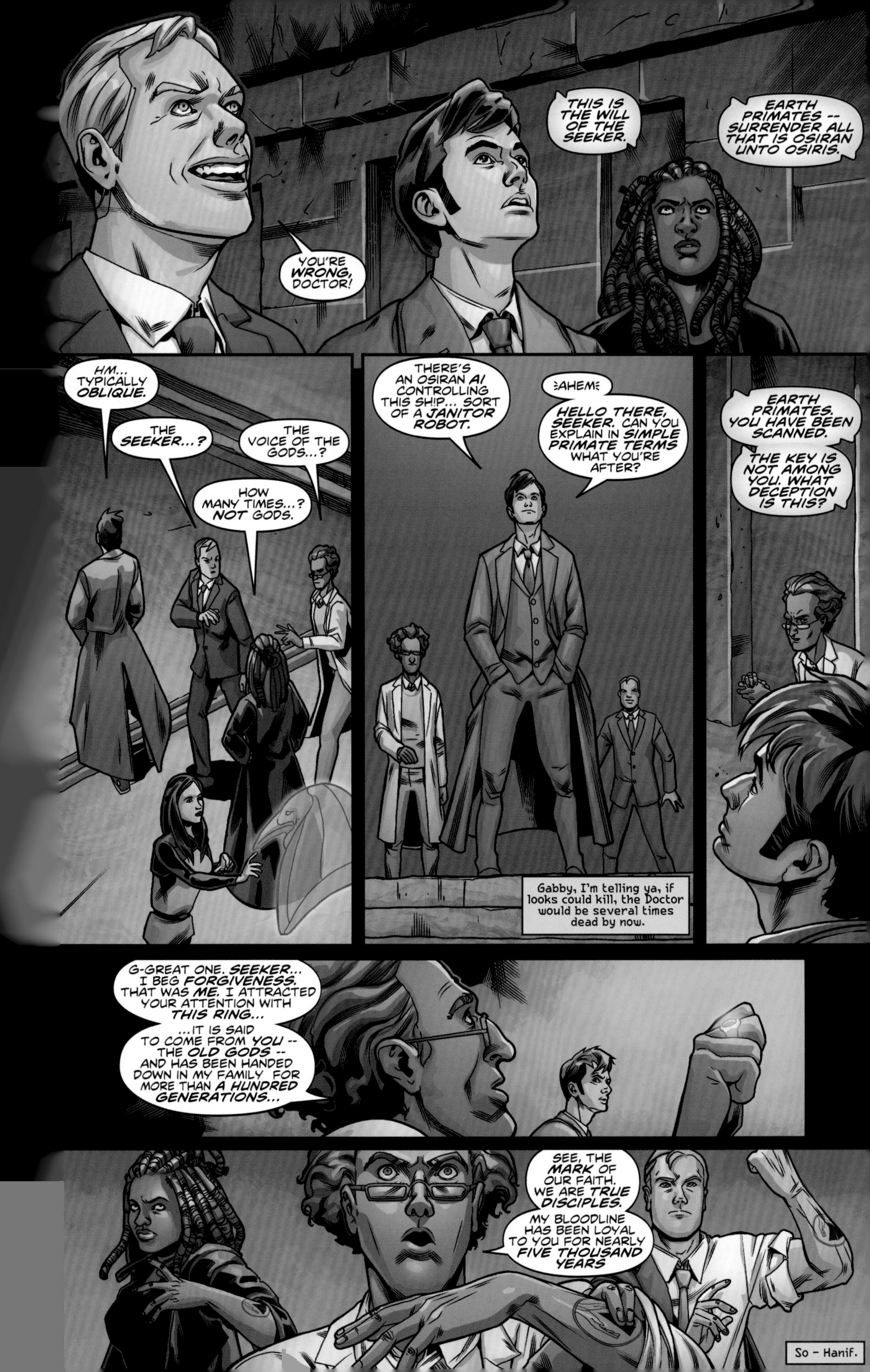
THIS IS THE WILL OF THE SEEKER.
EARTH PRIMATES -- SURRENDER ALL THAT IS OSIRAN UNTO OSIRIS.
YOU'RE WRONG, DOCTOR!
HM... TYPICALLY OBLIQUE.
THE SEEKER...?
THE VOICE OF THE GODS...?
HOW MANY TIMES...? NOT GODS.
THERE'S AN OSIRAN AI CONTROLLING THIS SHIP... SORT OF A JANITOR ROBOT.
AHEM
HELLO THERE, SEEKER. CAN YOU EXPLAIN IN SIMPLE PRIMATE TERMS WHAT YOU'RE AFTER?
Gabby, I'm telling ya, if looks could kill, the Doctor would be several times dead by now.
EARTH PRIMATES. YOU HAVE BEEN SCANNED.
THE KEY IS NOT AMONG YOU. WHAT DECEPTION IS THIS?
G-GREAT ONE. SEEKER... I BEG FORGIVENESS. THAT WAS ME. I ATTRACTED YOUR ATTENTION WITH THIS RING...
...IT IS SAID TO COME FROM YOU -- THE OLD GODS -- AND HAS BEEN HANDED DOWN IN MY FAMILY FOR MORE THAN A HUNDRED GENERATIONS...
SEE, THE MARK OF OUR FAITH. WE ARE TRUE DISCIPLES.
MY BLOODLINE HAS BEEN LOYAL TO YOU FOR NEARLY FIVE THOUSAND YEARS
So - Hanif.

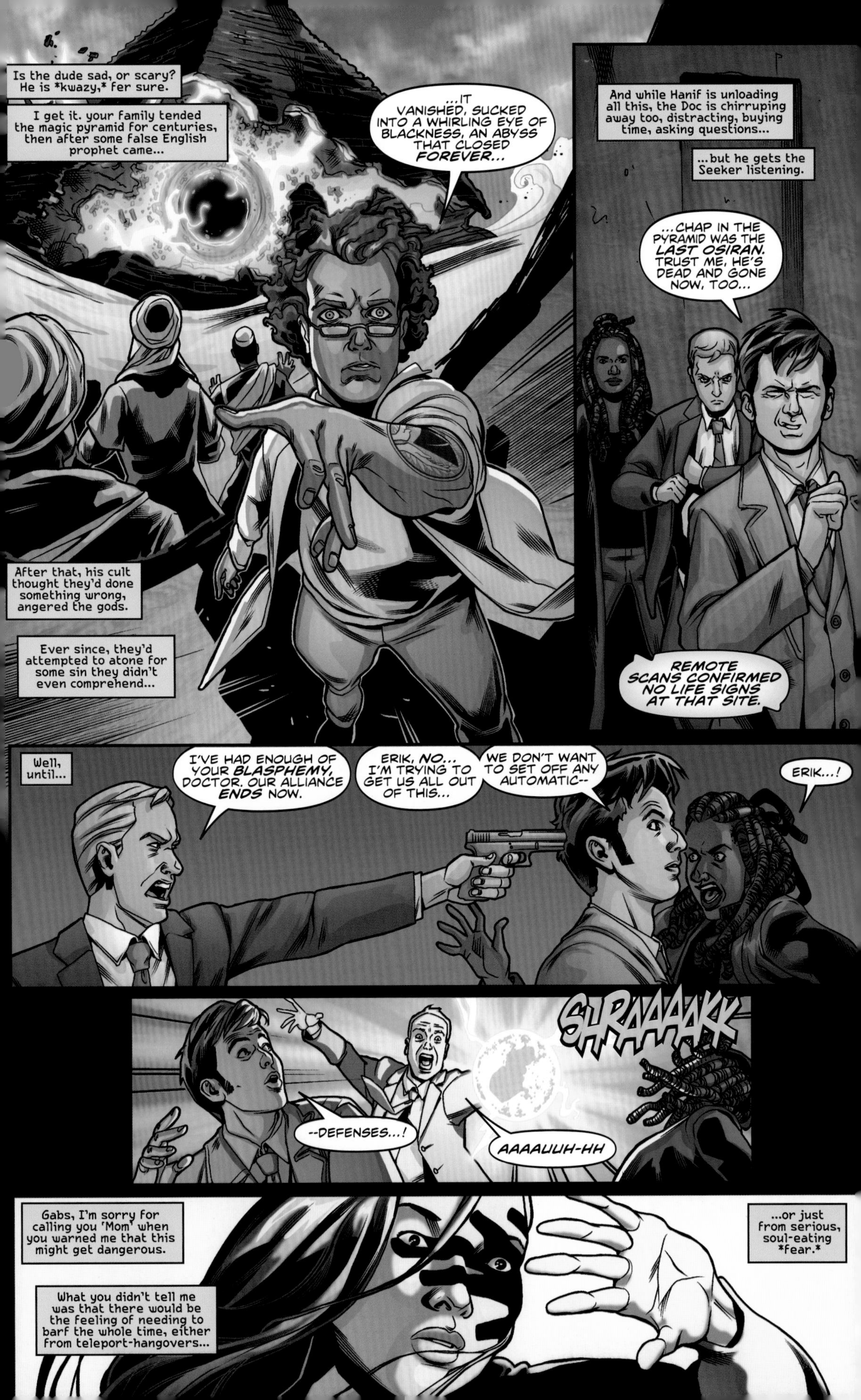

Is the dude sad, or scary? He is *kwazy,* fer sure.
I get it. your family tended the magic pyramid for centuries, then after some false English prophet came...
...IT VANISHED, SUCKED INTO A WHIRLING EYE OF BLACKNESS, AN ABYSS THAT CLOSED FOREVER...
After that, his cult thought they'd done something wrong, angered the gods.
Ever since, they'd attempted to atone for some sin they didn't even comprehend...
And while Hanif is unloading all this, the Doc is chirruping away too, distracting, buying time, asking questions...
...but he gets the Seeker listening.
...CHAP IN THE PYRAMID WAS THE LAST OSIRAN. TRUST ME, HE'S DEAD AND GONE NOW, TOO...
REMOTE SCANS CONFIRMED NO LIFE SIGNS AT THAT SITE.
Well, until...
I'VE HAD ENOUGH OF YOUR BLASPHEMY, DOCTOR. OUR ALLIANCE ENDS NOW.
ERIK, NO... I'M TRYING TO GET US ALL OUT OF THIS...
WE DON'T WANT TO SET OFF ANY AUTOMATIC--
ERIK...!
SHRAAAKK
--DEFENSES...!
AAAAUUH-HH
Gabs, I'm sorry for calling you 'Mom' when you warned me that this might get dangerous.
What you didn't tell me was that there would be the feeling of needing to barf the whole time, either from teleport-hangovers...
...or just from serious, soul-eating *fear.*

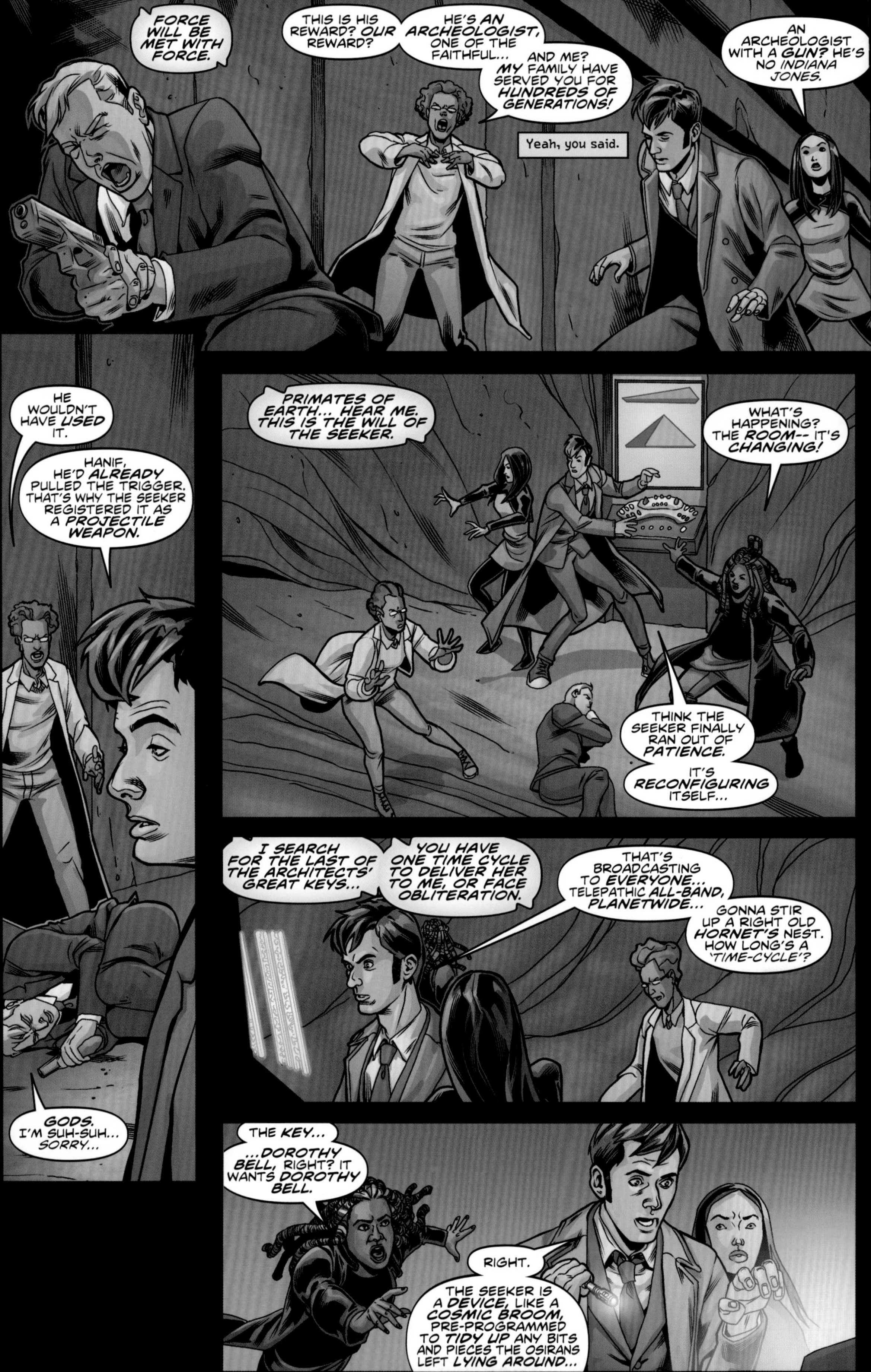
FORCE WILL BE MET WITH FORCE.
THIS IS HIS REWARD? OUR REWARD?
HE'S AN ARCHEOLOGIST, ONE OF THE FAITHFUL...
AND ME? MY FAMILY HAVE SERVED YOU FOR HUNDREDS OF GENERATIONS!
Yeah, you said.
AN ARCHEOLOGIST WITH A GUN? HE'S NO INDIANA JONES.
HE WOULDN'T HAVE USED IT.
HANIF, HE'D ALREADY PULLED THE TRIGGER. THAT'S WHY THE SEEKER REGISTERED IT AS A PROJECTILE WEAPON.
GODS. I'M SUH-SUH... SORRY...
PRIMATES OF EARTH... HEAR ME. THIS IS THE WILL OF THE SEEKER.
WHAT'S HAPPENING? THE ROOM-- IT'S CHANGING!
THINK THE SEEKER FINALLY RAN OUT OF PATIENCE.
IT'S RECONFIGURING ITSELF...
I SEARCH FOR THE LAST OF THE ARCHITECTS' GREAT KEYS...
YOU HAVE ONE TIME CYCLE TO DELIVER HER TO ME, OR FACE OBLITERATION.
THAT'S BROADCASTING TO EVERYONE... TELEPATHIC ALL-BAND, PLANETWIDE...
GONNA STIR UP A RIGHT OLD HORNET'S NEST. HOW LONG'S A 'TIME-CYCLE'?
THE KEY...
...DOROTHY BELL, RIGHT? IT WANTS DOROTHY BELL.
RIGHT.
THE SEEKER IS A DEVICE, LIKE A COSMIC BROOM, PRE-PROGRAMMED TO TIDY UP ANY BITS AND PIECES THE OSIRANS LEFT LYING AROUND...

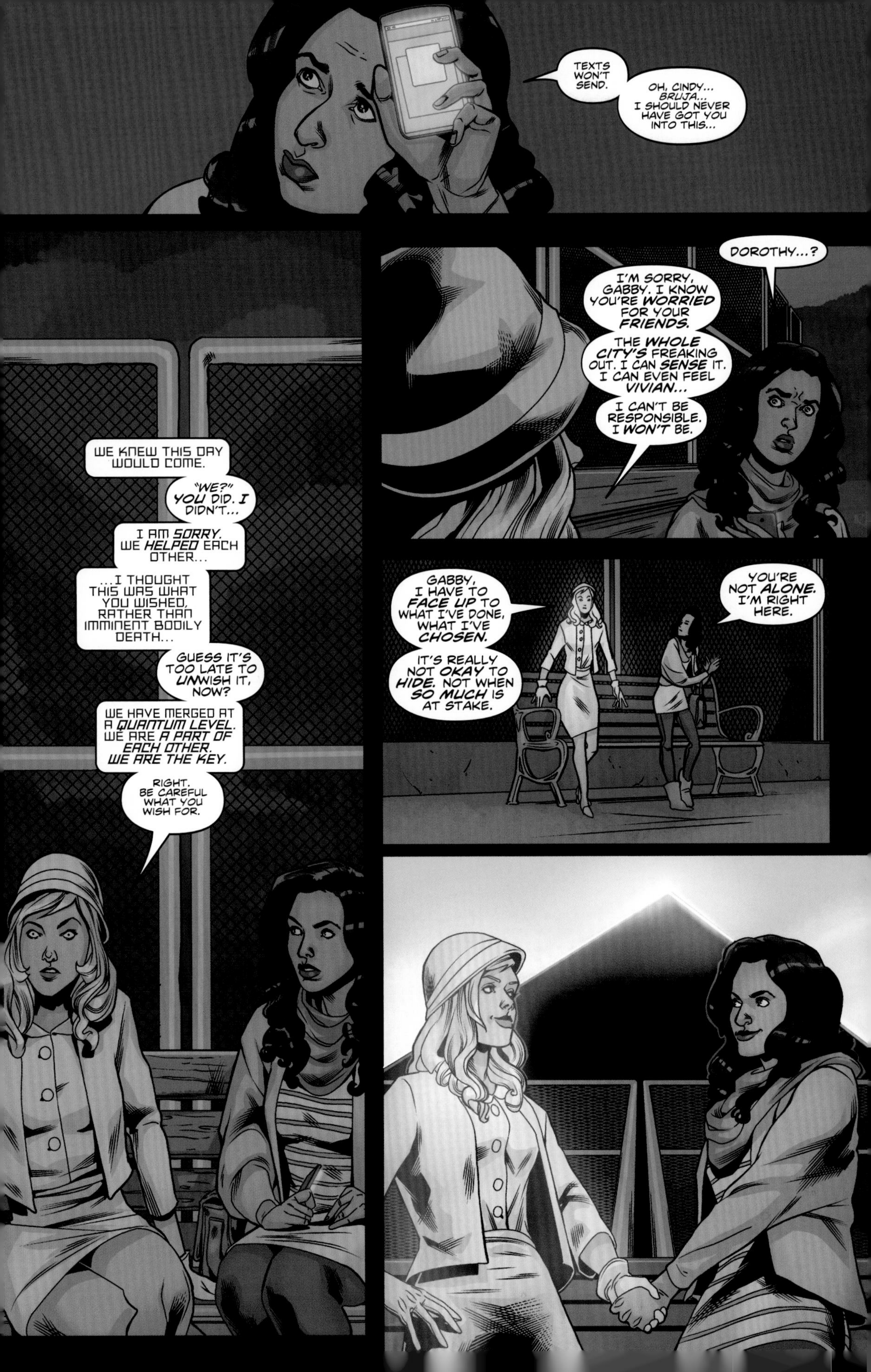
TEXTS WON'T SEND.
OH, CINDY... BRUJA... I SHOULD NEVER HAVE GOT YOU INTO THIS...
WE KNEW THIS DAY WOULD COME.
"WE?" YOU DID. I DIDN'T...
I AM SORRY. WE HELPED EACH OTHER...
...I THOUGHT THIS WAS WHAT YOU WISHED, RATHER THAN IMMINENT BODILY DEATH...
GUESS IT'S TOO LATE TO UNWISH IT, NOW?
WE HAVE MERGED AT A QUANTUM LEVEL. WE ARE A PART OF EACH OTHER. WE ARE THE KEY.
RIGHT. BE CAREFUL WHAT YOU WISH FOR.
DOROTHY...?
I'M SORRY, GABBY. I KNOW YOU'RE WORRIED FOR YOUR FRIENDS.
THE WHOLE CITY'S FREAKING OUT. I CAN SENSE IT. I CAN EVEN FEEL VIVIAN...
I CAN'T BE RESPONSIBLE. I WON'T BE.
GABBY, I HAVE TO FACE UP TO WHAT I'VE DONE, WHAT I'VE CHOSEN.
IT'S REALLY NOT OKAY TO HIDE. NOT WHEN SO MUCH IS AT STAKE.
YOU'RE NOT ALONE. I'M RIGHT HERE.

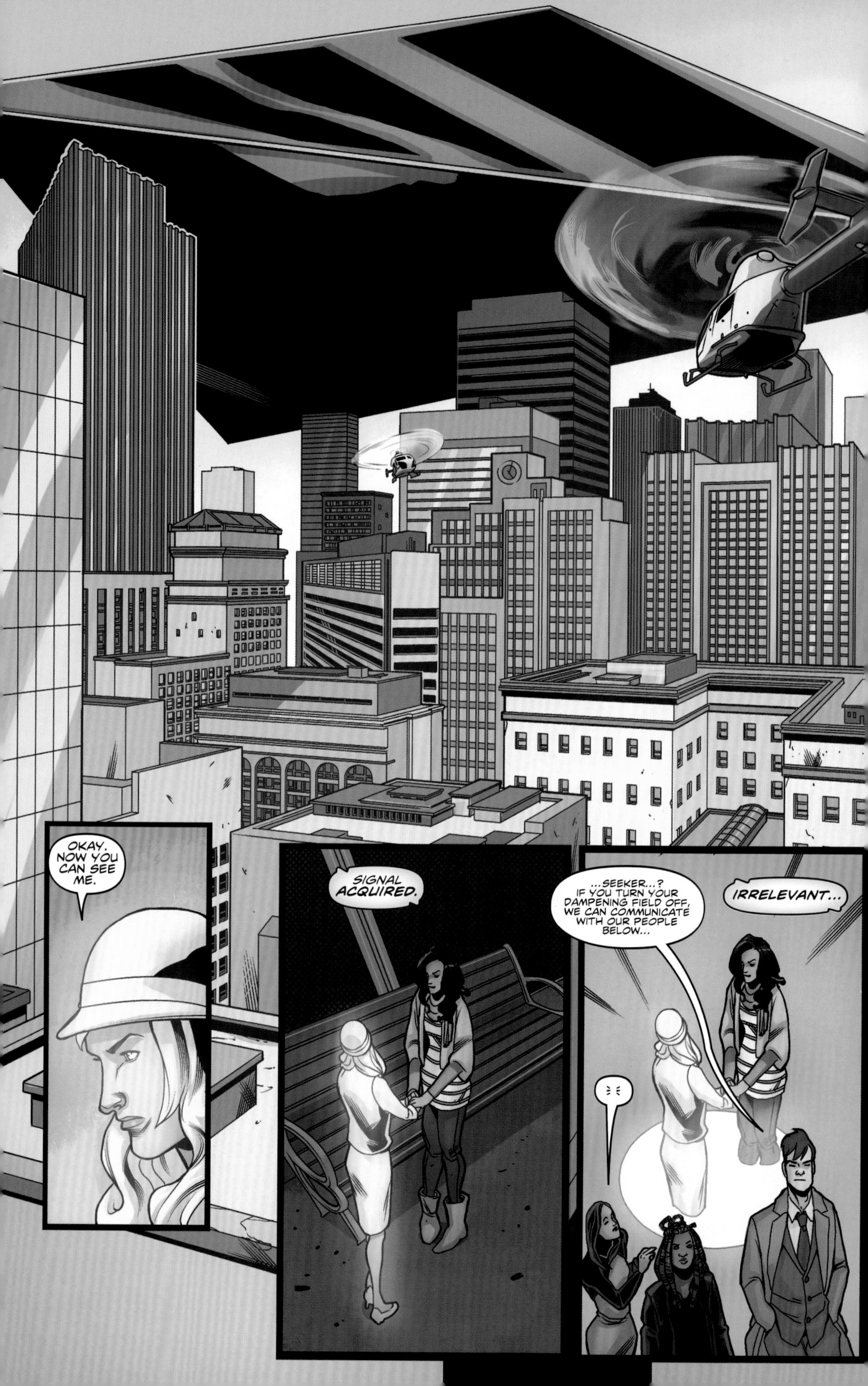
OKAY. NOW YOU CAN SEE ME.
SIGNAL ACQUIRED.
...SEEKER...? IF YOU TURN YOUR DAMPENING FIELD OFF, WE CAN COMMUNICATE WITH OUR PEOPLE BELOW...
IRRELEVANT...

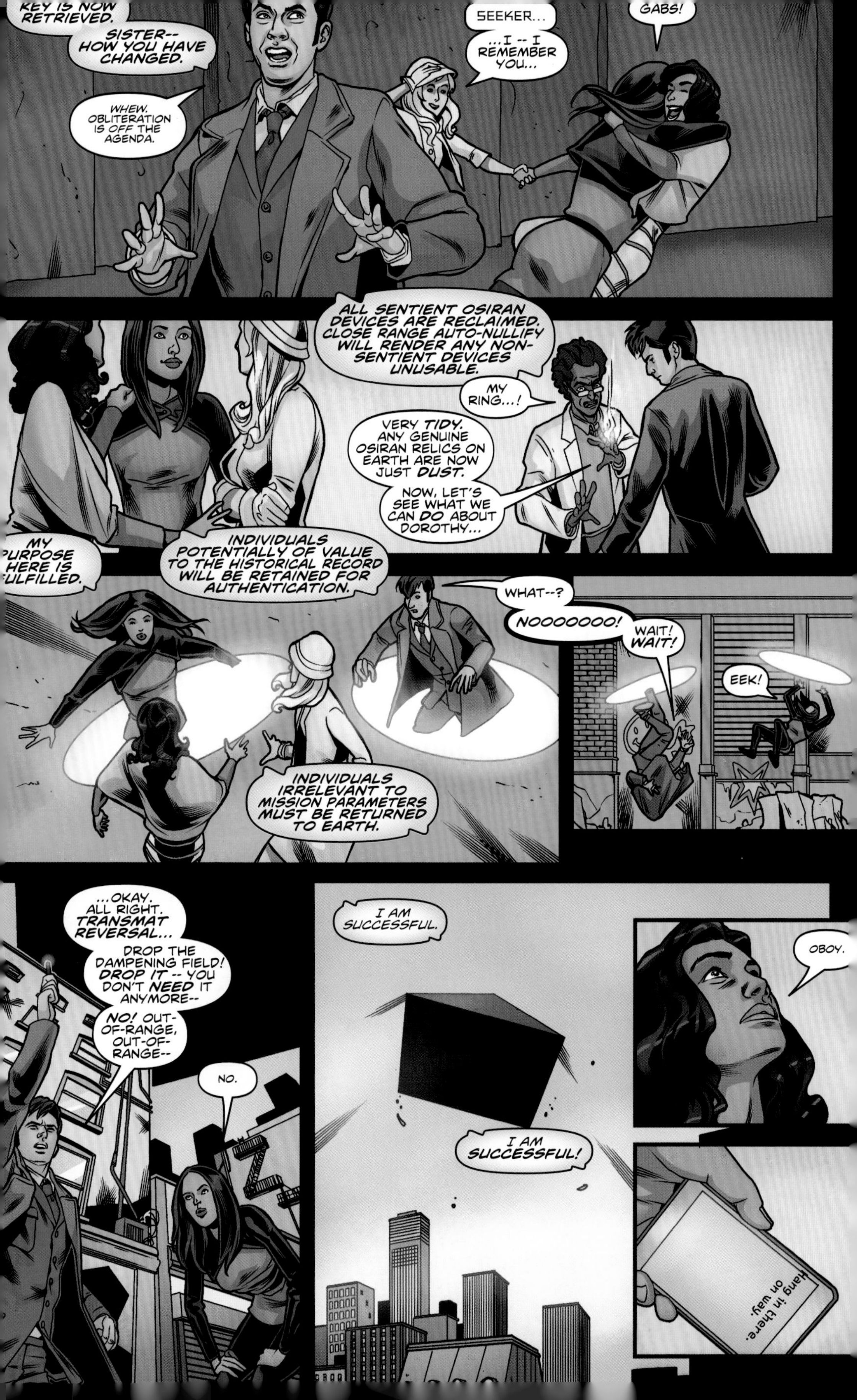
KEY IS NOW RETRIEVED.
SISTER-- HOW YOU HAVE CHANGED.
WHEW. OBLITERATION IS OFF THE AGENDA.
SEEKER...
...I -- I REMEMBER YOU...
GABS!
ALL SENTIENT OSIRAN DEVICES ARE RECLAIMED. CLOSE RANGE AUTO-NULLIFY WILL RENDER ANY NON-SENTIENT DEVICES UNUSABLE.
MY RING...!
VERY TIDY. ANY GENUINE OSIRAN RELICS ON EARTH ARE NOW JUST DUST.
NOW, LET'S SEE WHAT WE CAN DO ABOUT DOROTHY...
MY PURPOSE HERE IS FULFILLED.
INDIVIDUALS POTENTIALLY OF VALUE TO THE HISTORICAL RECORD WILL BE RETAINED FOR AUTHENTICATION.
WHAT--?
INDIVIDUALS IRRELEVANT TO MISSION PARAMETERS MUST BE RETURNED TO EARTH.
NOOOOOOO!
WAIT! WAIT!
EEK!
...OKAY. ALL RIGHT. TRANSMAT REVERSAL...
DROP THE DAMPENING FIELD! DROP IT -- YOU DON'T NEED IT ANYMORE--
NO! OUT-OF-RANGE, OUT-OF-RANGE--
NO.
I AM SUCCESSFUL.
I AM SUCCESSFUL!
OBOY.
Hang in there. On way.

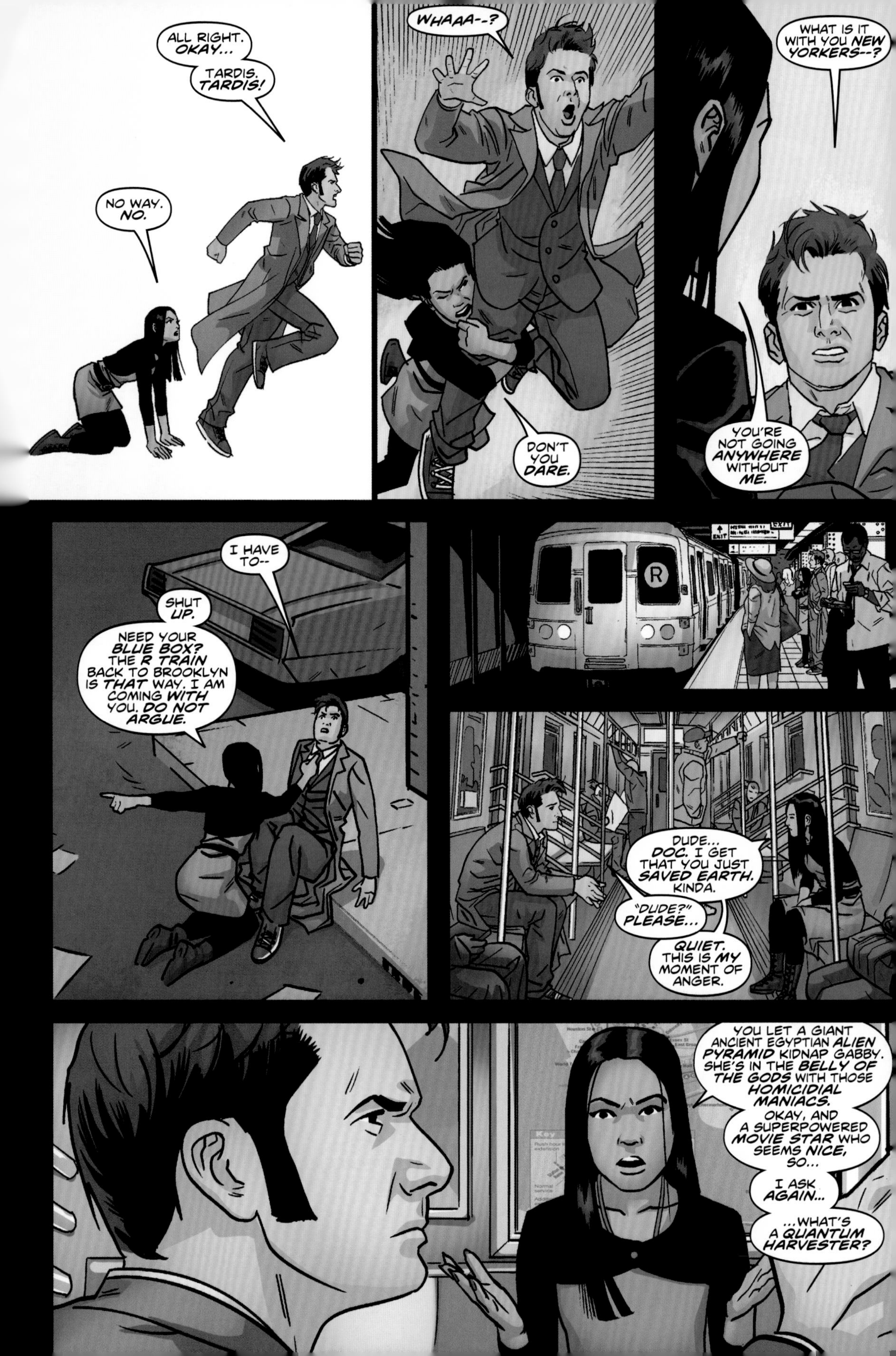
ALL RIGHT. OKAY...
TARDIS. TARDIS!
NO WAY. NO.
WHAAA--?
DON'T YOU DARE.
WHAT IS IT WITH YOU NEW YORKERS--?
YOU'RE NOT GOING ANYWHERE WITHOUT ME.
I HAVE TO--
SHUT UP.
NEED YOUR BLUE BOX? THE R TRAIN BACK TO BROOKLYN IS THAT WAY. I AM COMING WITH YOU. DO NOT ARGUE.
DUDE... DOC. I GET THAT YOU JUST SAVED EARTH. KINDA.
"DUDE?" PLEASE...
QUIET. THIS IS MY MOMENT OF ANGER.
YOU LET A GIANT ANCIENT EGYPTIAN ALIEN PYRAMID KIDNAP GABBY. SHE'S IN THE BELLY OF THE GODS WITH THOSE HOMICIDIAL MANIACS.
OKAY, AND A SUPERPOWERED MOVIE STAR WHO SEEMS NICE, SO...
I ASK AGAIN...
...WHAT'S A QUANTUM HARVESTER?

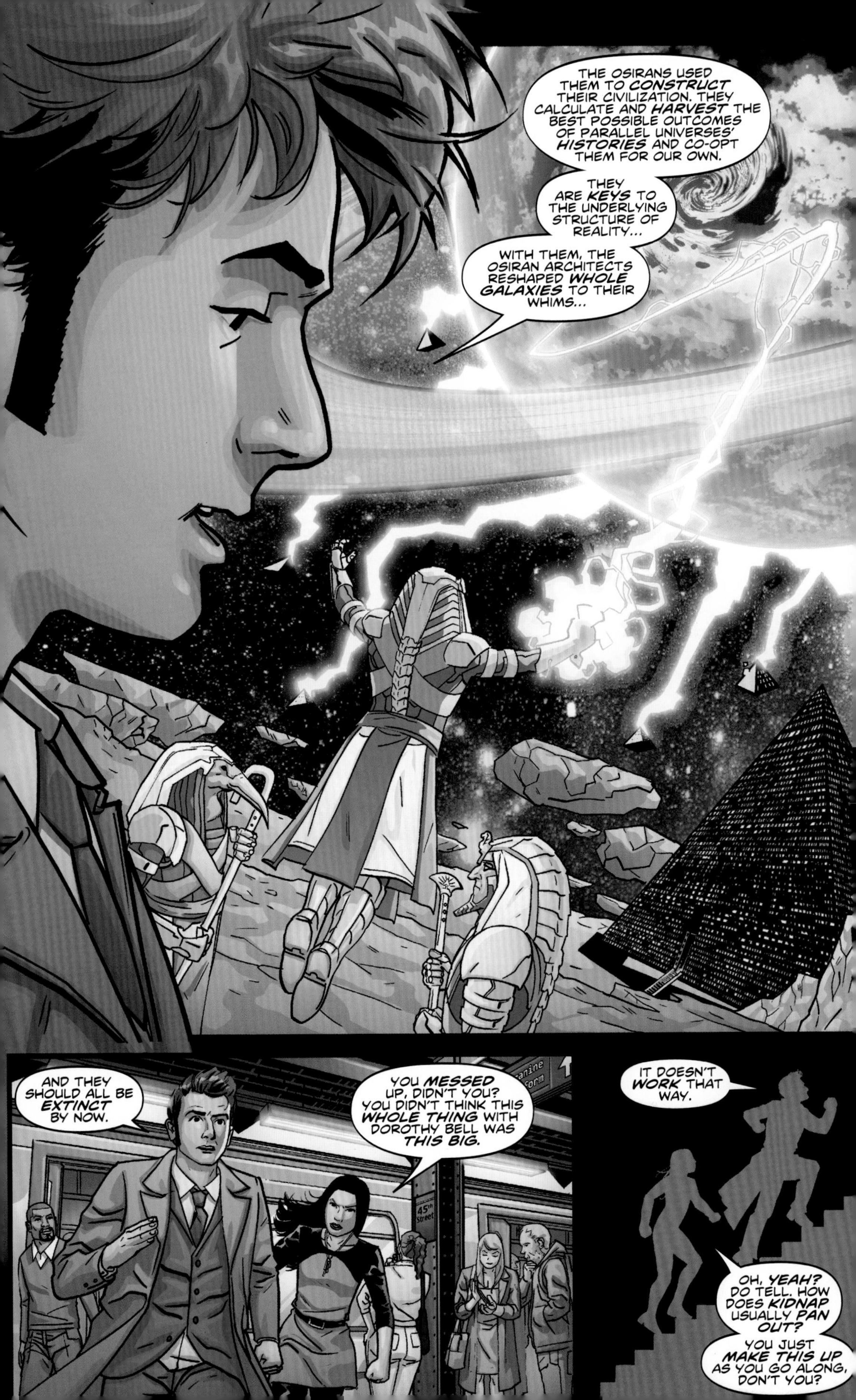
THE OSIRANS USED THEM TO CONSTRUCT THEIR CIVILIZATION. THEY CALCULATE AND HARVEST THE BEST POSSIBLE OUTCOMES OF PARALLEL UNIVERSES' HISTORIES AND CO-OPT THEM FOR OUR OWN.
THEY ARE KEYS TO THE UNDERLYING STRUCTURE OF REALITY...
WITH THEM, THE OSIRAN ARCHITECTS RESHAPED WHOLE GALAXIES TO THEIR WHIMS...
AND THEY SHOULD ALL BE EXTINCT BY NOW.
YOU MESSED UP, DIDN'T YOU? YOU DIDN'T THINK THIS WHOLE THING WITH DOROTHY BELL WAS THIS BIG.
45th Street
IT DOESN'T WORK THAT WAY.
OH, YEAH? DO TELL. HOW DOES KIDNAP USUALLY PAN OUT?
YOU JUST MAKE THIS UP AS YOU GO ALONG, DON'T YOU?

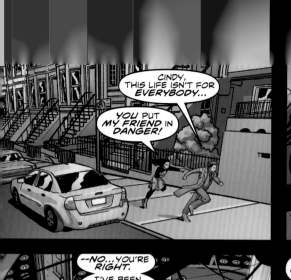

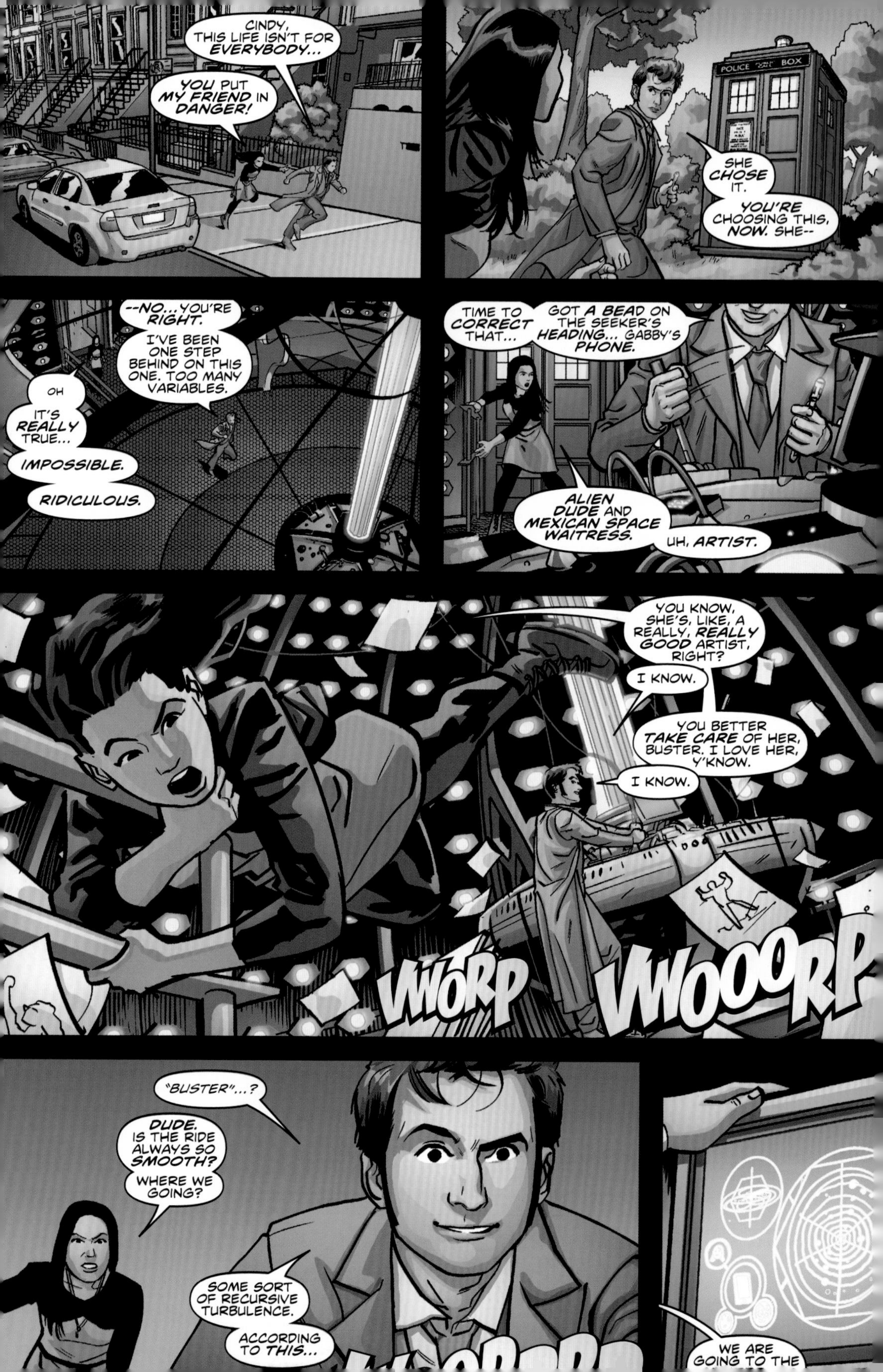
CINDY, THIS LIFE ISN'T FOR EVERYBODY...
YOU PUT MY FRIEND IN DANGER!
SHE CHOSE IT.
YOU'RE CHOOSING THIS, NOW. SHE--
--NO... YOU'RE RIGHT.
I'VE BEEN ONE STEP BEHIND ON THIS ONE. TOO MANY VARIABLES.
OH
IT'S REALLY TRUE...
IMPOSSIBLE.
RIDICULOUS.
TIME TO CORRECT THAT...
GOT A BEAD ON THE SEEKER'S HEADING... GABBY'S PHONE.
ALIEN DUDE AND MEXICAN SPACE WAITRESS.
UH, ARTIST.
YOU KNOW, SHE'S, LIKE, A REALLY, REALLY GOOD ARTIST, RIGHT?
I KNOW.
YOU BETTER TAKE CARE OF HER, BUSTER. I LOVE HER, Y'KNOW.
I KNOW.
VWORP
VWOOORP
"BUSTER"...?
DUDE. IS THE RIDE ALWAYS SO SMOOTH?
WHERE WE GOING?
SOME SORT OF RECURSIVE TURBULENCE.
ACCORDING TO THIS...
WE ARE GOING TO THE

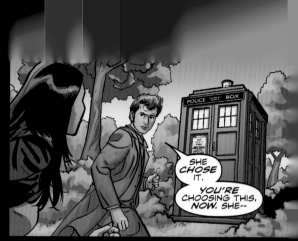

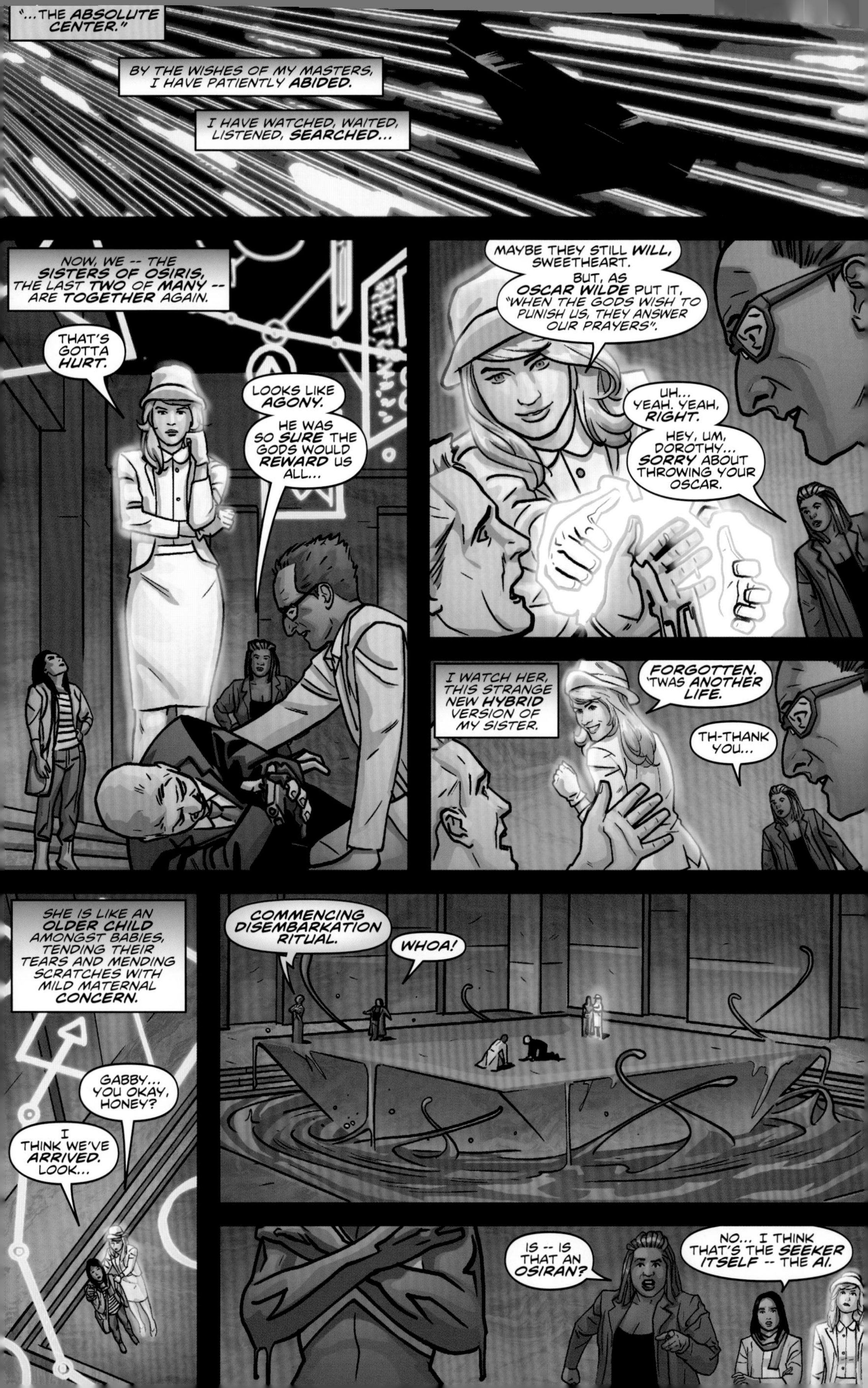
"...THE ABSOLUTE CENTER."
BY THE WISHES OF MY MASTERS, I HAVE PATIENTLY ABIDED.
I HAVE WATCHED, WAITED, LISTENED, SEARCHED...
NOW, WE -- THE SISTERS OF OSIRIS, THE LAST TWO OF MANY -- ARE TOGETHER AGAIN.
THAT'S GOTTA HURT.
LOOKS LIKE AGONY.
HE WAS SO SURE THE GODS WOULD REWARD US ALL...
MAYBE THEY STILL WILL, SWEETHEART.
BUT, AS OSCAR WILDE PUT IT, "WHEN THE GODS WISH TO PUNISH US, THEY ANSWER OUR PRAYERS".
UH... YEAH. YEAH, RIGHT.
HEY, UM, DOROTHY... SORRY ABOUT THROWING YOUR OSCAR.
I WATCH HER, THIS STRANGE NEW HYBRID VERSION OF MY SISTER.
FORGOTTEN. 'TWAS ANOTHER LIFE.
TH-THANK YOU...
SHE IS LIKE AN OLDER CHILD AMONGST BABIES, TENDING THEIR TEARS AND MENDING SCRATCHES WITH MILD MATERNAL CONCERN.
GABBY... YOU OKAY, HONEY?
I THINK WE'VE ARRIVED. LOOK...
COMMENCING DISEMBARKATION RITUAL.
WHOA!
IS -- IS THAT AN OSIRAN?
NO... I THINK THAT'S THE SEEKER ITSELF -- THE AI.

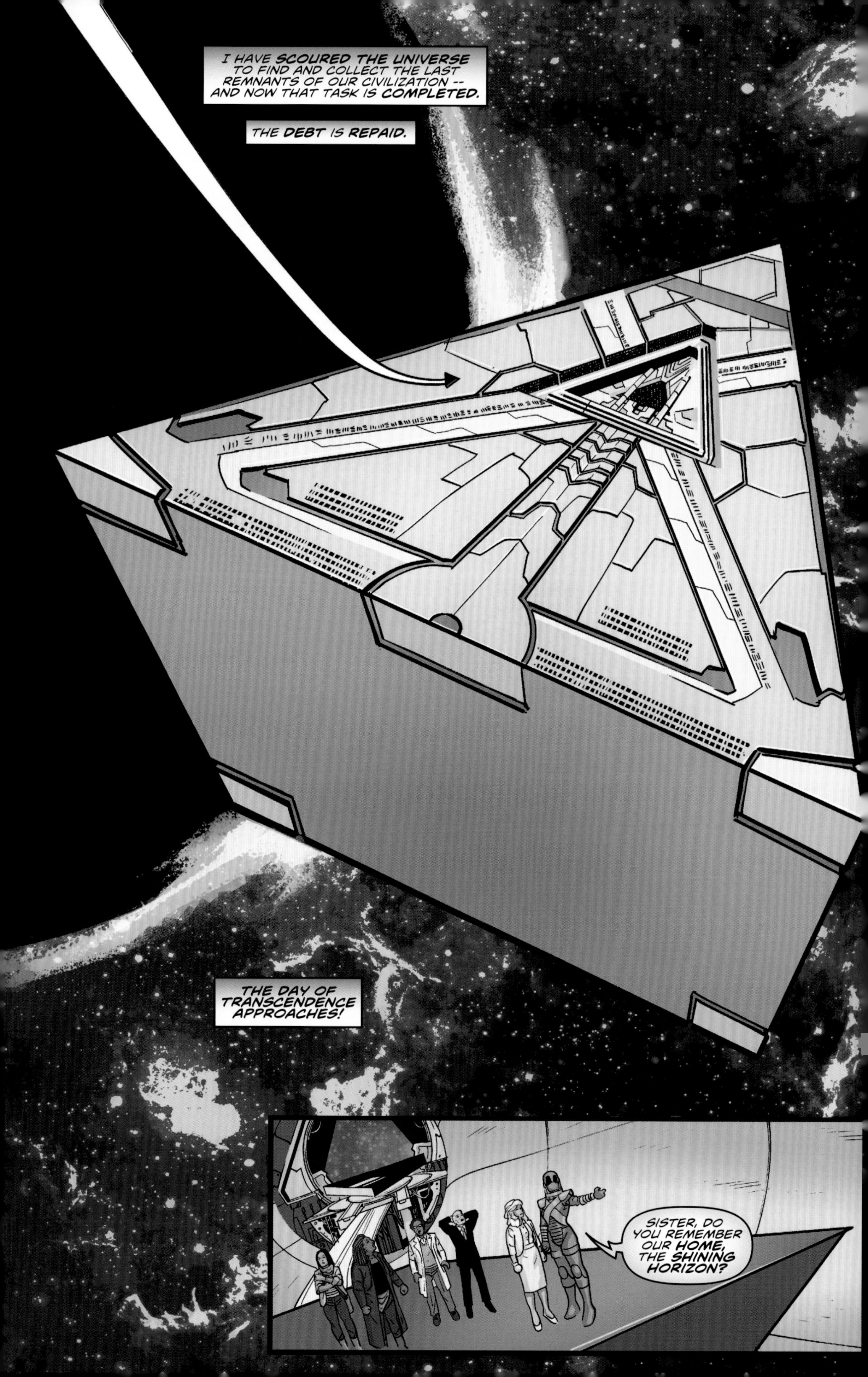
I HAVE SCOURED THE UNIVERSE TO FIND AND COLLECT THE LAST REMNANTS OF OUR CIVILIZATION -- AND NOW THAT TASK IS COMPLETED.
THE DEBT IS REPAID.
THE DAY OF TRANSCENDENCE APPROACHES!
SISTER, DO YOU REMEMBER OUR HOME, THE SHINING HORIZON?

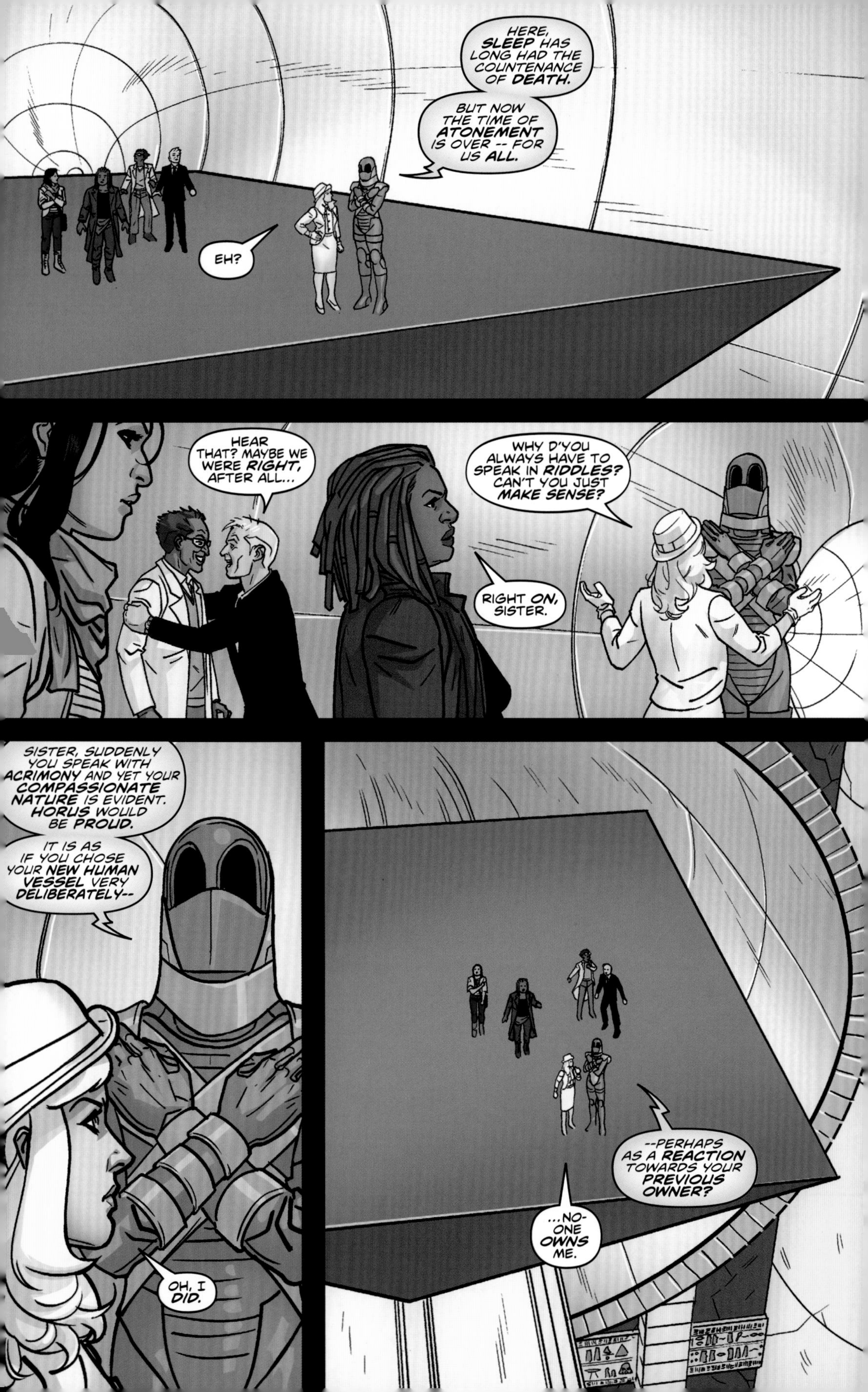
HERE, SLEEP HAS LONG HAD THE COUNTENANCE OF DEATH.
BUT NOW THE TIME OF ATONEMENT IS OVER -- FOR US ALL.
EH?
HEAR THAT? MAYBE WE WERE RIGHT, AFTER ALL...
WHY D'YOU ALWAYS HAVE TO SPEAK IN RIDDLES? CAN'T YOU JUST MAKE SENSE?
RIGHT ON, SISTER.
SISTER, SUDDENLY YOU SPEAK WITH ACRIMONY AND YET YOUR COMPASSIONATE NATURE IS EVIDENT. HORUS WOULD BE PROUD.
IT IS AS IF YOU CHOSE YOUR NEW HUMAN VESSEL VERY DELIBERATELY--
OH, I DID.
--PERHAPS AS A REACTION TOWARDS YOUR PREVIOUS OWNER?
...NO-ONE OWNS ME.

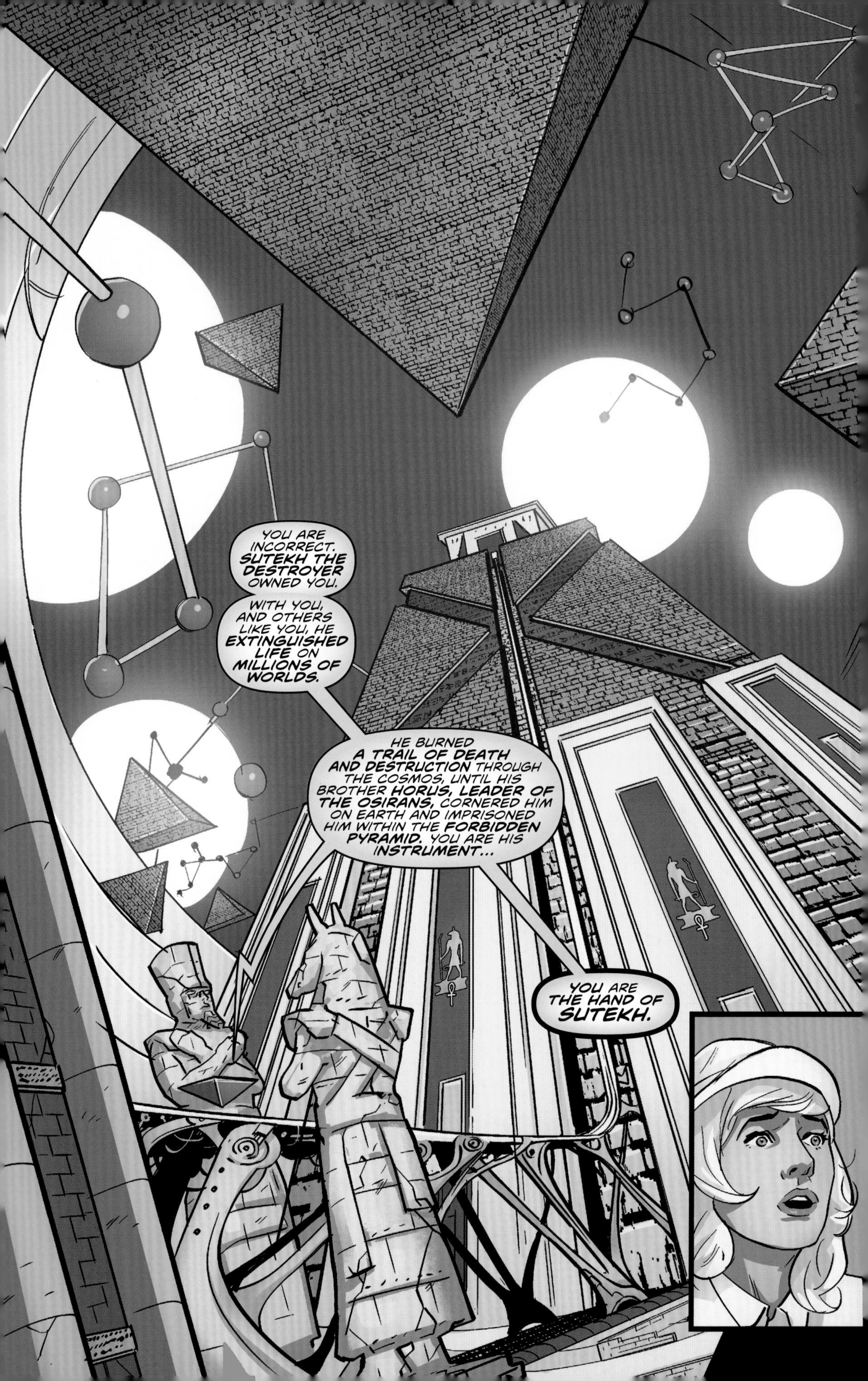
YOU ARE INCORRECT. SUTEKH THE DESTROYER OWNED YOU.
WITH YOU, AND OTHERS LIKE YOU, HE EXTINGUISHED LIFE ON MILLIONS OF WORLDS.
HE BURNED A TRAIL OF DEATH AND DESTRUCTION THROUGH THE COSMOS, UNTIL HIS BROTHER HORUS, LEADER OF THE OSIRANS, CORNERED HIM ON EARTH AND IMPRISONED HIM WITHIN THE FORBIDDEN PYRAMID. YOU ARE HIS INSTRUMENT...
YOU ARE THE HAND OF SUTEKH.

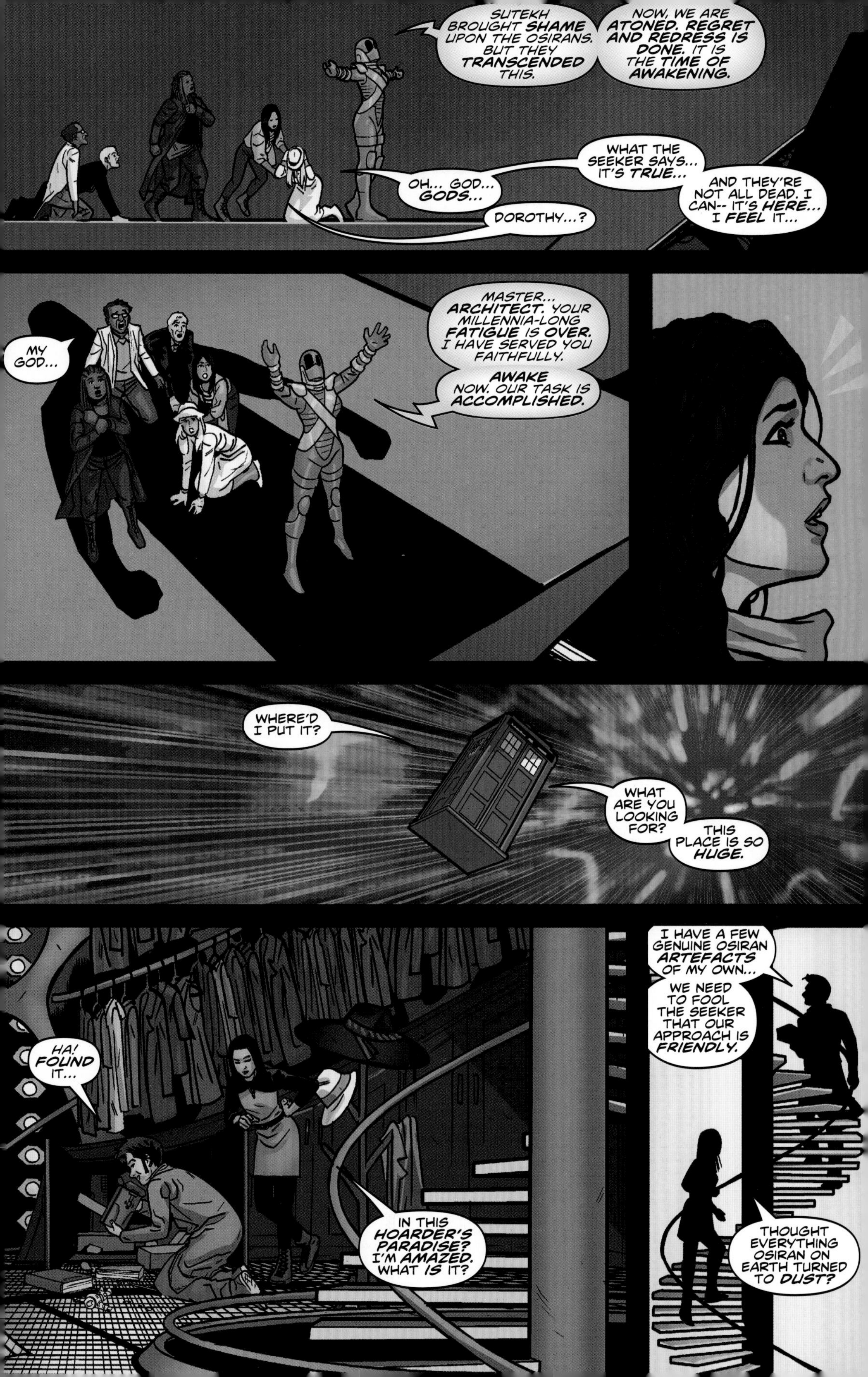
SUTEKH BROUGHT SHAME UPON THE OSIRANS. BUT THEY TRANSCENDED THIS.
NOW, WE ARE ATONED. REGRET AND REDRESS IS DONE. IT IS THE TIME OF AWAKENING.
OH... GOD... GODS...
WHAT THE SEEKER SAYS... IT'S TRUE...
AND THEY'RE NOT ALL DEAD. I CAN-- IT'S HERE... I FEEL IT...
DOROTHY...?
MY GOD...
MASTER... ARCHITECT. YOUR MILLENNIA-LONG FATIGUE IS OVER. I HAVE SERVED YOU FAITHFULLY.
AWAKE NOW. OUR TASK IS ACCOMPLISHED.
WHERE'D I PUT IT?
WHAT ARE YOU LOOKING FOR?
THIS PLACE IS SO HUGE.
HA! FOUND IT...
IN THIS HOARDER'S PARADISE? I'M AMAZED. WHAT IS IT?
I HAVE A FEW GENUINE OSIRAN ARTEFACTS OF MY OWN...
WE NEED TO FOOL THE SEEKER THAT OUR APPROACH IS FRIENDLY.
THOUGHT EVERYTHING OSIRAN ON EARTH TURNED TO DUST?

TARDIS REMAINED **PROTECTED.**

PROTECTED, UNAFFECTED AND UNSEEN...

THIS SHOULD ALLOW US TO *SLIP PAST* THEIR *CLOSED TIMELIKE DEFENSE MANIFOLD...*

WHAT?

VREEE

VWOORP

THOUGHT YOU **UNDERSTOOD SCIENCE?**

THAT'S NOT FAIR.

ALL RIGHT, PAY ATTENTION -- WE'RE IN...

VWOORP KTHUNN OORP

I THOUGHT THE *DALEKS'* ENGINEERING OF *THE MEDUSA CASCADE* WAS *IMPRESSIVE,* BUT THIS...

...THIS IS **PHENOMENAL.**

WHAT *IS* IT?

A STRUCTURE. A *GATEWAY...?*

SPACE-TIME DEFECTS HIDDEN INSIDE *FOLDS OF ARTICULATED QUANTUM FOAM...*

IMPOSSIBLE TO FIND UNLESS YOU *KNEW* IT WAS THERE -- OR HAD A WAY OF FOLLOWING THE SEEKER.

COULD *THAT* BE WHERE THE OSIRANS WENT?

YOU SAYING GABBY'S IN THERE?

NO, GABBY'S INSIDE *THIS* -- ALSO NOT SOMETHING YOU SEE *EVERY DAY.*

AN *OSIRAN MOTHERSHIP...*

WHAT ARE WE WAITING FOR?

HER SIGNAL'S RIGHT OUTSIDE. STAY HERE.

I WILL *NOT.*

CINDY, *NO--* DON'T OPEN THE--

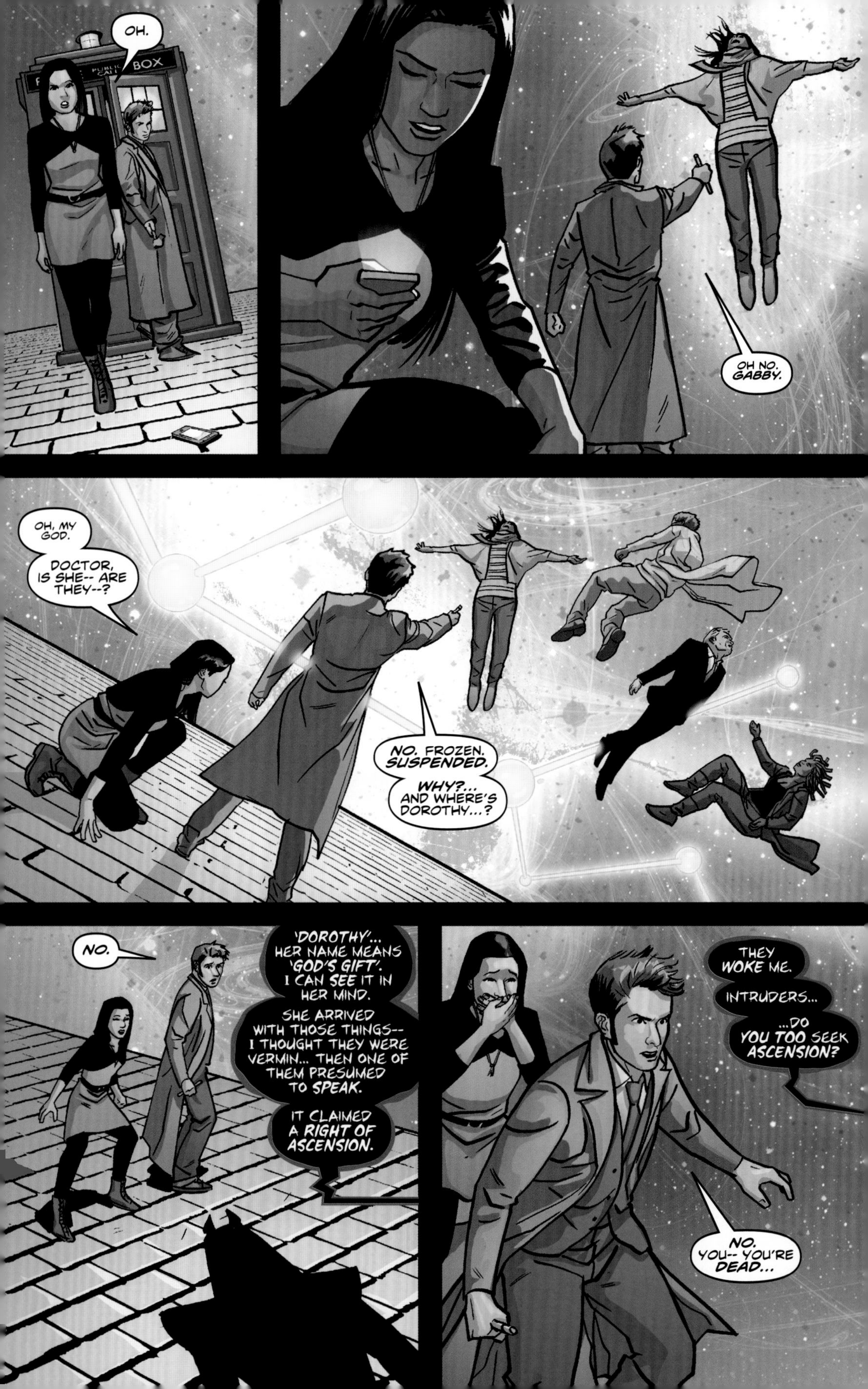

OH.
BOX
OH NO. GABBY.
OH, MY GOD.
DOCTOR, IS SHE-- ARE THEY--?
NO. FROZEN. SUSPENDED.
WHY?... AND WHERE'S DOROTHY...?
NO.
'DOROTHY'... HER NAME MEANS 'GOD'S GIFT'. I CAN SEE IT IN HER MIND.
SHE ARRIVED WITH THOSE THINGS-- I THOUGHT THEY WERE VERMIN... THEN ONE OF THEM PRESUMED TO SPEAK.
IT CLAIMED A RIGHT OF ASCENSION.
THEY WOKE ME.
INTRUDERS...
...DO YOU TOO SEEK ASCENSION?
NO. YOU-- YOU'RE DEAD...

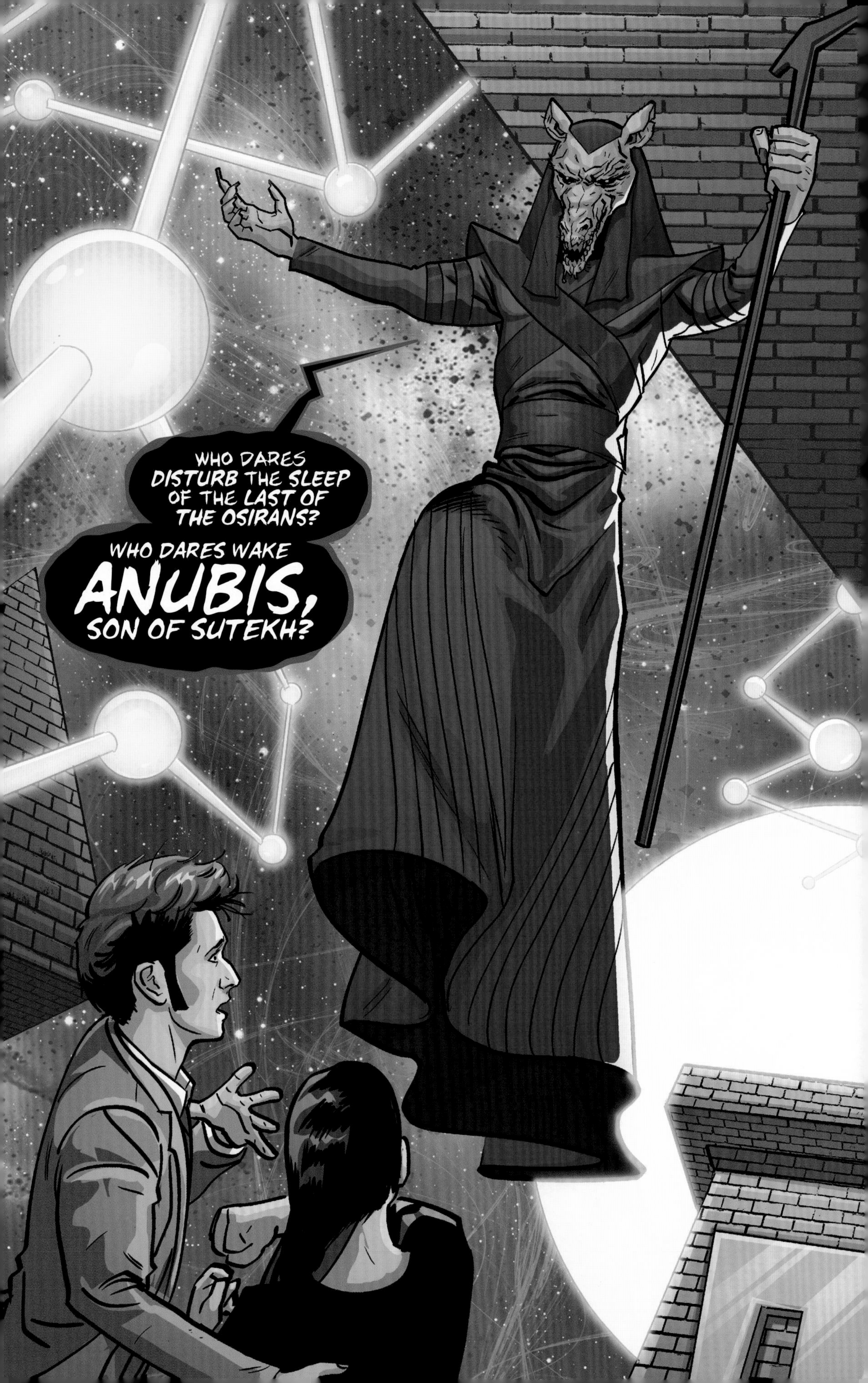
WHO DARES DISTURB THE SLEEP OF THE LAST OF THE OSIRANS?
WHO DARES WAKE ANUBIS, SON OF SUTEKH?

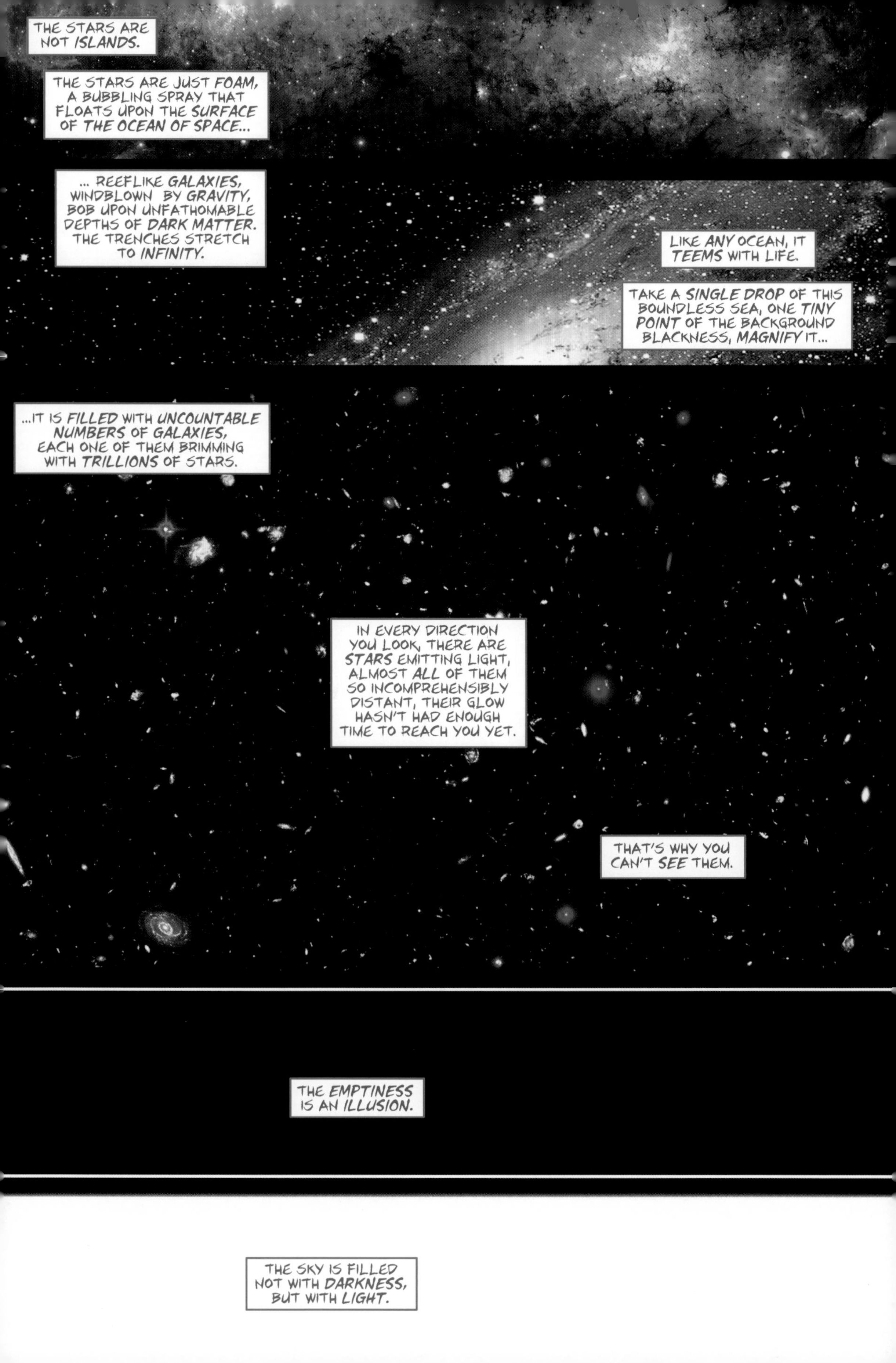
THE STARS ARE NOT ISLANDS.
THE STARS ARE JUST FOAM, A BUBBLING SPRAY THAT FLOATS UPON THE SURFACE OF THE OCEAN OF SPACE...
... REEFLIKE GALAXIES, WINDBLOWN BY GRAVITY, BOB UPON UNFATHOMABLE DEPTHS OF DARK MATTER. THE TRENCHES STRETCH TO INFINITY.
LIKE ANY OCEAN, IT TEEMS WITH LIFE.
TAKE A SINGLE DROP OF THIS BOUNDLESS SEA, ONE TINY POINT OF THE BACKGROUND BLACKNESS, MAGNIFY IT...
...IT IS FILLED WITH UNCOUNTABLE NUMBERS OF GALAXIES, EACH ONE OF THEM BRIMMING WITH TRILLIONS OF STARS.
IN EVERY DIRECTION YOU LOOK, THERE ARE STARS EMITTING LIGHT, ALMOST ALL OF THEM SO INCOMPREHENSIBLY DISTANT, THEIR GLOW HASN'T HAD ENOUGH TIME TO REACH YOU YET.
THAT'S WHY YOU CAN'T SEE THEM.
THE EMPTINESS IS AN ILLUSION.
THE SKY IS FILLED NOT WITH DARKNESS, BUT WITH LIGHT.

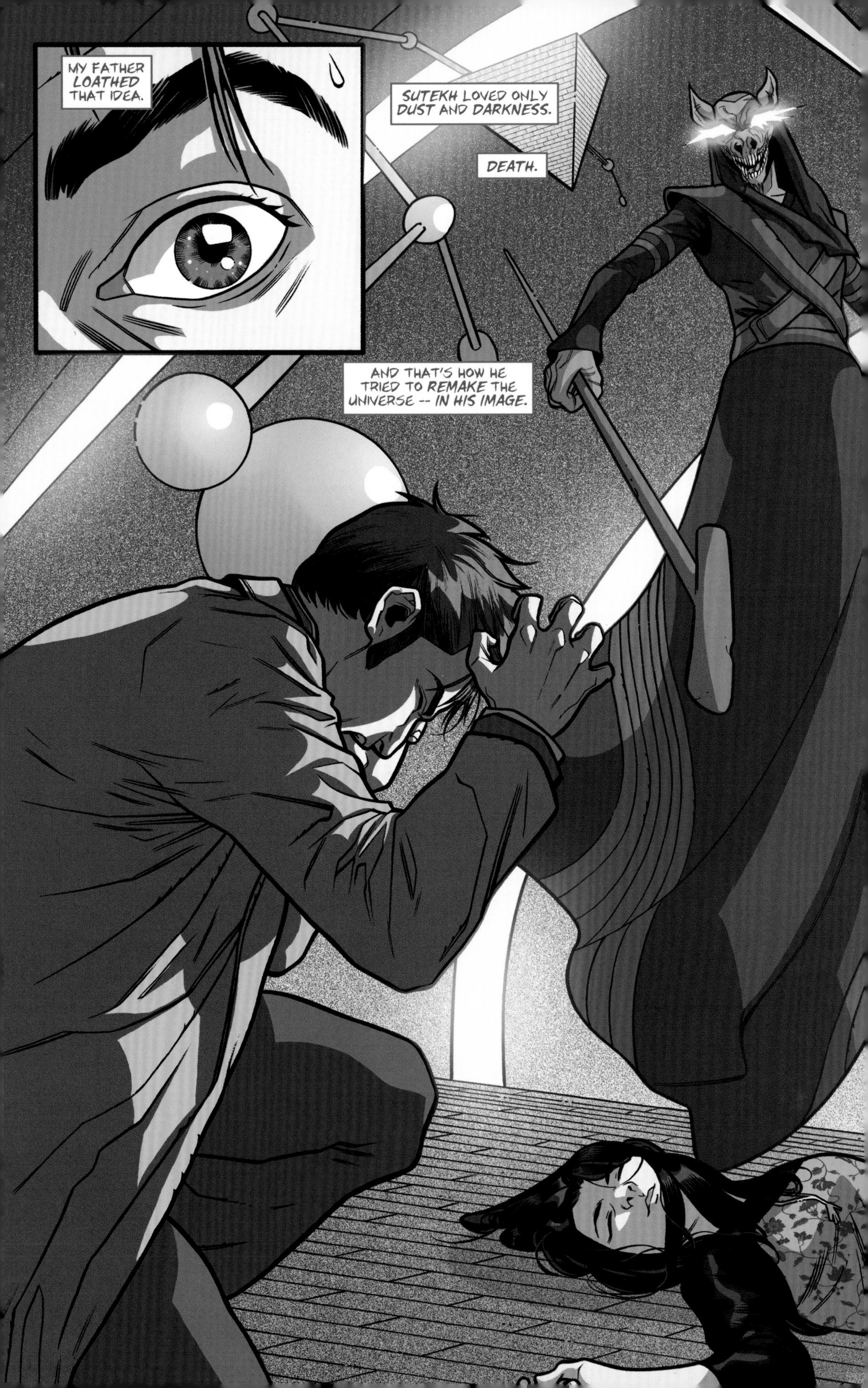
MY FATHER LOATHED THAT IDEA.
SUTEKH LOVED ONLY DUST AND DARKNESS.
DEATH.
AND THAT'S HOW HE TRIED TO REMAKE THE UNIVERSE -- IN HIS IMAGE.

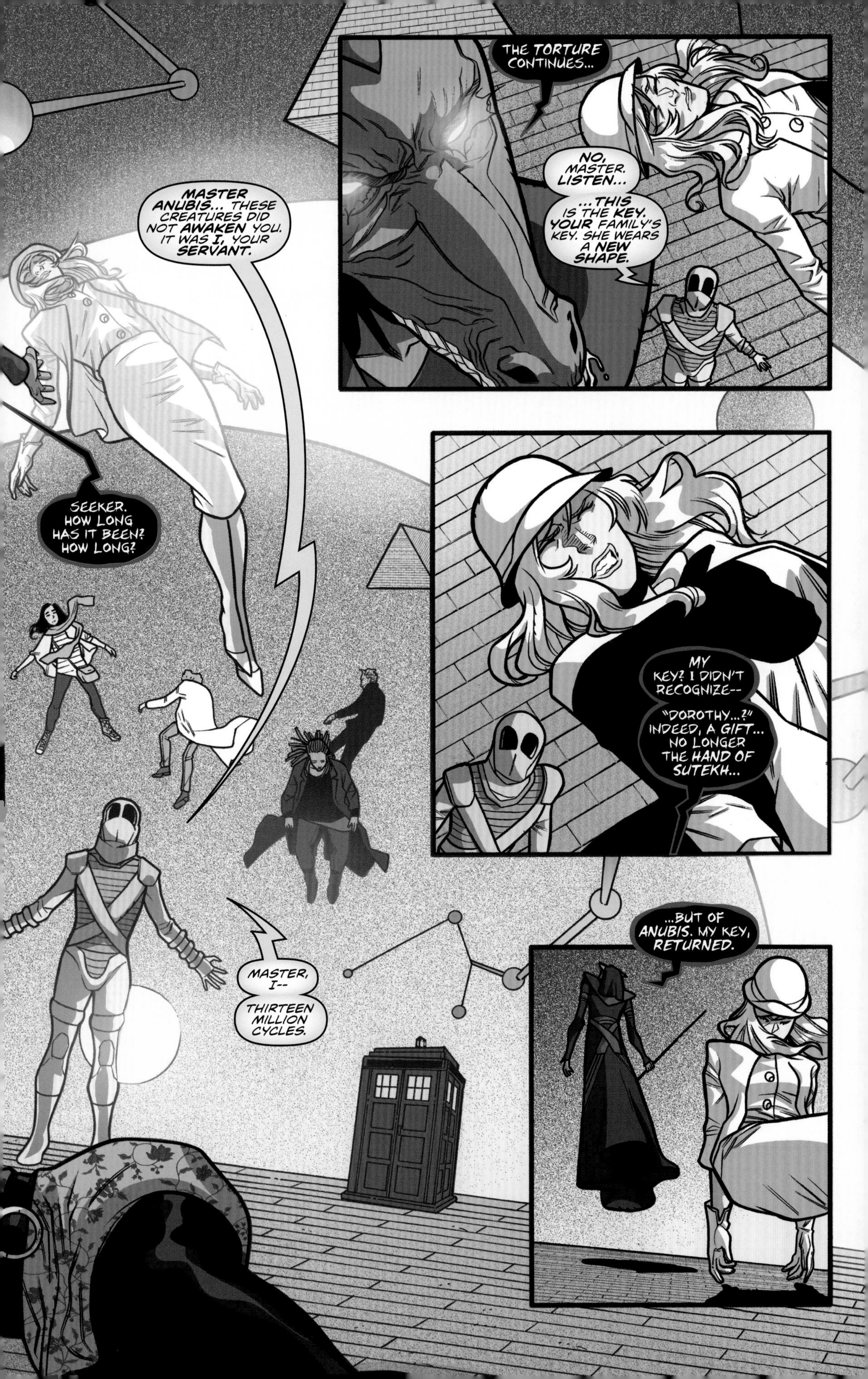
THE TORTURE CONTINUES...
NO, MASTER. LISTEN...
...THIS IS THE KEY. YOUR FAMILY'S KEY. SHE WEARS A NEW SHAPE.
MASTER ANUBIS... THESE CREATURES DID NOT AWAKEN YOU. IT WAS I, YOUR SERVANT.
SEEKER. HOW LONG HAS IT BEEN? HOW LONG?
MASTER, I--
THIRTEEN MILLION CYCLES.
MY KEY? I DIDN'T RECOGNIZE--
"DOROTHY...?" INDEED, A GIFT... NO LONGER THE HAND OF SUTEKH...
...BUT OF ANUBIS. MY KEY, RETURNED.

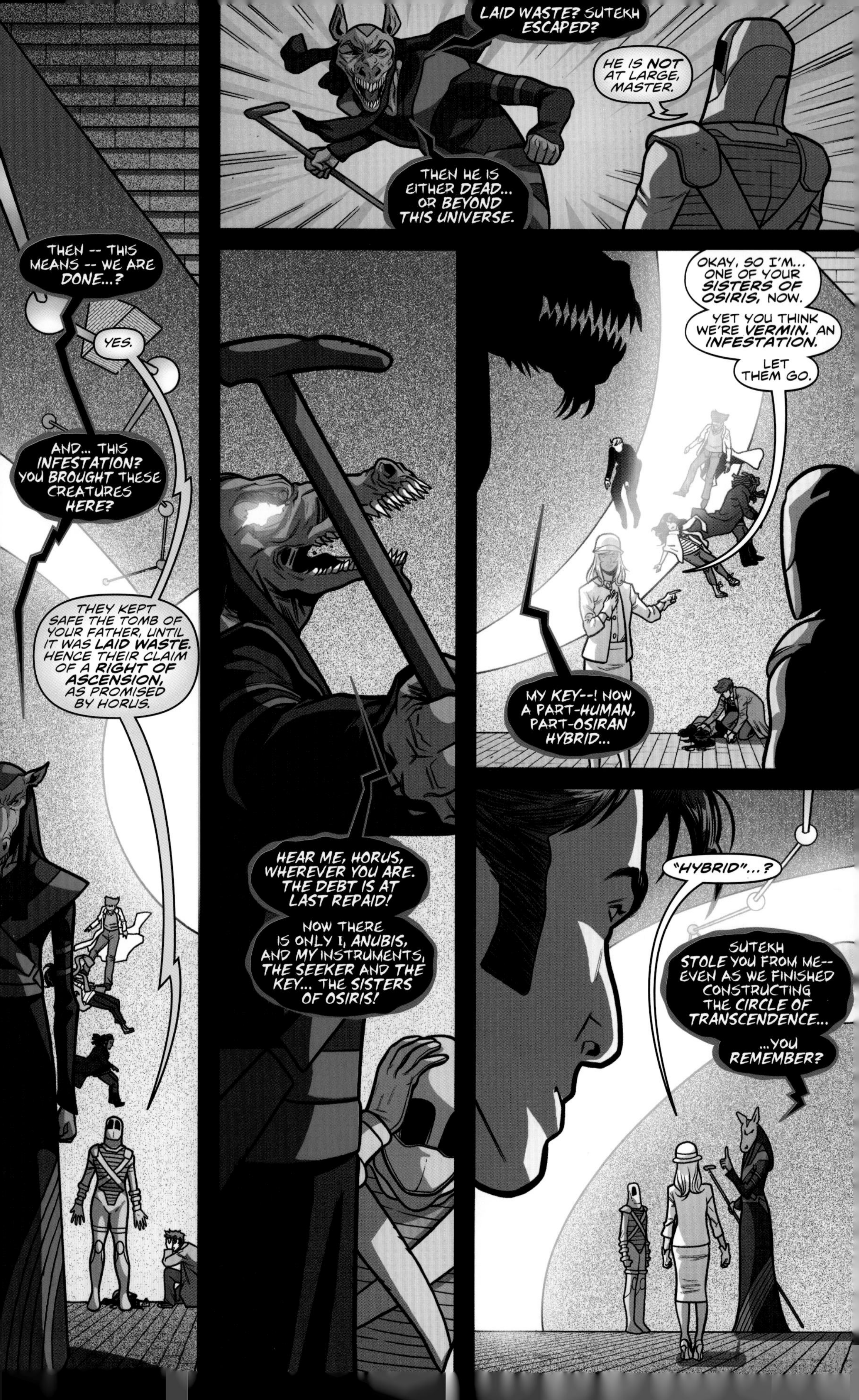

LAID WASTE? SUTEKH ESCAPED?
HE IS NOT AT LARGE, MASTER.
THEN HE IS EITHER DEAD... OR BEYOND THIS UNIVERSE.
THEN -- THIS MEANS -- WE ARE DONE...?
YES.
AND... THIS INFESTATION? YOU BROUGHT THESE CREATURES HERE?
THEY KEPT SAFE THE TOMB OF YOUR FATHER, UNTIL IT WAS LAID WASTE. HENCE THEIR CLAIM OF A RIGHT OF ASCENSION, AS PROMISED BY HORUS.
HEAR ME, HORUS, WHEREVER YOU ARE. THE DEBT IS AT LAST REPAID!
NOW THERE IS ONLY I, ANUBIS, AND MY INSTRUMENTS, THE SEEKER AND THE KEY... THE SISTERS OF OSIRIS!
OKAY, SO I'M... ONE OF YOUR SISTERS OF OSIRIS, NOW.
YET YOU THINK WE'RE VERMIN. AN INFESTATION.
LET THEM GO.
MY KEY--! NOW A PART-HUMAN, PART-OSIRAN HYBRID...
"HYBRID"...?
SUTEKH STOLE YOU FROM ME-- EVEN AS WE FINISHED CONSTRUCTING THE CIRCLE OF TRANSCENDENCE...
...YOU REMEMBER?

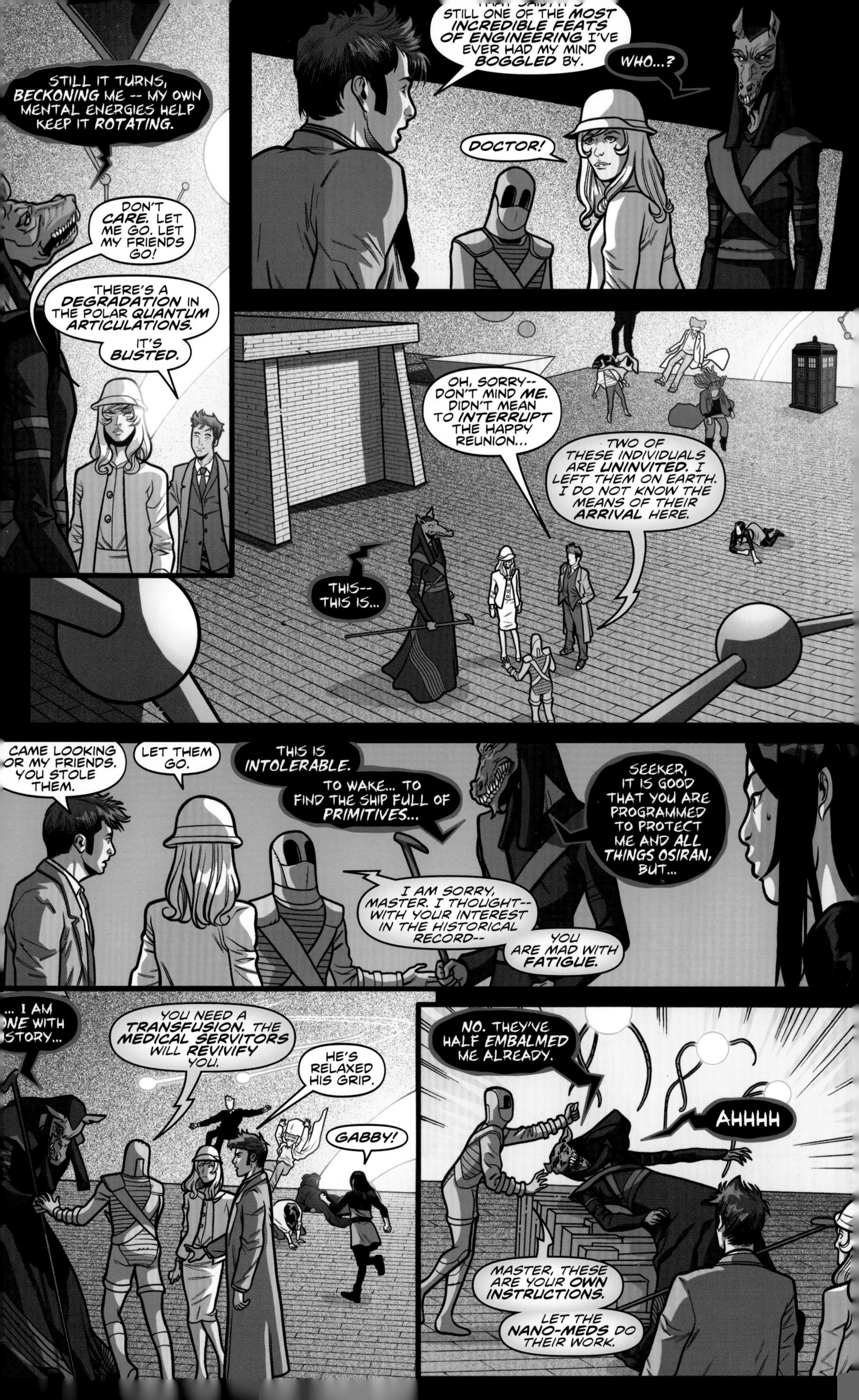
STILL IT TURNS, BECKONING ME -- MY OWN MENTAL ENERGIES HELP KEEP IT ROTATING.
DON'T CARE. LET ME GO. LET MY FRIENDS GO!
THERE'S A DEGRADATION IN THE POLAR QUANTUM ARTICULATIONS.
IT'S BUSTED.
STILL ONE OF THE MOST INCREDIBLE FEATS OF ENGINEERING I'VE EVER HAD MY MIND BOGGLED BY.
WHO...?
DOCTOR!
OH, SORRY-- DON'T MIND ME. DIDN'T MEAN TO INTERRUPT THE HAPPY REUNION...
TWO OF THESE INDIVIDUALS ARE UNINVITED. I LEFT THEM ON EARTH. I DO NOT KNOW THE MEANS OF THEIR ARRIVAL HERE.
THIS-- THIS IS...
CAME LOOKING OR MY FRIENDS. YOU STOLE THEM.
LET THEM GO.
THIS IS INTOLERABLE.
TO WAKE... TO FIND THE SHIP FULL OF PRIMITIVES...
SEEKER, IT IS GOOD THAT YOU ARE PROGRAMMED TO PROTECT ME AND ALL THINGS OSIRAN, BUT...
I AM SORRY, MASTER. I THOUGHT-- WITH YOUR INTEREST IN THE HISTORICAL RECORD--
YOU ARE MAD WITH FATIGUE.
... I AM ONE WITH STORY...
YOU NEED A TRANSFUSION. THE MEDICAL SERVITORS WILL REVIVIFY YOU.
HE'S RELAXED HIS GRIP.
GABBY!
NO. THEY'VE HALF EMBALMED ME ALREADY.
AHHHH
MASTER, THESE ARE YOUR OWN INSTRUCTIONS.
LET THE NANO-MEDS DO THEIR WORK.

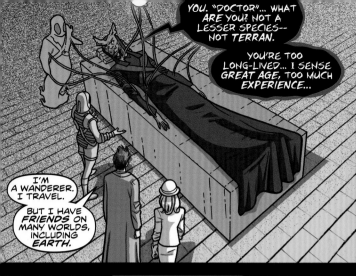

YOU. "DOCTOR"... WHAT ARE YOU? NOT A LESSER SPECIES-- NOT TERRAN.

YOU'RE TOO LONG-LIVED... I SENSE GREAT AGE, TOO MUCH EXPERIENCE...

I'M A WANDERER. I TRAVEL.

BUT I HAVE FRIENDS ON MANY WORLDS, INCLUDING EARTH.

DON'T OBFUSCATE, DOCTOR. WHAT ARE YOU?

AH. A... GALLIFREYAN...?

AAAAH! YES!-- YES! A TIME LORD.

VORSSSH

MASTER -- DO NOT EXERT YOURSELF UNTIL THE REJUVENATION PROCESS IS COMPLETED.

PFFFFT. LAST I WAS AWARE, THE TIME LORDS WERE ENGAGED IN SOME PETTY SQUABBLE WITH THE DALEKS...

GUILTY AS CHARGED. ALL FINISHED NOW.

INDEED -- THOUGH THE AFFAIRS OF THE LOWER ORDERS ARE NO CONCERN OF MINE.

IT'S TIME FOR ME TO ASCEND-- TO TRAVEL BEYOND THIS UNIVERSE...

WHAT-- THROUGH THAT?

NO CHANCE. YOUR 'CIRCLE OF TRANSCENDENCE' ISN'T STABLE ANYMORE.

THIS IS A FOUR-DIMENSIONAL CONSTRUCTION HERE IN OUR THREE-DIMENSIONAL COSMOS. IT REALLY IS A WAY THROUGH TO A HIGHER UNIVERSE...

YOU'RE ANUBIS... ISN'T THAT WHAT YOU DO, PRESIDE OVER THE GATEWAY TO THE AFTERLIFE?

IS THAT WHAT THIS IS -- FOR OSIRANS?

WHY'D HORUS LEAVE YOU HERE, ANUBIS?

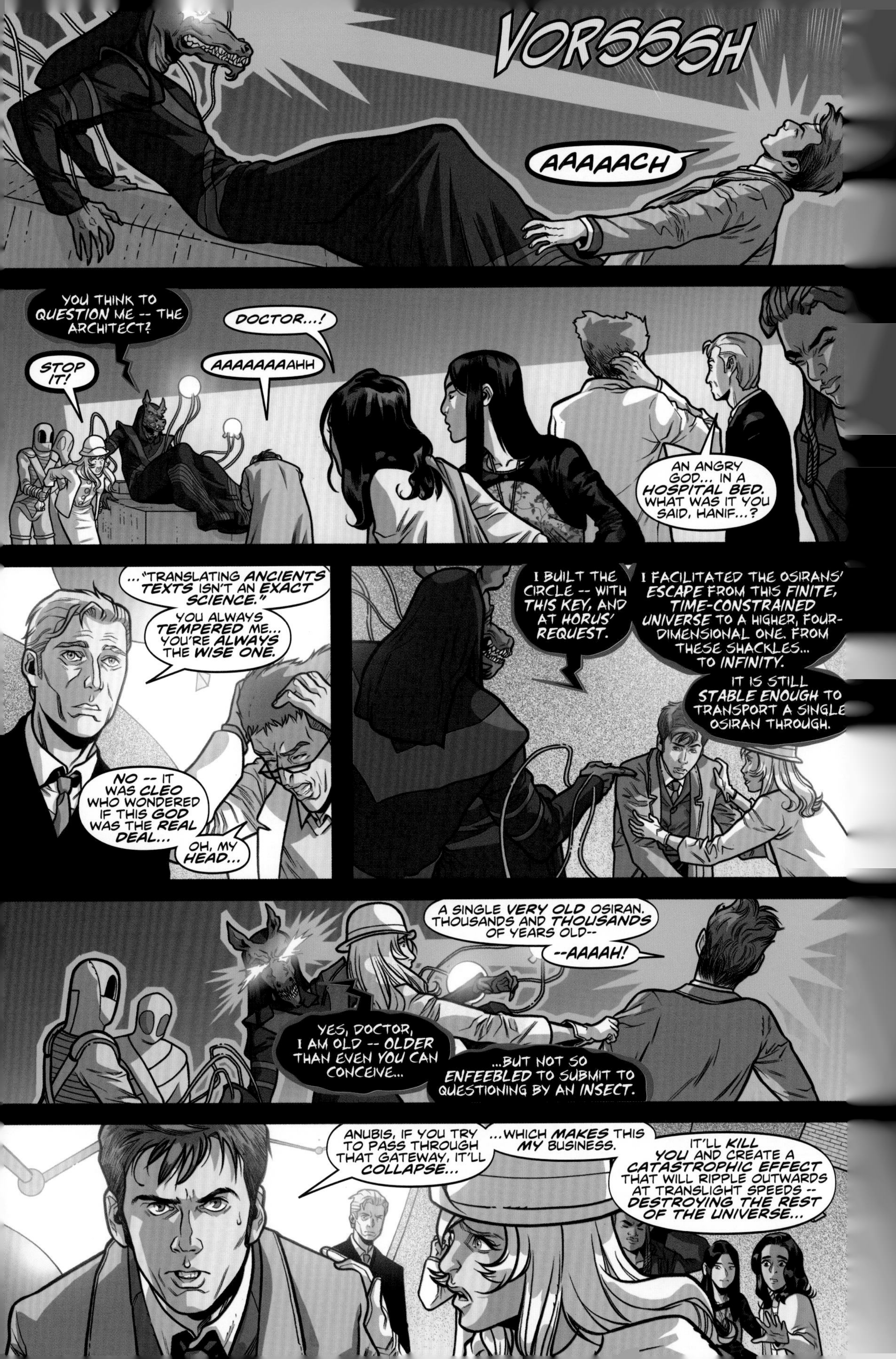
VORSSSH
AAAAACH
YOU THINK TO QUESTION ME -- THE ARCHITECT?
STOP IT!
DOCTOR...!
AAAAAAAAHH
AN ANGRY GOD... IN A HOSPITAL BED. WHAT WAS IT YOU SAID, HANIF...?
..."TRANSLATING ANCIENTS TEXTS ISN'T AN EXACT SCIENCE."
YOU ALWAYS TEMPERED ME... YOU'RE ALWAYS THE WISE ONE.
NO -- IT WAS CLEO WHO WONDERED IF THIS GOD WAS THE REAL DEAL...
OH, MY HEAD...
I BUILT THE CIRCLE -- WITH THIS KEY, AND AT HORUS' REQUEST.
I FACILITATED THE OSIRANS' ESCAPE FROM THIS FINITE, TIME-CONSTRAINED UNIVERSE TO A HIGHER, FOUR-DIMENSIONAL ONE. FROM THESE SHACKLES... TO INFINITY.
IT IS STILL STABLE ENOUGH TO TRANSPORT A SINGLE OSIRAN THROUGH.
A SINGLE VERY OLD OSIRAN. THOUSANDS AND THOUSANDS OF YEARS OLD--
--AAAAH!
YES, DOCTOR, I AM OLD -- OLDER THAN EVEN YOU CAN CONCEIVE...
...BUT NOT SO ENFEEBLED TO SUBMIT TO QUESTIONING BY AN INSECT.
ANUBIS, IF YOU TRY TO PASS THROUGH THAT GATEWAY, IT'LL COLLAPSE...
...WHICH MAKES THIS MY BUSINESS.
IT'LL KILL YOU AND CREATE A CATASTROPHIC EFFECT THAT WILL RIPPLE OUTWARDS AT TRANSLIGHT SPEEDS -- DESTROYING THE REST OF THE UNIVERSE...

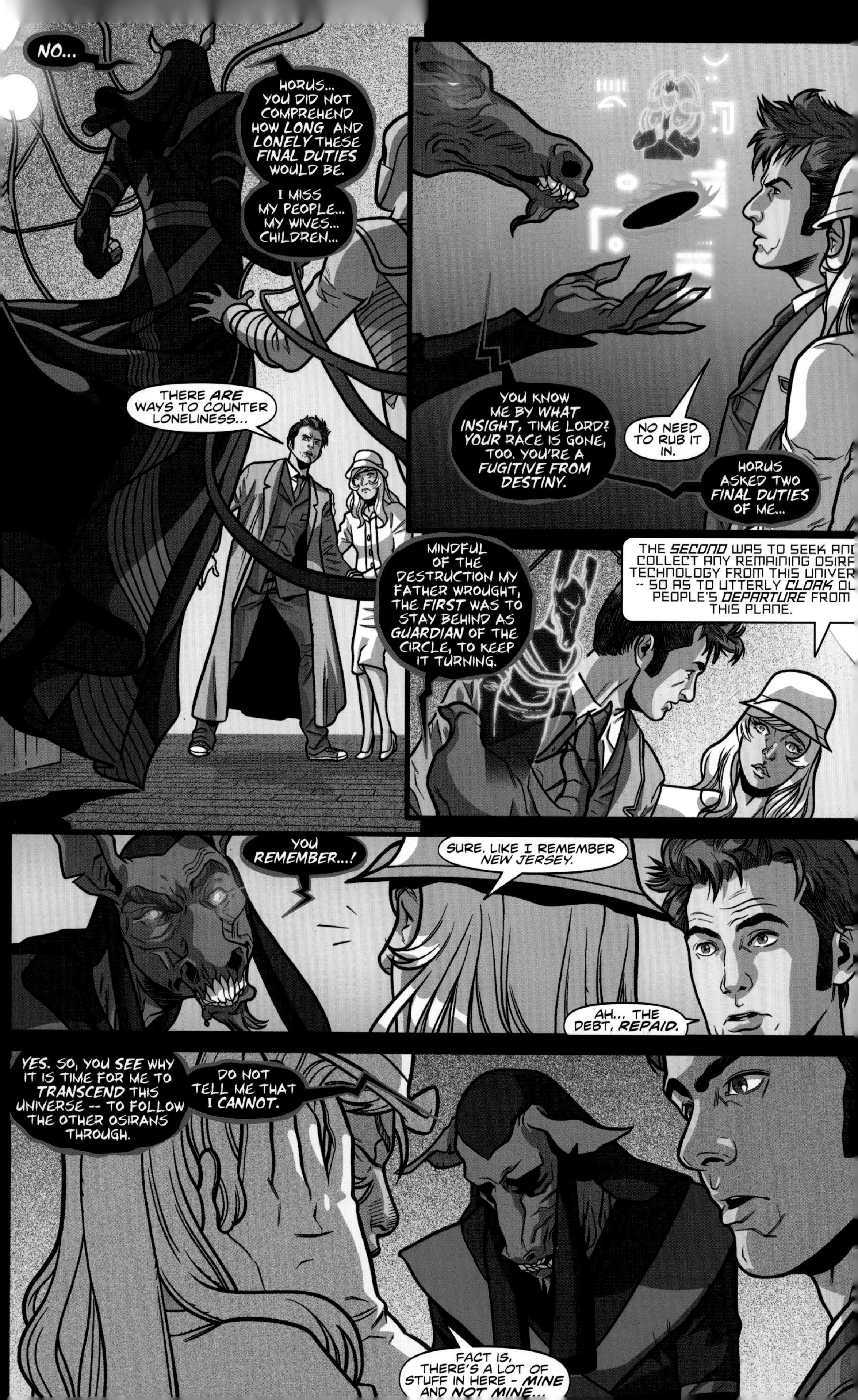
NO...
HORUS... YOU DID NOT COMPREHEND HOW LONG AND LONELY THESE FINAL DUTIES WOULD BE.
I MISS MY PEOPLE... MY WIVES... CHILDREN...
THERE ARE WAYS TO COUNTER LONELINESS...
YOU KNOW ME BY WHAT INSIGHT, TIME LORD? YOUR RACE IS GONE, TOO. YOU'RE A FUGITIVE FROM DESTINY.
NO NEED TO RUB IT IN.
HORUS ASKED TWO FINAL DUTIES OF ME...
MINDFUL OF THE DESTRUCTION MY FATHER WROUGHT, THE FIRST WAS TO STAY BEHIND AS GUARDIAN OF THE CIRCLE, TO KEEP IT TURNING.
THE SECOND WAS TO SEEK AND COLLECT ANY REMAINING OSIRA TECHNOLOGY FROM THIS UNIVER -- SO AS TO UTTERLY CLOAK OU PEOPLE'S DEPARTURE FROM THIS PLANE.
YOU REMEMBER...!
SURE. LIKE I REMEMBER NEW JERSEY.
AH... THE DEBT, REPAID.
YES. SO, YOU SEE WHY IT IS TIME FOR ME TO TRANSCEND THIS UNIVERSE -- TO FOLLOW THE OTHER OSIRANS THROUGH.
DO NOT TELL ME THAT I CANNOT.
FACT IS, THERE'S A LOT OF STUFF IN HERE - MINE AND NOT MINE...

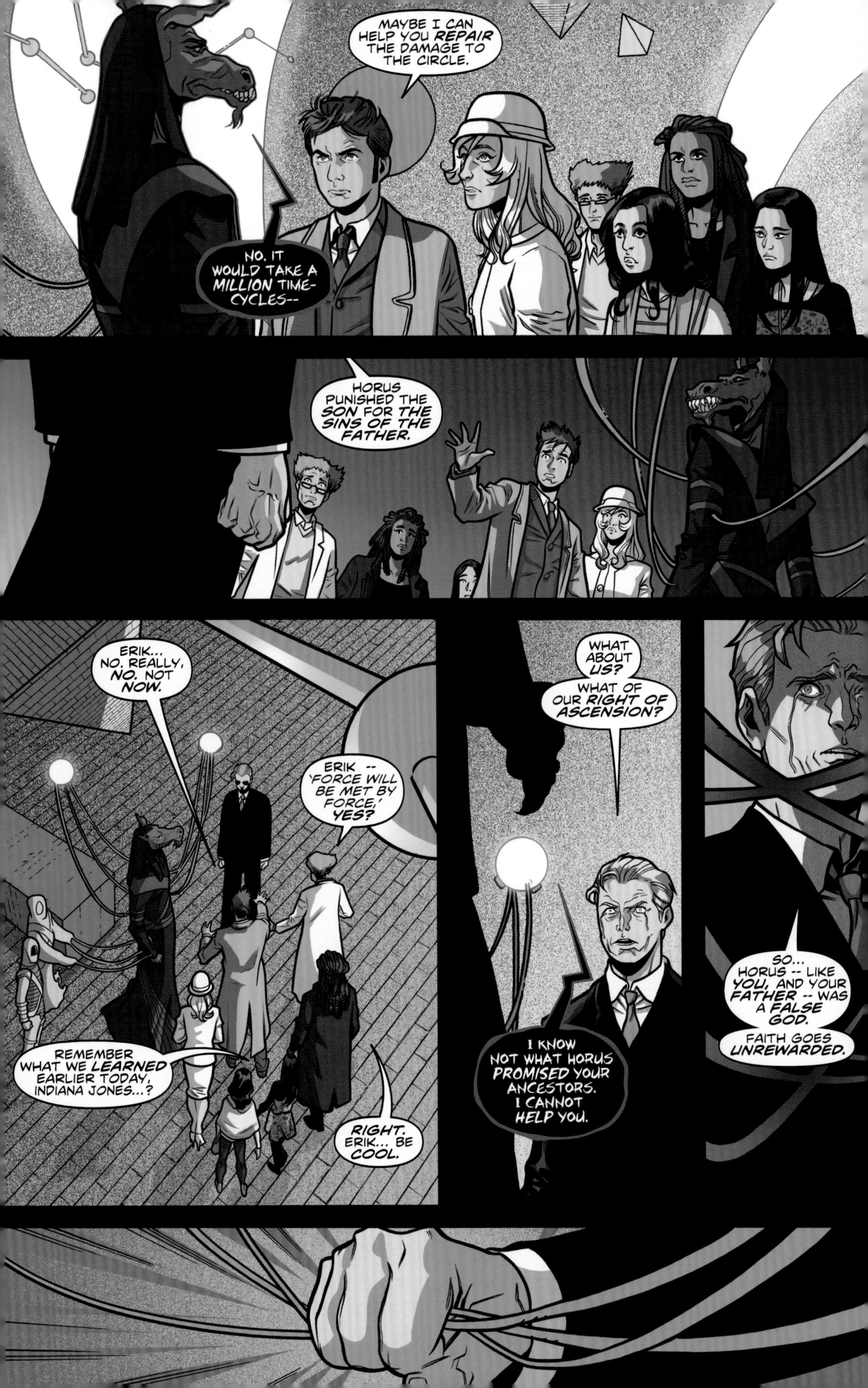
MAYBE I CAN HELP YOU REPAIR THE DAMAGE TO THE CIRCLE.
NO. IT WOULD TAKE A MILLION TIME-CYCLES--
HORUS PUNISHED THE SON FOR THE SINS OF THE FATHER.
ERIK... NO. REALLY, NO. NOT NOW.
ERIK -- 'FORCE WILL BE MET BY FORCE,' YES?
REMEMBER WHAT WE LEARNED EARLIER TODAY, INDIANA JONES...?
RIGHT. ERIK... BE COOL.
WHAT ABOUT US?
WHAT OF OUR RIGHT OF ASCENSION?
I KNOW NOT WHAT HORUS PROMISED YOUR ANCESTORS. I CANNOT HELP YOU.
SO... HORUS -- LIKE YOU, AND YOUR FATHER -- WAS A FALSE GOD.
FAITH GOES UNREWARDED.

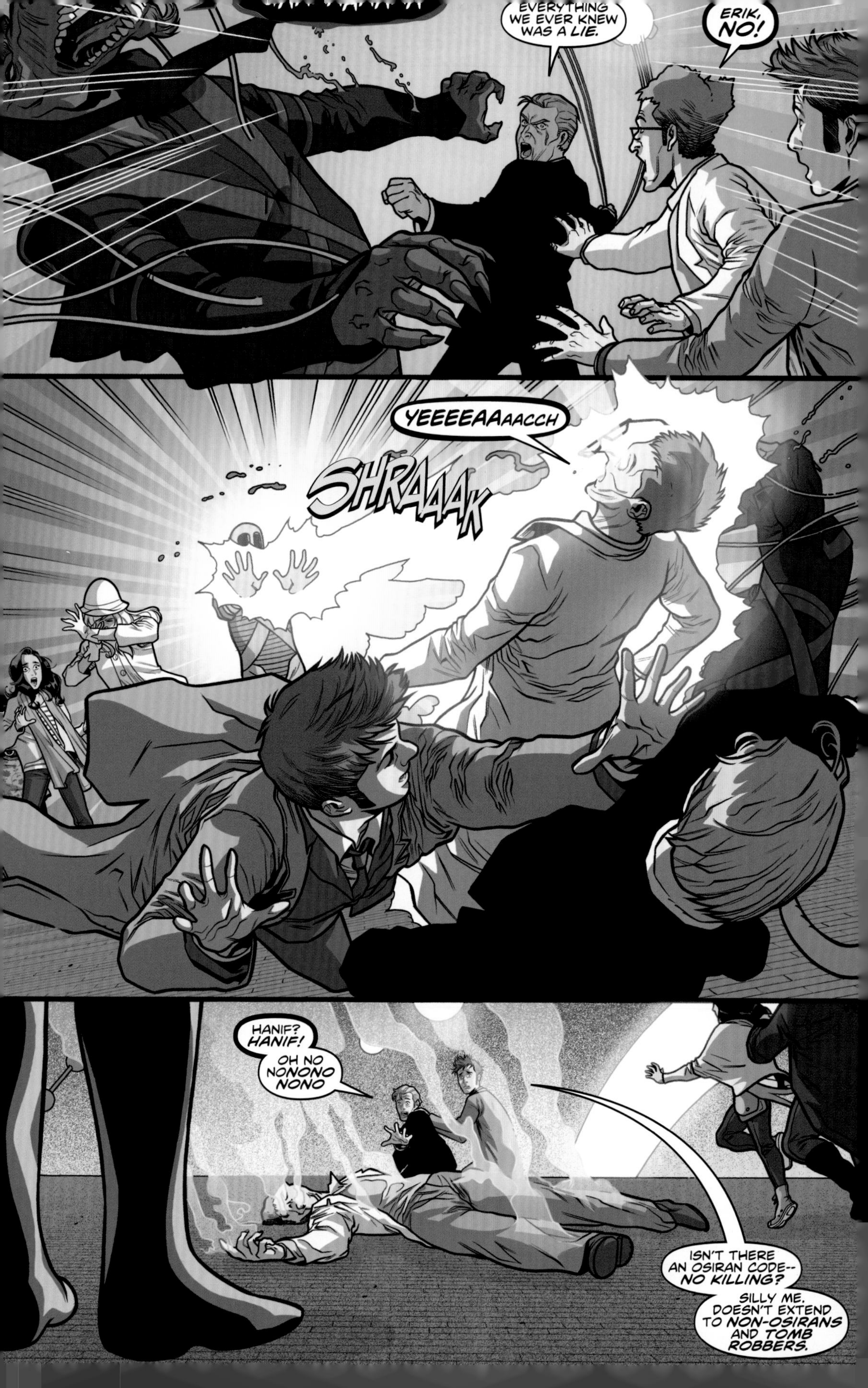
EVERYTHING WE EVER KNEW WAS A LIE.
ERIK, NO!
YEEEEAAAACCH
SHRAAAK
HANIF? HANIF!
OH NO NONONO NONO
ISN'T THERE AN OSIRAN CODE-- NO KILLING?
SILLY ME. DOESN'T EXTEND TO NON-OSIRANS AND TOMB ROBBERS.

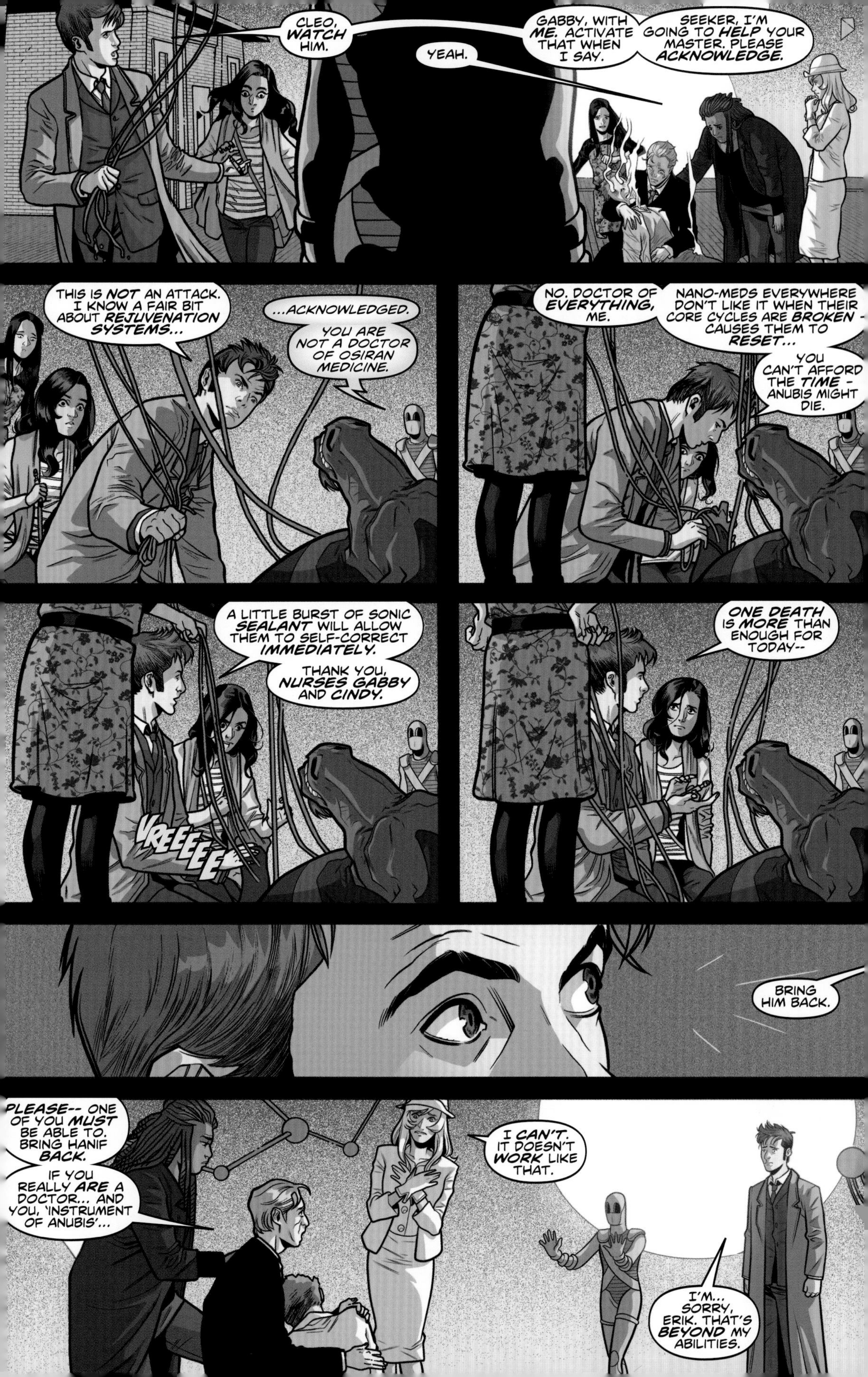
CLEO, WATCH HIM.
GABBY, WITH ME. ACTIVATE THAT WHEN I SAY.
YEAH.
SEEKER, I'M GOING TO HELP YOUR MASTER. PLEASE ACKNOWLEDGE.
THIS IS NOT AN ATTACK. I KNOW A FAIR BIT ABOUT REJUVENATION SYSTEMS...
...ACKNOWLEDGED.
YOU ARE NOT A DOCTOR OF OSIRAN MEDICINE.
NO. DOCTOR OF EVERYTHING, ME.
NANO-MEDS EVERYWHERE DON'T LIKE IT WHEN THEIR CORE CYCLES ARE BROKEN - CAUSES THEM TO RESET...
YOU CAN'T AFFORD THE TIME - ANUBIS MIGHT DIE.
A LITTLE BURST OF SONIC SEALANT WILL ALLOW THEM TO SELF-CORRECT IMMEDIATELY.
THANK YOU, NURSES GABBY AND CINDY.
VREEEEE
ONE DEATH IS MORE THAN ENOUGH FOR TODAY--
BRING HIM BACK.
PLEASE-- ONE OF YOU MUST BE ABLE TO. BRING HANIF BACK.
IF YOU REALLY ARE A DOCTOR... AND YOU, 'INSTRUMENT OF ANUBIS'...
I CAN'T. IT DOESN'T WORK LIKE THAT.
I'M... SORRY, ERIK. THAT'S BEYOND MY ABILITIES.

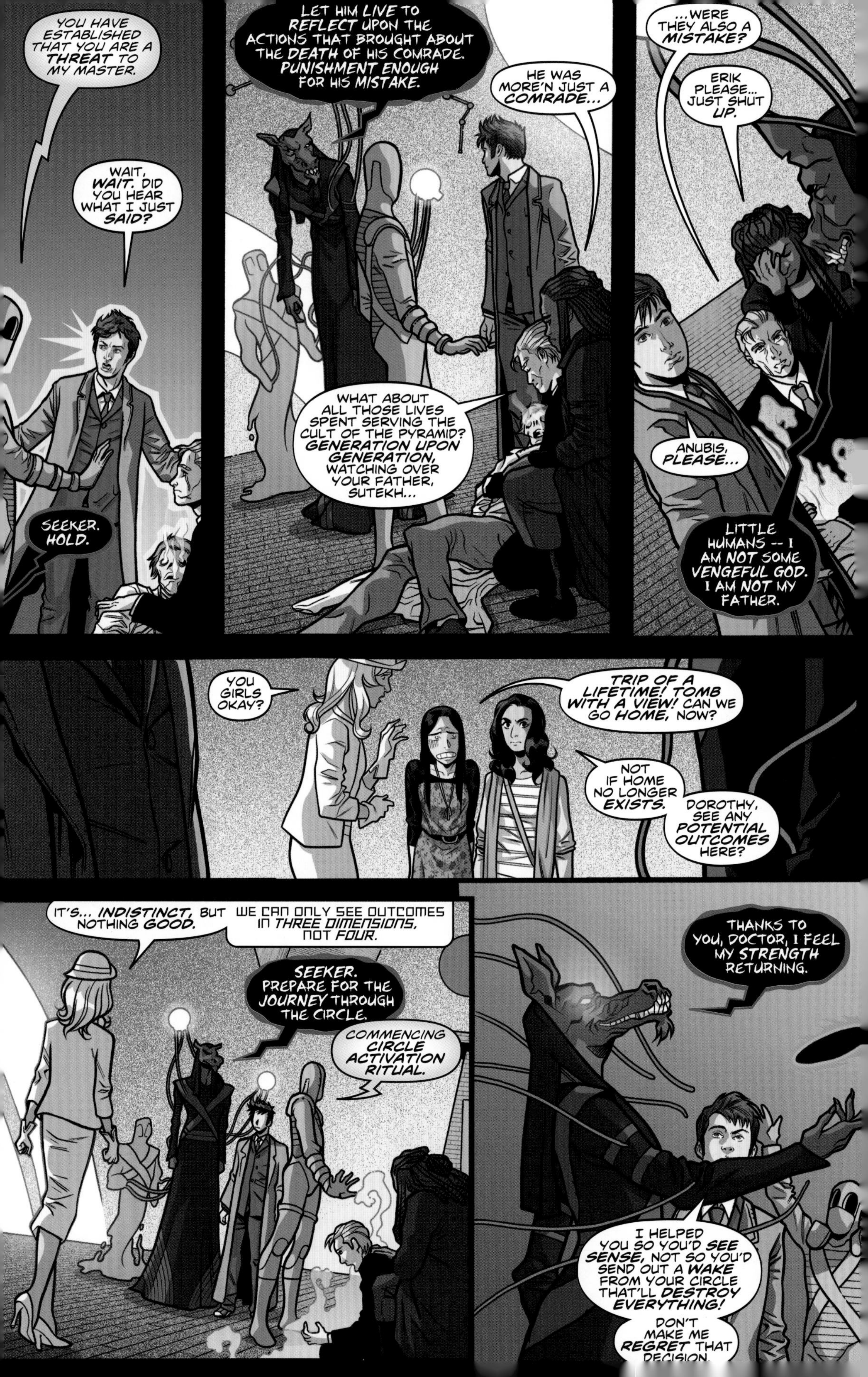

YOU HAVE ESTABLISHED THAT YOU ARE A THREAT TO MY MASTER.
WAIT, WAIT. DID YOU HEAR WHAT I JUST SAID?
SEEKER. HOLD.
LET HIM LIVE TO REFLECT UPON THE ACTIONS THAT BROUGHT ABOUT THE DEATH OF HIS COMRADE. PUNISHMENT ENOUGH FOR HIS MISTAKE.
HE WAS MORE'N JUST A COMRADE...
WHAT ABOUT ALL THOSE LIVES SPENT SERVING THE CULT OF THE PYRAMID? GENERATION UPON GENERATION, WATCHING OVER YOUR FATHER, SUTEKH...
...WERE THEY ALSO A MISTAKE?
ERIK PLEASE... JUST SHUT UP.
ANUBIS, PLEASE...
LITTLE HUMANS -- I AM NOT SOME VENGEFUL GOD. I AM NOT MY FATHER.
YOU GIRLS OKAY?
TRIP OF A LIFETIME! TOMB WITH A VIEW! CAN WE GO HOME, NOW?
NOT IF HOME NO LONGER EXISTS.
DOROTHY, SEE ANY POTENTIAL OUTCOMES HERE?
IT'S... INDISTINCT, BUT NOTHING GOOD.
WE CAN ONLY SEE OUTCOMES IN THREE DIMENSIONS, NOT FOUR.
SEEKER. PREPARE FOR THE JOURNEY THROUGH THE CIRCLE.
COMMENCING CIRCLE ACTIVATION RITUAL.
THANKS TO YOU, DOCTOR, I FEEL MY STRENGTH RETURNING.
I HELPED YOU SO YOU'D SEE SENSE, NOT SO YOU'D SEND OUT A WAKE FROM YOUR CIRCLE THAT'LL DESTROY EVERYTHING!
DON'T MAKE ME REGRET THAT DECISION.

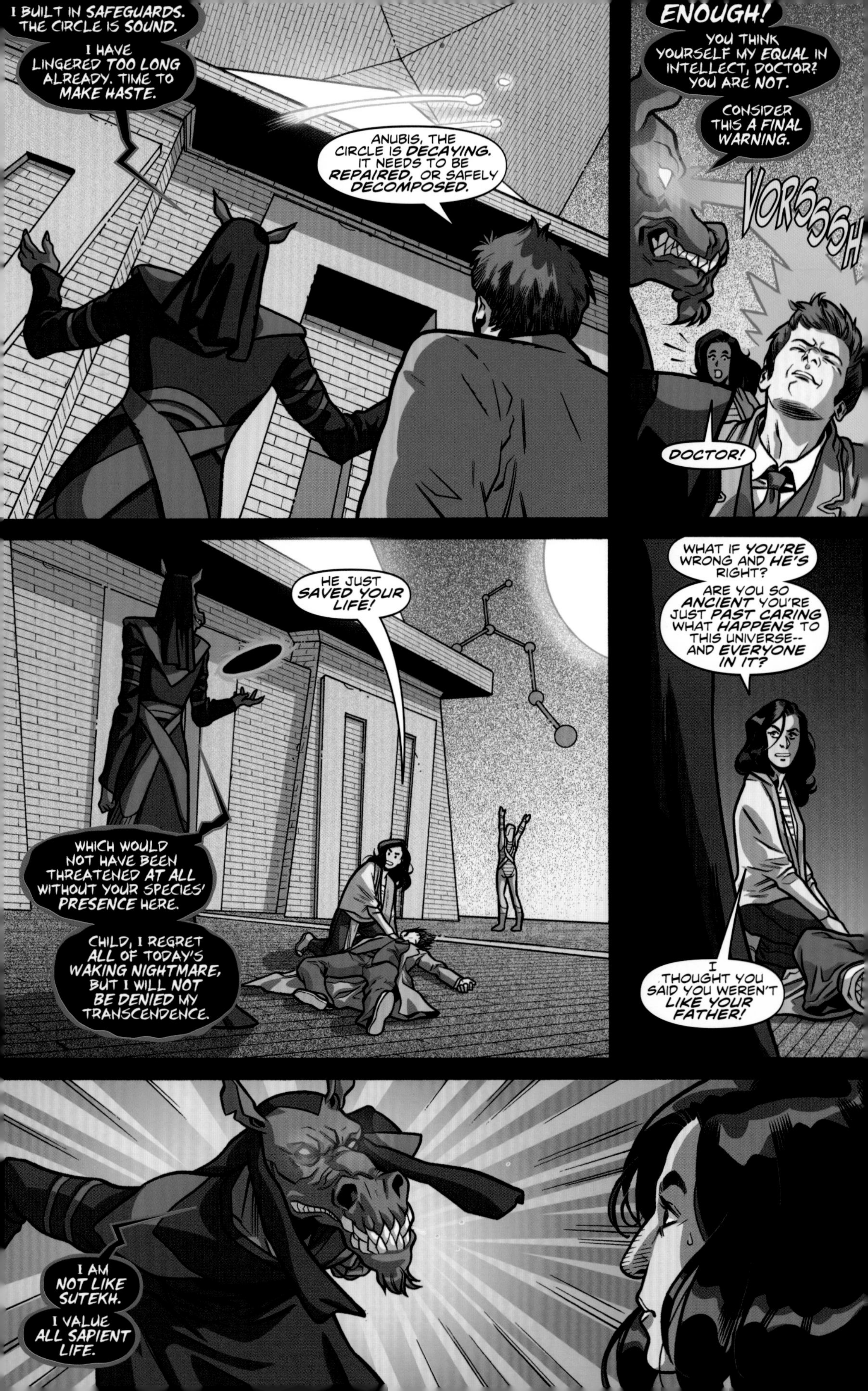
I BUILT IN SAFEGUARDS. THE CIRCLE IS SOUND.
I HAVE LINGERED TOO LONG ALREADY. TIME TO MAKE HASTE.
ANUBIS, THE CIRCLE IS DECAYING. IT NEEDS TO BE REPAIRED, OR SAFELY DECOMPOSED.
ENOUGH!
YOU THINK YOURSELF MY EQUAL IN INTELLECT, DOCTOR? YOU ARE NOT.
CONSIDER THIS A FINAL WARNING.
VORSSSH
DOCTOR!
HE JUST SAVED YOUR LIFE!
WHICH WOULD NOT HAVE BEEN THREATENED AT ALL WITHOUT YOUR SPECIES' PRESENCE HERE.
CHILD, I REGRET ALL OF TODAY'S WAKING NIGHTMARE, BUT I WILL NOT BE DENIED MY TRANSCENDENCE.
WHAT IF YOU'RE WRONG AND HE'S RIGHT?
ARE YOU SO ANCIENT YOU'RE JUST PAST CARING WHAT HAPPENS TO THIS UNIVERSE-- AND EVERYONE IN IT?
I THOUGHT YOU SAID YOU WEREN'T LIKE YOUR FATHER!
I AM NOT LIKE SUTEKH.
I VALUE ALL SAPIENT LIFE.

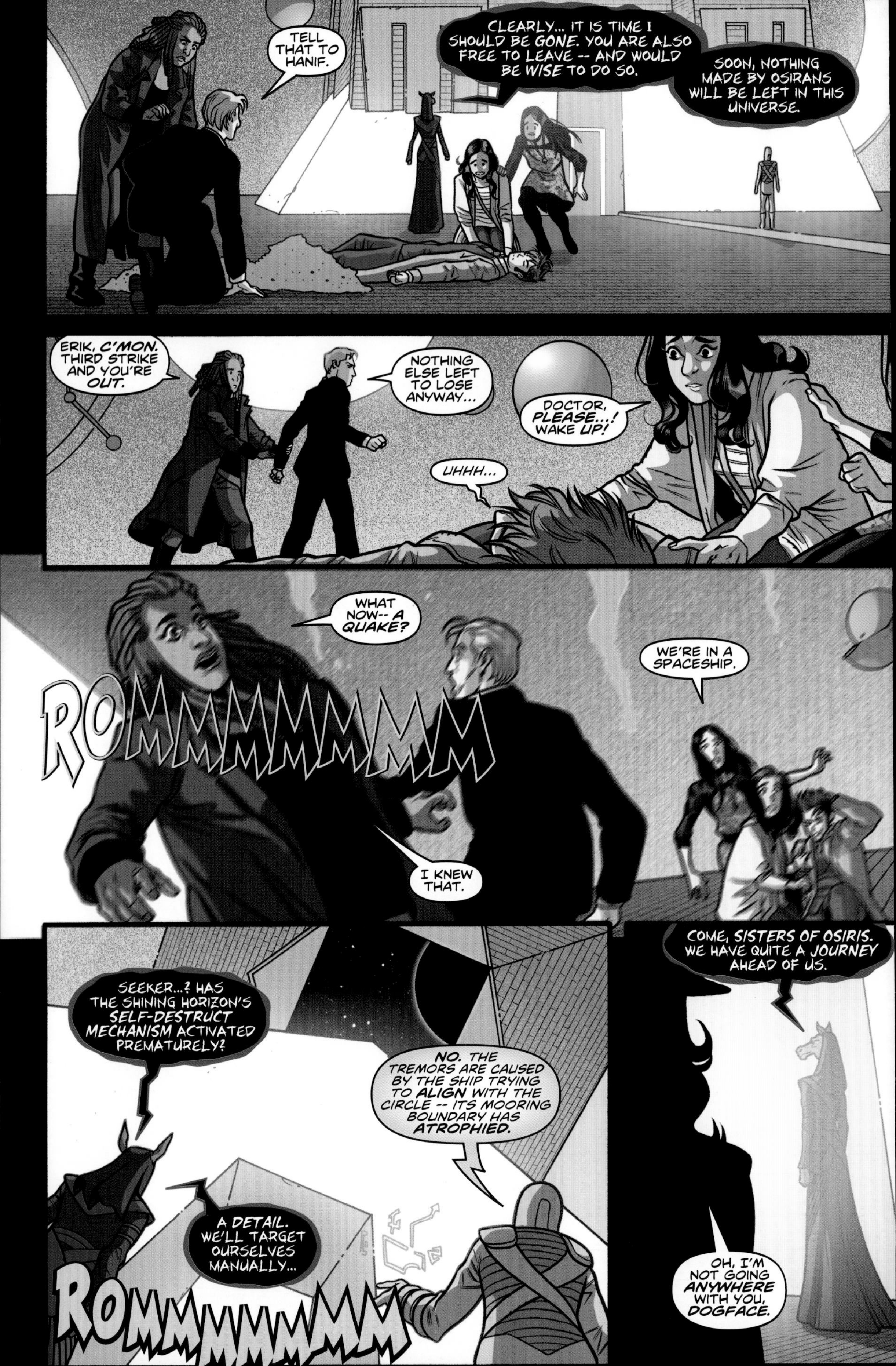
TELL THAT TO HANIF.
CLEARLY... IT IS TIME I SHOULD BE GONE. YOU ARE ALSO FREE TO LEAVE -- AND WOULD BE WISE TO DO SO.
SOON, NOTHING MADE BY OSIRANS WILL BE LEFT IN THIS UNIVERSE.
ERIK, C'MON. THIRD STRIKE AND YOU'RE OUT.
NOTHING ELSE LEFT TO LOSE ANYWAY...
DOCTOR, PLEASE...! WAKE UP!
UHHH...
WHAT NOW-- A QUAKE?
ROMMMMMMMM
WE'RE IN A SPACESHIP.
I KNEW THAT.
SEEKER...? HAS THE SHINING HORIZON'S SELF-DESTRUCT MECHANISM ACTIVATED PREMATURELY?
NO. THE TREMORS ARE CAUSED BY THE SHIP TRYING TO ALIGN WITH THE CIRCLE -- ITS MOORING BOUNDARY HAS ATROPHIED.
A DETAIL. WE'LL TARGET OURSELVES MANUALLY...
ROMMMMMMMM
COME, SISTERS OF OSIRIS. WE HAVE QUITE A JOURNEY AHEAD OF US.
OH, I'M NOT GOING ANYWHERE WITH YOU, DOGFACE.

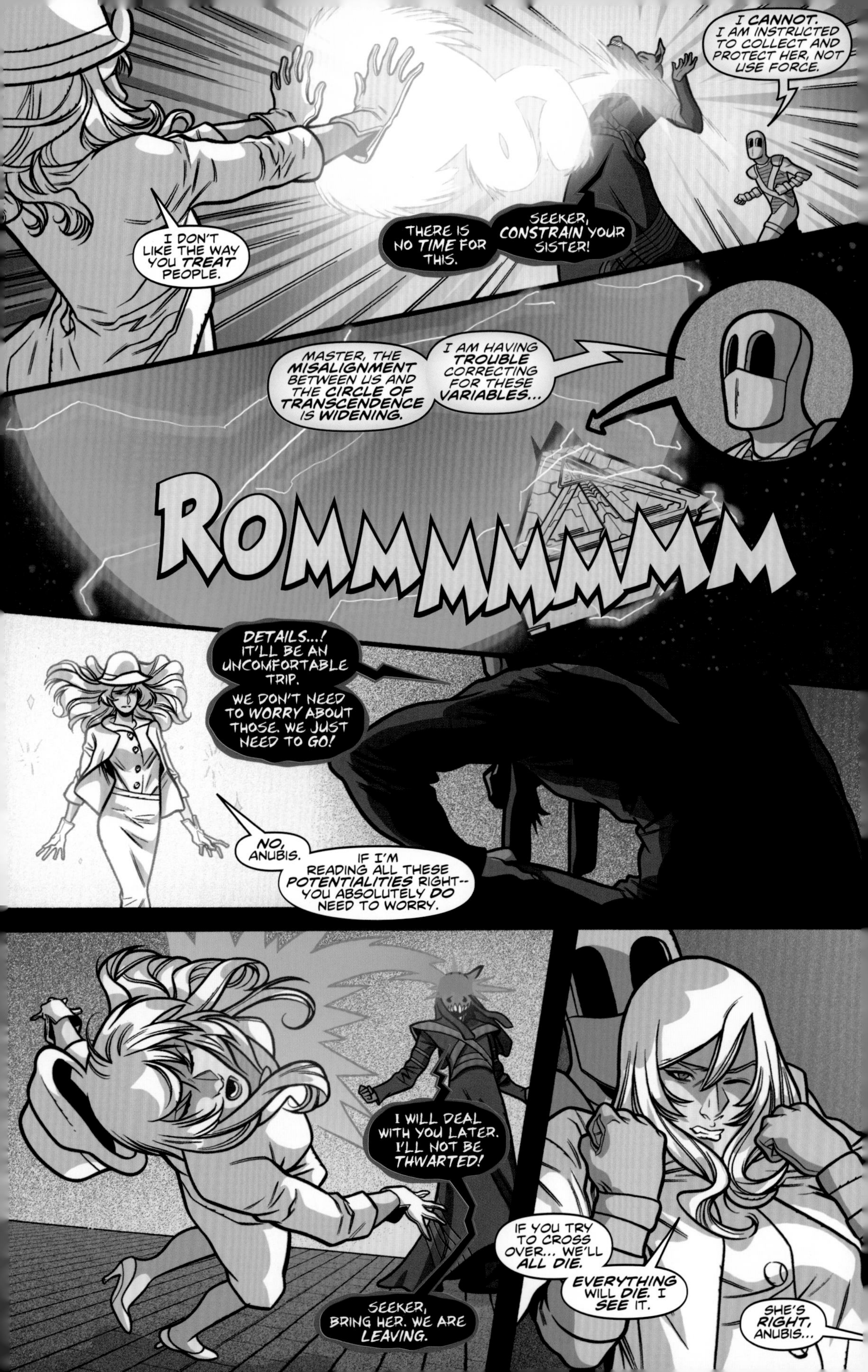
I CANNOT. I AM INSTRUCTED TO COLLECT AND PROTECT HER, NOT USE FORCE.
I DON'T LIKE THE WAY YOU TREAT PEOPLE.
THERE IS NO TIME FOR THIS.
SEEKER, CONSTRAIN YOUR SISTER!
MASTER, THE MISALIGNMENT BETWEEN US AND THE CIRCLE OF TRANSCENDENCE IS WIDENING.
I AM HAVING TROUBLE CORRECTING FOR THESE VARIABLES...
ROMMMMMMMM
DETAILS...! IT'LL BE AN UNCOMFORTABLE TRIP.
WE DON'T NEED TO WORRY ABOUT THOSE. WE JUST NEED TO GO!
NO, ANUBIS.
IF I'M READING ALL THESE POTENTIALITIES RIGHT-- YOU ABSOLUTELY DO NEED TO WORRY.
I WILL DEAL WITH YOU LATER. I'LL NOT BE THWARTED!
SEEKER, BRING HER. WE ARE LEAVING.
IF YOU TRY TO CROSS OVER... WE'LL ALL DIE.
EVERYTHING WILL DIE. I SEE IT.
SHE'S RIGHT, ANUBIS...

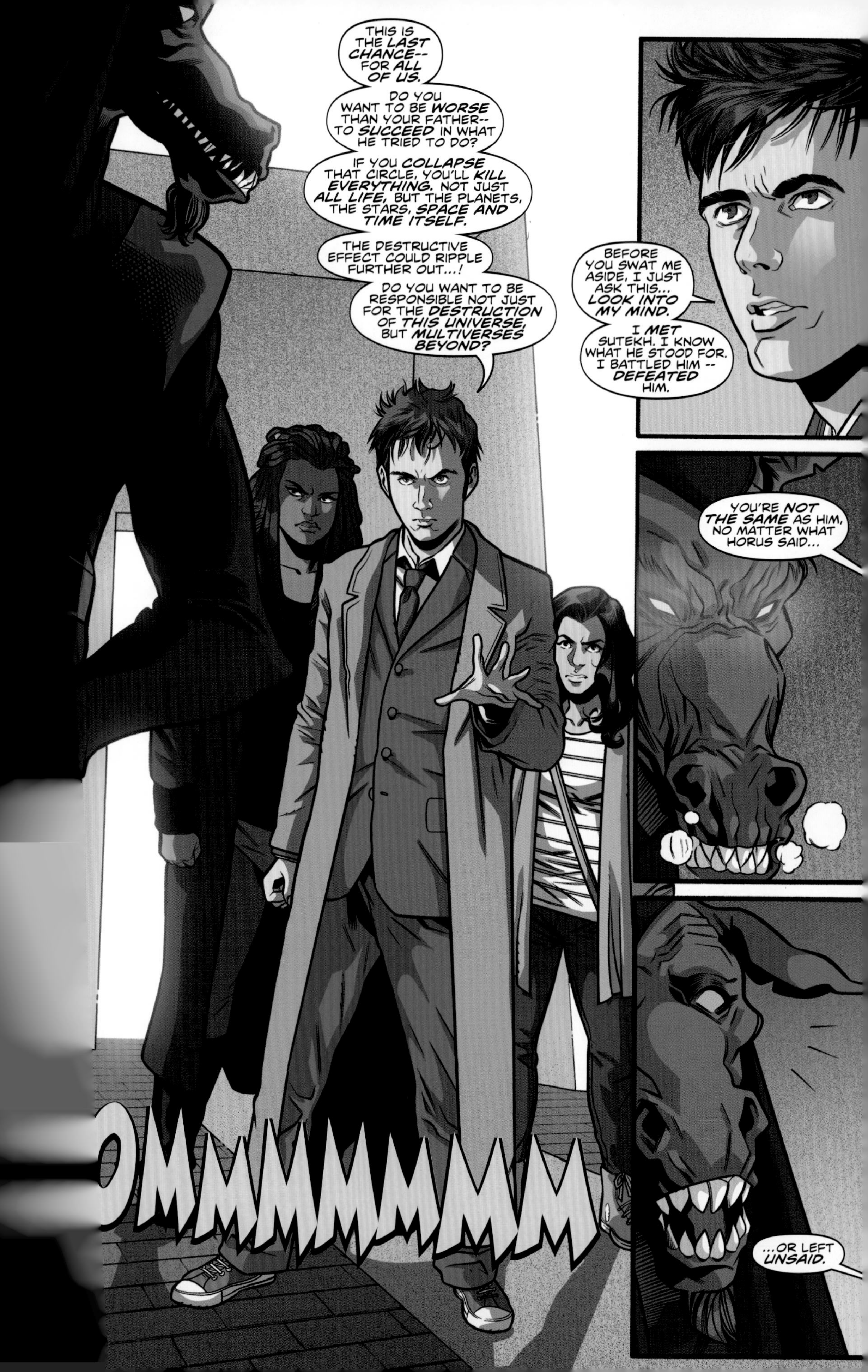
THIS IS THE LAST CHANCE-- FOR ALL OF US.
DO YOU WANT TO BE WORSE THAN YOUR FATHER-- TO SUCCEED IN WHAT HE TRIED TO DO?
IF YOU COLLAPSE THAT CIRCLE, YOU'LL KILL EVERYTHING. NOT JUST ALL LIFE, BUT THE PLANETS, THE STARS, SPACE AND TIME ITSELF.
THE DESTRUCTIVE EFFECT COULD RIPPLE FURTHER OUT...!
DO YOU WANT TO BE RESPONSIBLE NOT JUST FOR THE DESTRUCTION OF THIS UNIVERSE, BUT MULTIVERSES BEYOND?
OMMMMMMMMM
BEFORE YOU SWAT ME ASIDE, I JUST ASK THIS... LOOK INTO MY MIND.
I MET SUTEKH. I KNOW WHAT HE STOOD FOR. I BATTLED HIM -- DEFEATED HIM.
YOU'RE NOT THE SAME AS HIM, NO MATTER WHAT HORUS SAID...
...OR LEFT UNSAID.

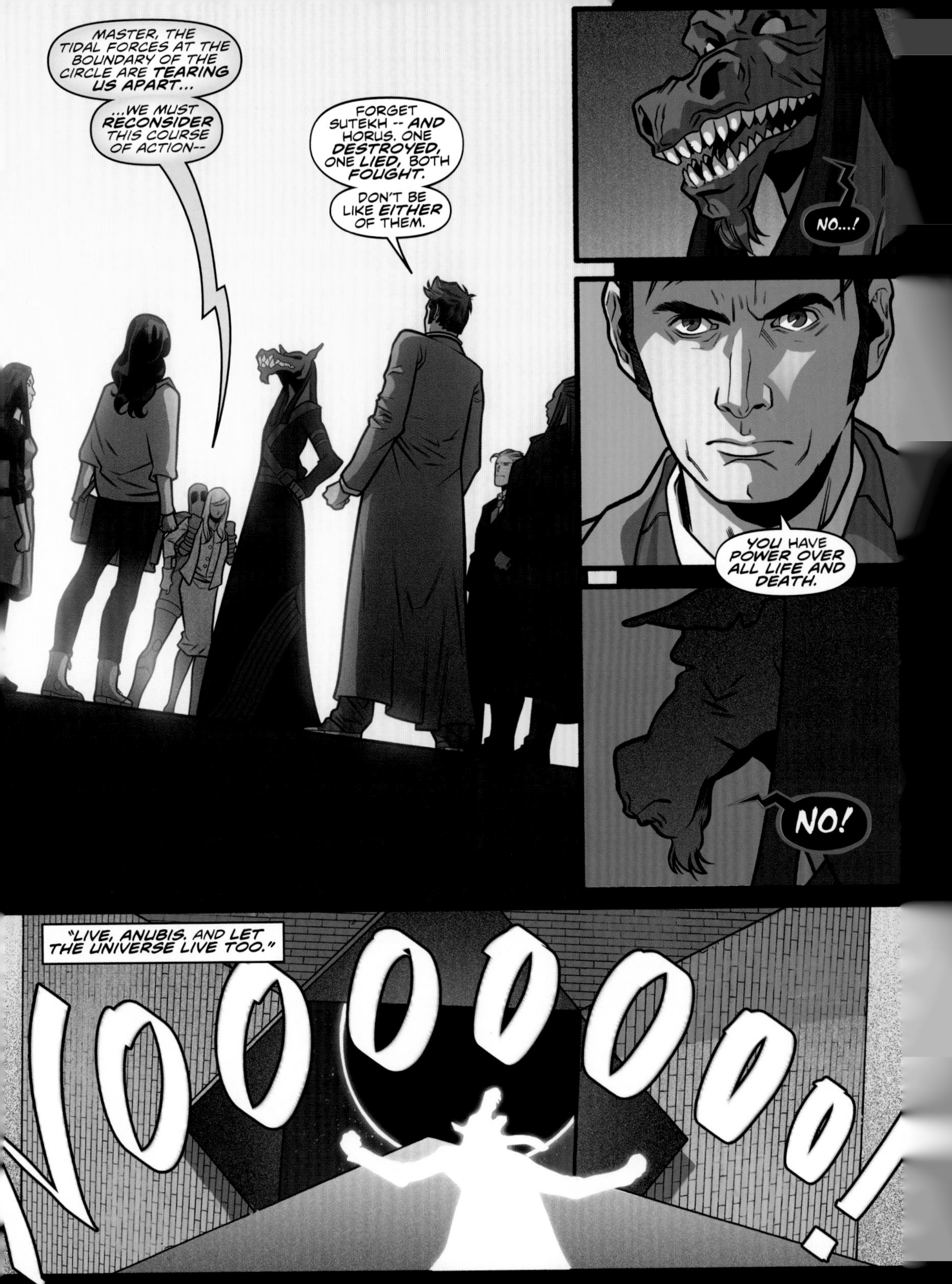

MASTER, THE TIDAL FORCES AT THE BOUNDARY OF THE CIRCLE ARE TEARING US APART...
...WE MUST RECONSIDER THIS COURSE OF ACTION--
FORGET SUTEKH -- AND HORUS. ONE DESTROYED, ONE LIED, BOTH FOUGHT.
DON'T BE LIKE EITHER OF THEM.
NO...!
YOU HAVE POWER OVER ALL LIFE AND DEATH.
NO!
"LIVE, ANUBIS. AND LET THE UNIVERSE LIVE TOO."
NOOOOOOOO!

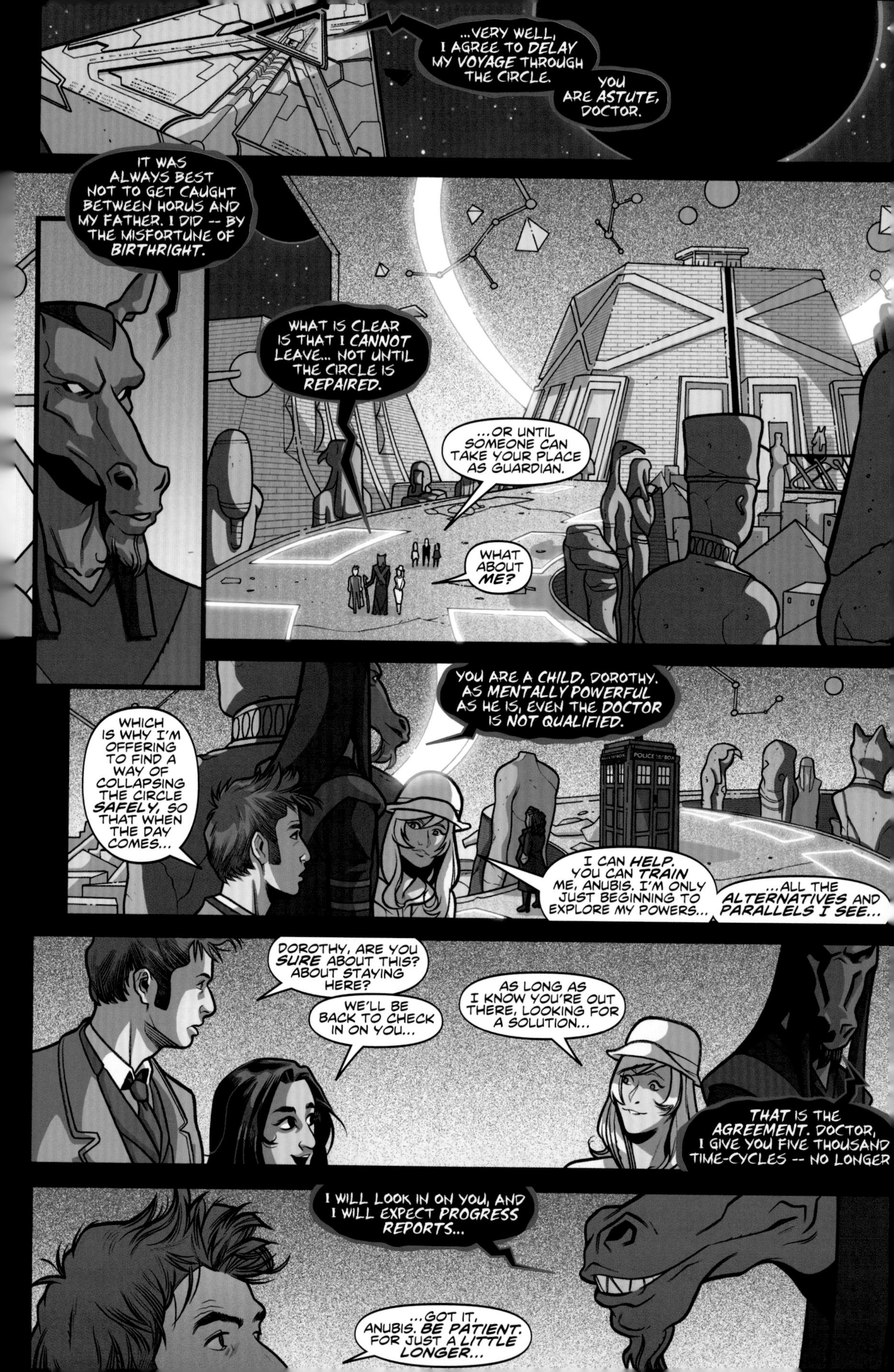
...VERY WELL, I AGREE TO DELAY MY VOYAGE THROUGH THE CIRCLE.
YOU ARE ASTUTE, DOCTOR.
IT WAS ALWAYS BEST NOT TO GET CAUGHT BETWEEN HORUS AND MY FATHER. I DID -- BY THE MISFORTUNE OF BIRTHRIGHT.
WHAT IS CLEAR IS THAT I CANNOT LEAVE... NOT UNTIL THE CIRCLE IS REPAIRED.
...OR UNTIL SOMEONE CAN TAKE YOUR PLACE AS GUARDIAN.
WHAT ABOUT ME?
YOU ARE A CHILD, DOROTHY. AS MENTALLY POWERFUL AS HE IS, EVEN THE DOCTOR IS NOT QUALIFIED.
POLICE BOX
WHICH IS WHY I'M OFFERING TO FIND A WAY OF COLLAPSING THE CIRCLE SAFELY, SO THAT WHEN THE DAY COMES...
I CAN HELP. YOU CAN TRAIN ME, ANUBIS. I'M ONLY JUST BEGINNING TO EXPLORE MY POWERS...
...ALL THE ALTERNATIVES AND PARALLELS I SEE...
DOROTHY, ARE YOU SURE ABOUT THIS? ABOUT STAYING HERE?
WE'LL BE BACK TO CHECK IN ON YOU...
AS LONG AS I KNOW YOU'RE OUT THERE, LOOKING FOR A SOLUTION...
THAT IS THE AGREEMENT. DOCTOR, I GIVE YOU FIVE THOUSAND TIME-CYCLES -- NO LONGER
I WILL LOOK IN ON YOU, AND I WILL EXPECT PROGRESS REPORTS...
...GOT IT, ANUBIS. BE PATIENT. FOR JUST A LITTLE LONGER...

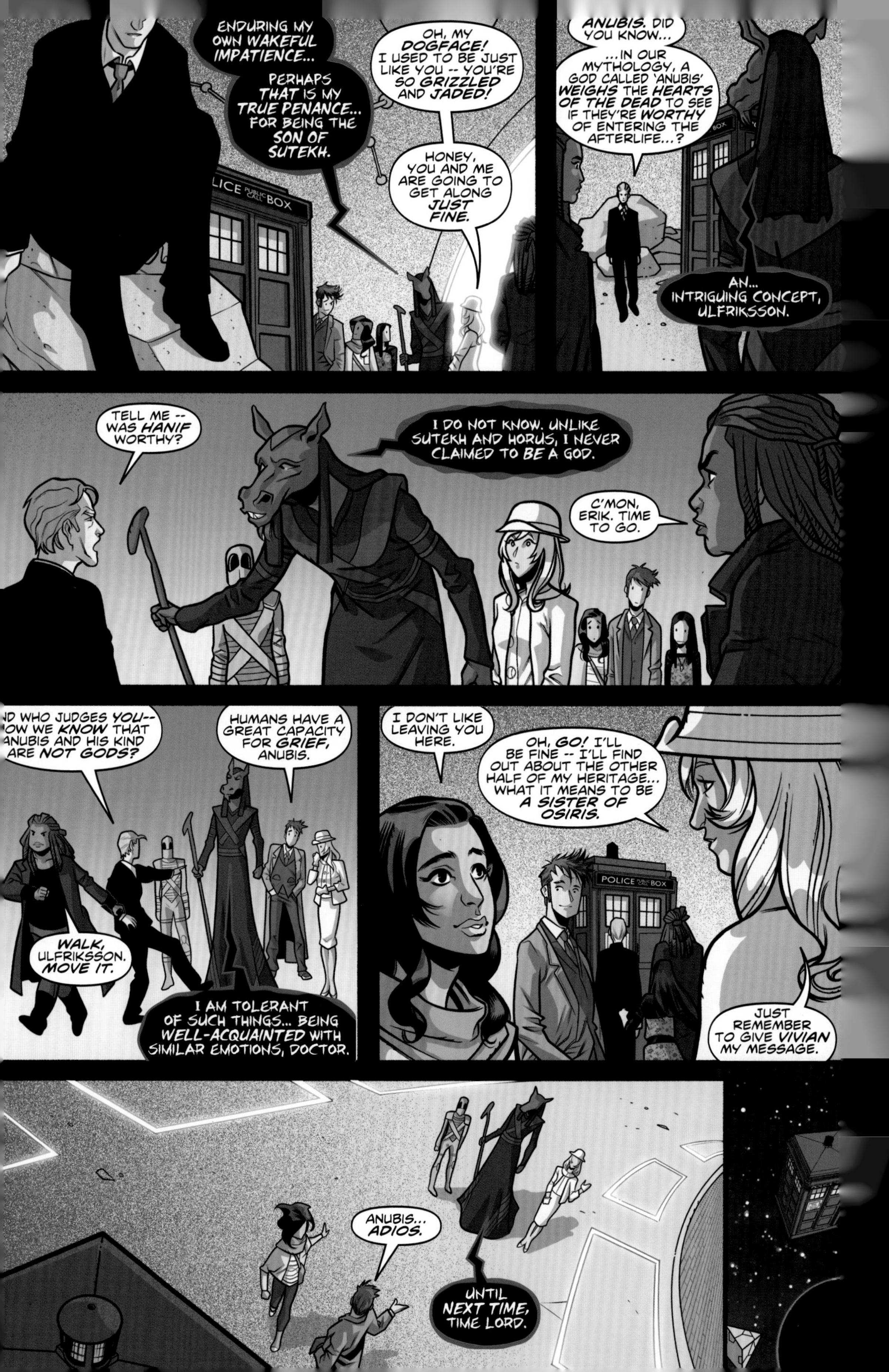
ENDURING MY OWN WAKEFUL IMPATIENCE...
PERHAPS THAT IS MY TRUE PENANCE... FOR BEING THE SON OF SUTEKH.
OH, MY DOGFACE! I USED TO BE JUST LIKE YOU -- YOU'RE SO GRIZZLED AND JADED!
HONEY, YOU AND ME ARE GOING TO GET ALONG JUST FINE.
POLICE PUBLIC CALL BOX
ANUBIS. DID YOU KNOW...
...IN OUR MYTHOLOGY, A GOD CALLED 'ANUBIS' WEIGHS THE HEARTS OF THE DEAD TO SEE IF THEY'RE WORTHY OF ENTERING THE AFTERLIFE...?
AN... INTRIGUING CONCEPT, ULFRIKSSON.
TELL ME -- WAS HANIF WORTHY?
I DO NOT KNOW. UNLIKE SUTEKH AND HORUS, I NEVER CLAIMED TO BE A GOD.
C'MON, ERIK. TIME TO GO.
ND WHO JUDGES YOU-- OW WE KNOW THAT ANUBIS AND HIS KIND ARE NOT GODS?
HUMANS HAVE A GREAT CAPACITY FOR GRIEF, ANUBIS.
WALK, ULFRIKSSON. MOVE IT.
I AM TOLERANT OF SUCH THINGS... BEING WELL-ACQUAINTED WITH SIMILAR EMOTIONS, DOCTOR.
I DON'T LIKE LEAVING YOU HERE.
OH, GO! I'LL BE FINE -- I'LL FIND OUT ABOUT THE OTHER HALF OF MY HERITAGE... WHAT IT MEANS TO BE A SISTER OF OSIRIS.
POLICE PUBLIC CALL BOX
JUST REMEMBER TO GIVE VIVIAN MY MESSAGE.
ANUBIS... ADIOS.
UNTIL NEXT TIME, TIME LORD.

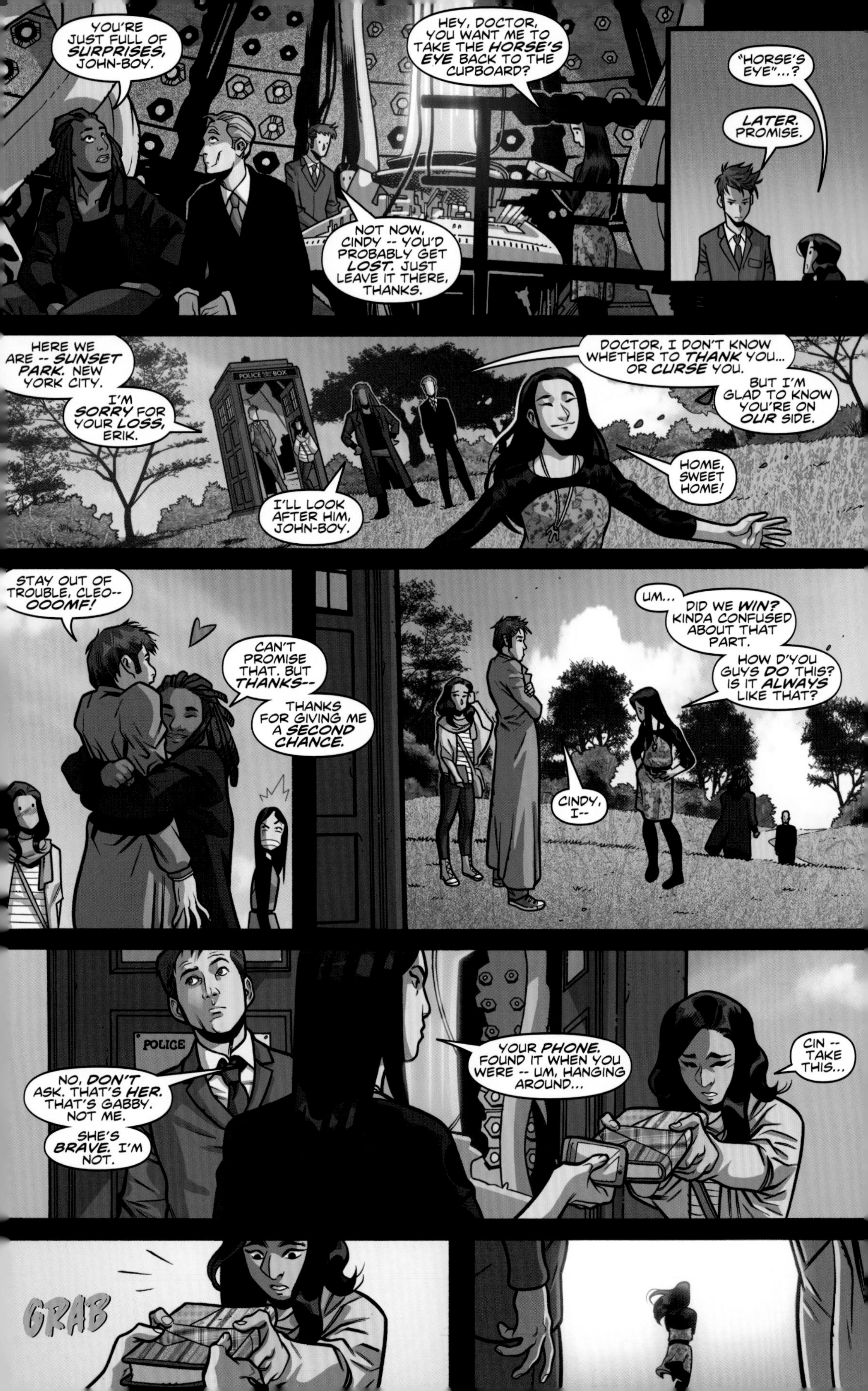
YOU'RE JUST FULL OF SURPRISES, JOHN-BOY.
HEY, DOCTOR, YOU WANT ME TO TAKE THE HORSE'S EYE BACK TO THE CUPBOARD?
NOT NOW, CINDY -- YOU'D PROBABLY GET LOST. JUST LEAVE IT THERE, THANKS.
"HORSE'S EYE"...?
LATER. PROMISE.
HERE WE ARE -- SUNSET PARK. NEW YORK CITY.
I'M SORRY FOR YOUR LOSS, ERIK.
I'LL LOOK AFTER HIM, JOHN-BOY.
DOCTOR, I DON'T KNOW WHETHER TO THANK YOU... OR CURSE YOU.
BUT I'M GLAD TO KNOW YOU'RE ON OUR SIDE.
HOME, SWEET HOME!
STAY OUT OF TROUBLE, CLEO-- OOOMF!
CAN'T PROMISE THAT. BUT THANKS--
THANKS FOR GIVING ME A SECOND CHANCE.
UM...
DID WE WIN? KINDA CONFUSED ABOUT THAT PART.
HOW D'YOU GUYS DO THIS? IS IT ALWAYS LIKE THAT?
CINDY, I--
POLICE
NO, DON'T ASK. THAT'S HER. THAT'S GABBY. NOT ME.
SHE'S BRAVE. I'M NOT.
YOUR PHONE. FOUND IT WHEN YOU WERE -- UM, HANGING AROUND...
CIN -- TAKE THIS...
GRAB

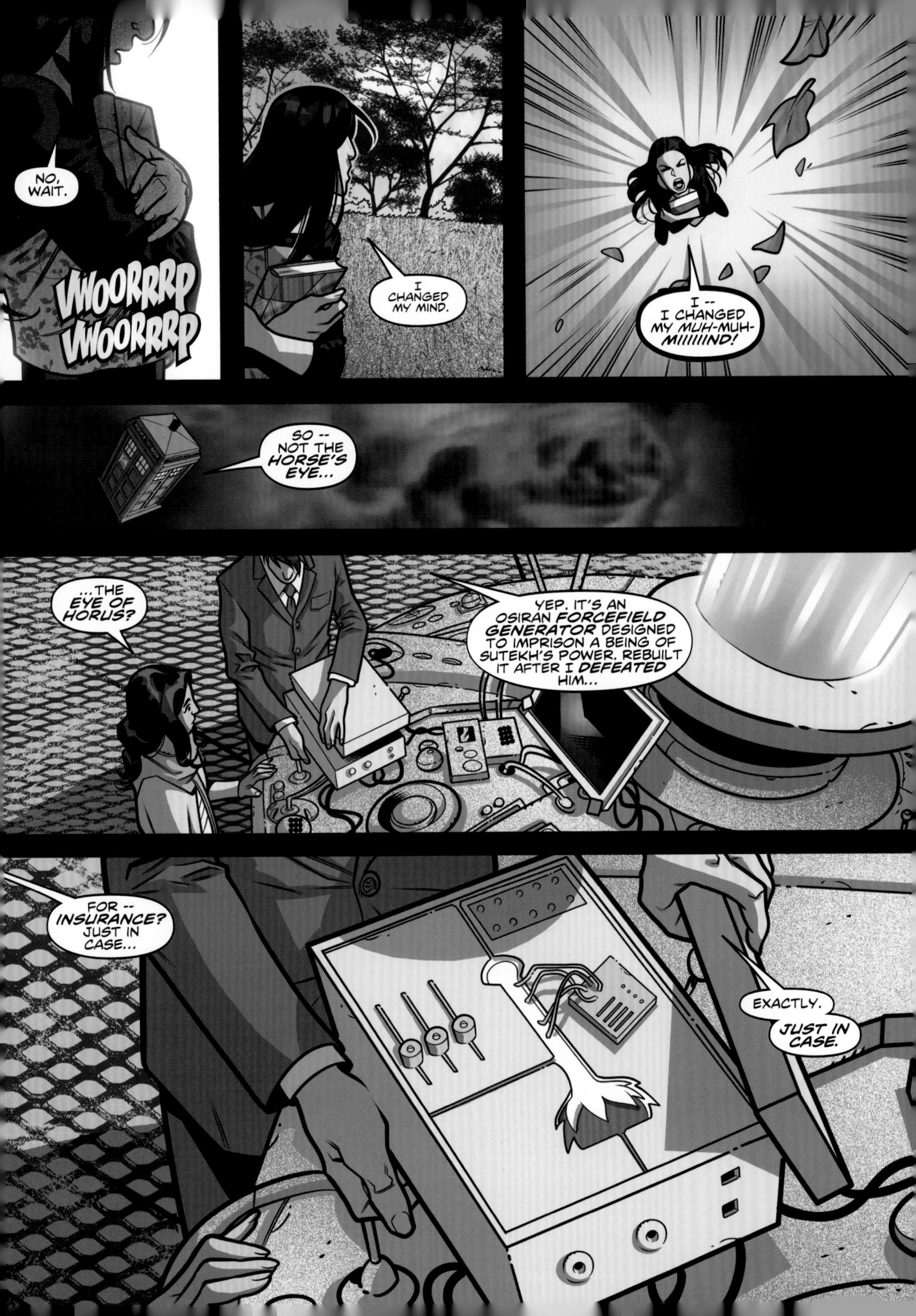
NO, WAIT.
VWOORRRP VWOORRRP
I CHANGED MY MIND.
I -- I CHANGED MY MUH-MUH-MIIIIIIND!
SO -- NOT THE HORSE'S EYE...
...THE EYE OF HORUS?
YEP. IT'S AN OSIRAN FORCEFIELD GENERATOR DESIGNED TO IMPRISON A BEING OF SUTEKH'S POWER. REBUILT IT AFTER I DEFEATED HIM...
FOR -- INSURANCE? JUST IN CASE...
EXACTLY. JUST IN CASE.

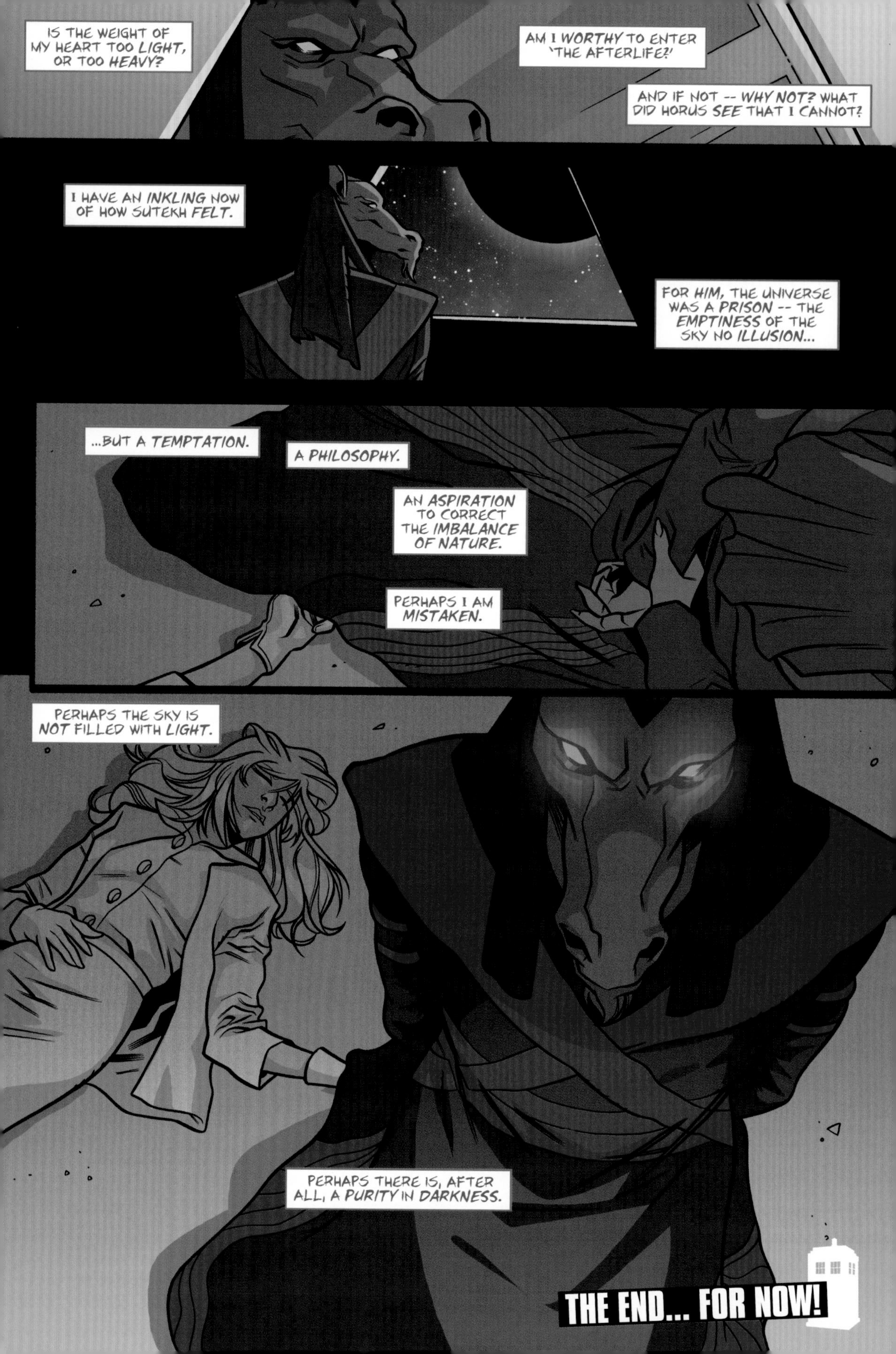
IS THE WEIGHT OF MY HEART TOO LIGHT, OR TOO HEAVY?
AM I WORTHY TO ENTER 'THE AFTERLIFE?'
AND IF NOT -- WHY NOT? WHAT DID HORUS SEE THAT I CANNOT?
I HAVE AN INKLING NOW OF HOW SUTEKH FELT.
FOR HIM, THE UNIVERSE WAS A PRISON -- THE EMPTINESS OF THE SKY NO ILLUSION...
...BUT A TEMPTATION.
A PHILOSOPHY.
AN ASPIRATION TO CORRECT THE IMBALANCE OF NATURE.
PERHAPS I AM MISTAKEN.
PERHAPS THE SKY IS NOT FILLED WITH LIGHT.
PERHAPS THERE IS, AFTER ALL, A PURITY IN DARKNESS.
THE END... FOR NOW!

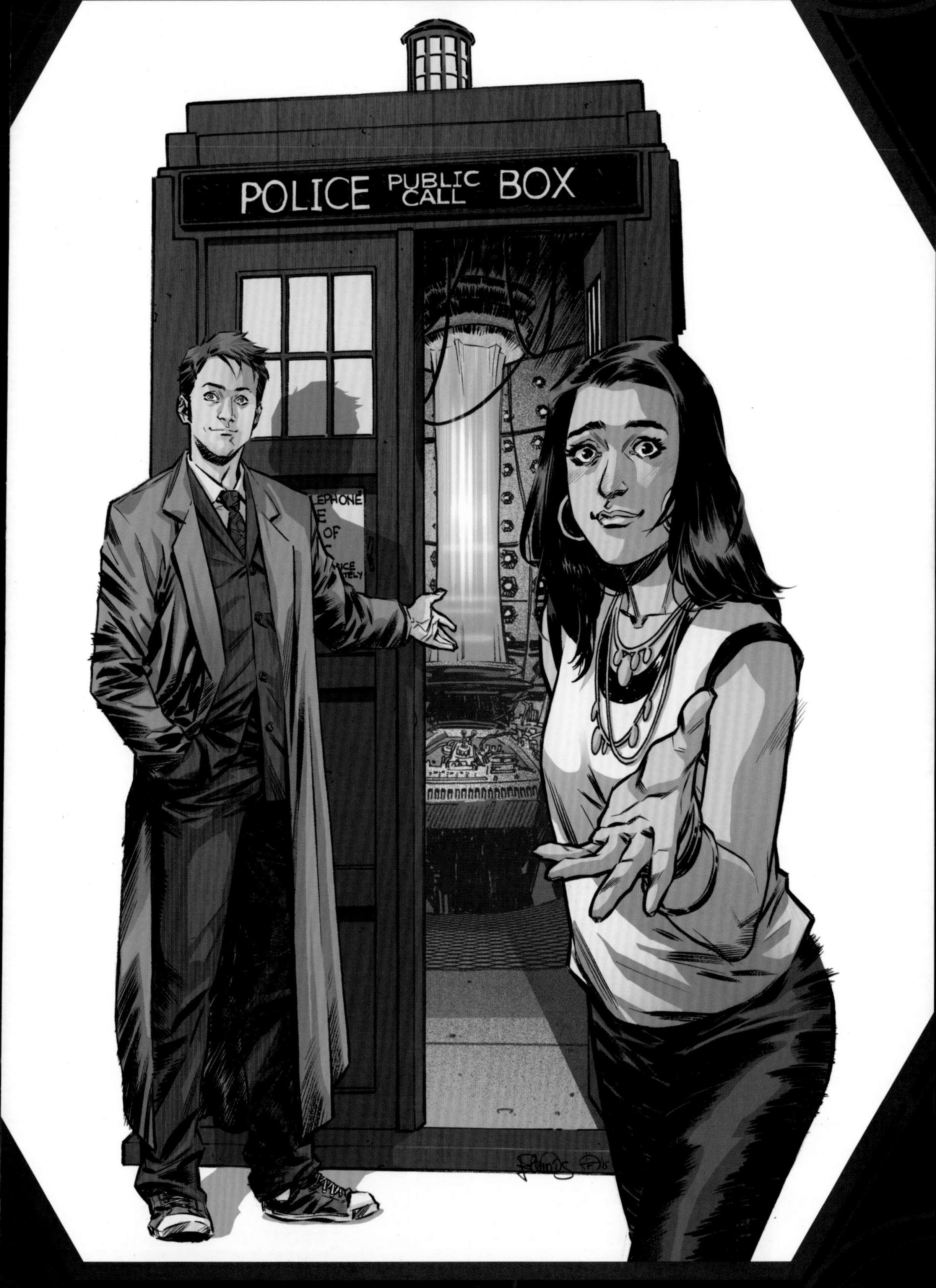
POLICE PUBLIC CALL BOX

10D #15 Cover A: ELENA CASAGRANDE & ARIANNA FLOREAN

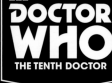

DOCTOR WHO
THE TENTH DOCTOR

COVER GALLERY

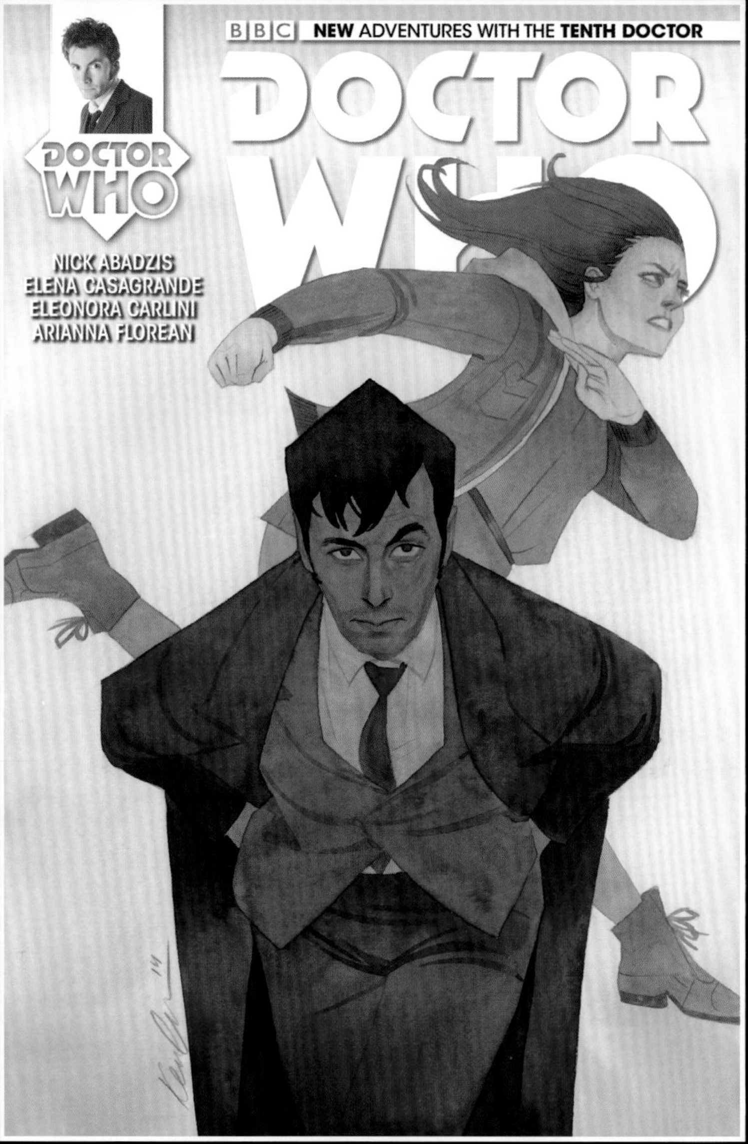
BBC NEW ADVENTURES WITH THE TENTH DOCTOR
DOCTOR WHO
DOCTOR WHO
NICK ABADZIS
ELENA CASAGRANDE
ELEONORA CARLINI
ARIANNA FLOREAN

A

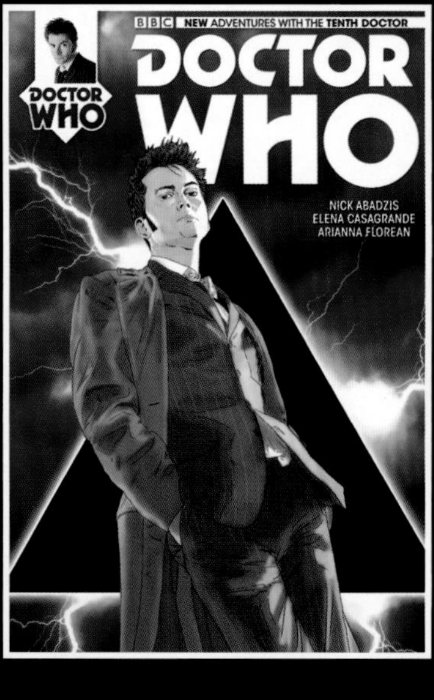
BBC NEW ADVENTURES WITH THE TENTH DOCTOR
DOCTOR WHO
DOCTOR WHO
NICK ABADZIS
ELENA CASAGRANDE
ARIANNA FLOREAN

B

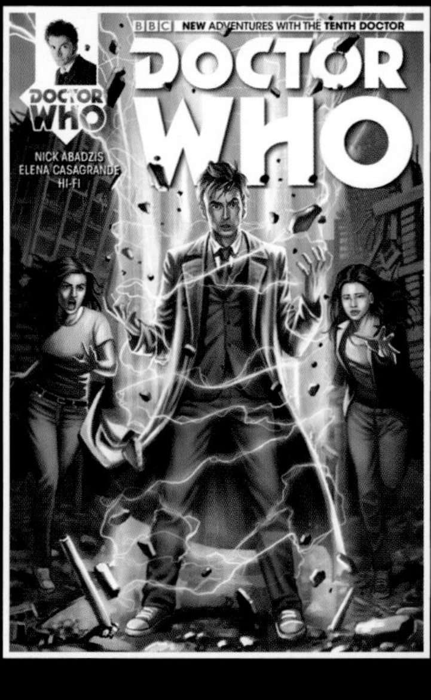
BBC NEW ADVENTURES WITH THE TENTH DOCTOR
DOCTOR WHO
DOCTOR WHO
NICK ABADZIS
ELENA CASAGRANDE
HI-FI

C

ISSUES #11-13

A: #12 Cover A – Kevin Wada
B: #11 Cover A – AJ
C: #13 Cover A – Mariano Laclaustra

BBC DOCTOR WHO THE TENTH DOCTOR

COVER GALLERY

BBC
NEW ADVENTURES WITH THE TENTH DOCTOR
DOCTOR WHO
DOCTOR WHO
NICK ABADZIS
RACHAEL STOTT
LEONARDO ROMERO
HI-FI

A

BBC
NEW ADVENTURES WITH THE TENTH DOCTOR
DOCTOR WHO
DOCTOR WHO
NICK ABADZIS
ELENA CASAGRANDE
ARIANNA FLOREAN

B

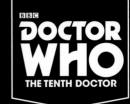

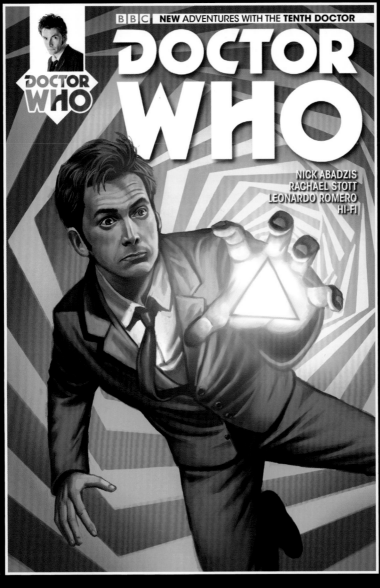

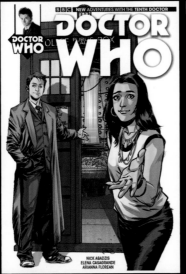

ISSUES #14-15

A: #14 Cover A – Mariano Laclaustra
B: #15 Cover A – Elena Casagrande & Arianna Florean

FOLLOW YOUR FAVORITE INCARNATIONS ACROSS THESE FANTASTIC COLLECTIONS!

DOCTOR WHO: THE TWELFTH DOCTOR
VOL. 1: TERRORFORMER

ISBN: 9781782761778
ON SALE NOW - $19.99 / $22.95 CAN / £10.99
(UK EDITION ISBN: 9781782763864)

DOCTOR WHO: THE TWELFTH DOCTOR
VOL. 2: FRACTURES

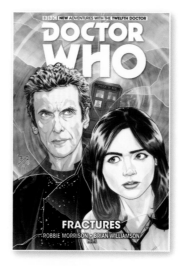

ISBN: 9781782763017
ON SALE NOW - $19.99 / $25.99 CAN / £10.99
(UK EDITION ISBN: 9781782766599)

DOCTOR WHO: THE TWELFTH DOCTOR
VOL. 3: HYPERION

ISBN: 9781782767473
COMING SOON - $19.99 / $25.99 CAN / £10.99
(UK EDITION ISBN: 9781782767442)

DOCTOR WHO: THE ELEVENTH DOCTOR
VOL. 1: AFTER LIFE

ISBN: 9781782761730
ON SALE NOW - $19.99 / $22.95 CAN / £10.99
(UK EDITION ISBN: 9781782763857)

DOCTOR WHO: THE ELEVENTH DOCTOR
VOL. 2: SERVE YOU

ISBN: 9781782761754
ON SALE NOW - $19.99 / $22.95 CAN / £10.99
(UK EDITION ISBN: 9781782766582)

DOCTOR WHO: THE ELEVENTH DOCTOR
VOL. 3: CONVERSION

ISBN: 9781782763024
COMING SOON - $19.99 / $25.99 CAN / £10.99
(UK EDITION ISBN: 9781782767435)

TITAN COMICS

For information on how to subscribe to our great Doctor Who titles, or to purchase them digitally, visit:
WWW.TITAN-COMICS.COM

COMPLETE YOUR COLLECTION!

DOCTOR WHO: THE TENTH DOCTOR
VOL. 1: REVOLUTIONS OF TERROR

ISBN: 9781782761747
ON SALE NOW - $19.99 / $22.95 CAN / £10.99
(UK EDITION ISBN: 9781782763840)

DOCTOR WHO: THE TENTH DOCTOR
VOL. 2: THE WEEPING ANGELS OF MONS

ISBN: 9781782761754
ON SALE NOW - $19.99 / $25.99 CAN / £10.99
(UK EDITION ISBN: 9781782766575)

COMING SOON!

DOCTOR WHO: THE NINTH DOCTOR
VOL. 1: WEAPONS OF PAST DESTRUCTION

ISBN: 9781782763369
COMING SOON - $19.99 / $25.99 CAN / £10.99
(UK EDITION ISBN: 9781782761056)

DOCTOR WHO EVENT 2015
FOUR DOCTORS

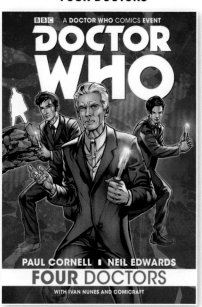

ISBN: 9781782765967
COMING SOON - $19.99 / $25.99 CAN / £10.99
(UK EDITION ISBN: 9781785851063)

AVAILABLE FROM ALL GOOD COMIC STORES, BOOK STORES, AND DIGITAL PROVIDERS!

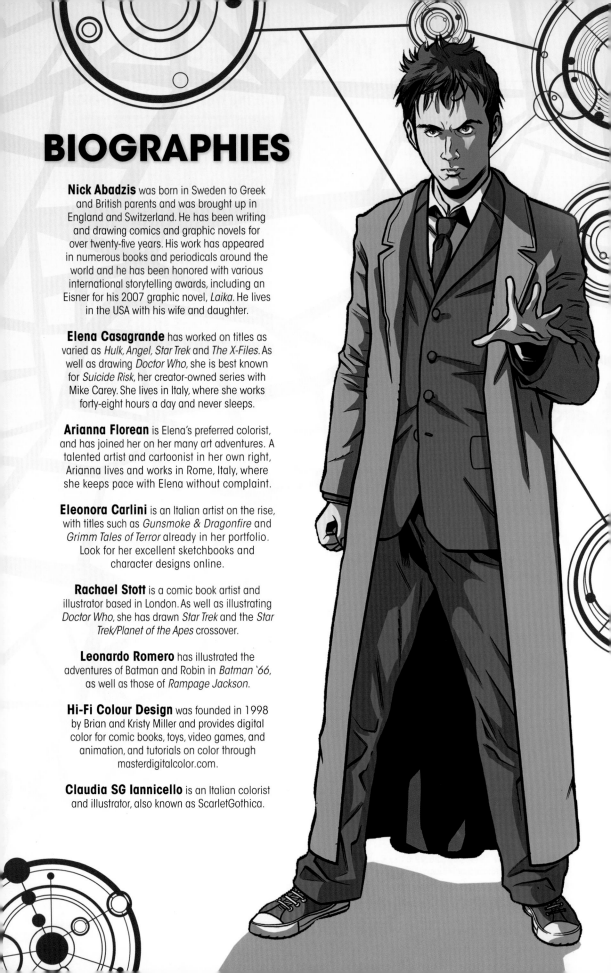

BIOGRAPHIES

Nick Abadzis was born in Sweden to Greek and British parents and was brought up in England and Switzerland. He has been writing and drawing comics and graphic novels for over twenty-five years. His work has appeared in numerous books and periodicals around the world and he has been honored with various international storytelling awards, including an Eisner for his 2007 graphic novel, *Laika*. He lives in the USA with his wife and daughter.

Elena Casagrande has worked on titles as varied as *Hulk, Angel, Star Trek* and *The X-Files*. As well as drawing *Doctor Who*, she is best known for *Suicide Risk*, her creator-owned series with Mike Carey. She lives in Italy, where she works forty-eight hours a day and never sleeps.

Arianna Florean is Elena's preferred colorist, and has joined her on her many art adventures. A talented artist and cartoonist in her own right, Arianna lives and works in Rome, Italy, where she keeps pace with Elena without complaint.

Eleonora Carlini is an Italian artist on the rise, with titles such as *Gunsmoke & Dragonfire* and *Grimm Tales of Terror* already in her portfolio. Look for her excellent sketchbooks and character designs online.

Rachael Stott is a comic book artist and illustrator based in London. As well as illustrating *Doctor Who*, she has drawn *Star Trek* and the *Star Trek/Planet of the Apes* crossover.

Leonardo Romero has illustrated the adventures of Batman and Robin in *Batman '66*, as well as those of *Rampage Jackson*.

Hi-Fi Colour Design was founded in 1998 by Brian and Kristy Miller and provides digital color for comic books, toys, video games, and animation, and tutorials on color through masterdigitalcolor.com.

Claudia SG Iannicello is an Italian colorist and illustrator, also known as ScarletGothica.